E-Government & E-Strategy

Explaining the Successful Korean E-Government Model and Strategies

Gi-Heon Kwon, Ph.D

PY
PUBLISHING
&COMPANY

E-Government & E-Strategy: SMART Revolution and IT Governance

The unfolding of the 21st century has brought the world into a new and different turn. It's an era of speed and change. Innovation is indispensable to achieve transformation of governance. The combination of ICT and Smart Revolution created the various social relationships (Social Network Services) and green growth, a new growth engine of national competitiveness. And therefore, the discussion of national competitiveness, quality of life, social relations, and competitiveness of enterprises is almost impracticable without touching e-Government based on SMART revolution.

While we are living in a chaotic and turbulent society, rapid changes have been evident in the 21stcentury. The blending of broadcasting, telecommunications and imaging in the information technology (IT) have created the SMART technological innovations such as Smartphone, PC Tablet, and Internet. Through internet, such amalgamation and conception of new technologies gives way to a new space for social experience and relationship using Twitter, Facebook, and other SNS devices.

The integration of SMART Information Technology (IT) and Green Revolution can lead to a low carbon market, thus, capable to commence a Cyber Civilization society. The advancement of digital technology and industrial development elevates the economic potential level of the whole society, and enables e-Government which is based on SMART revolution.

The full integration of knowledge and skills stacked in thousands of years can be attributed to digitization or advancement of information and communicationtechnology (ICT). The concept of time and space was totally obliterated due to the innovation of broadcasting and communication.

Currently existing government, market, and society's social relationships are completely changing due to the creation of new social network (SNS) such as Twitter,

Facebook, which are introduced through Smartphone, Tablet PC, and other new media-based electronic gadgets.

Such swirl of information revolution requires an unsullied evaluation of existing governance model and system. In particular, up until now, modern administrative bureaucracies that lead the development of science and technology reveal various limitations on responding and adapting to contemporary environmental changes. As a consequence, numerous scholars have suggested various forms of administrative governance models considering rapid environmental changes, such as increasing diversity and complexity of organizational activities, and increasing role of professional experts.

How these kinds of an enormous change and innovation, swirling from the high-technological environmental changes such as SMART revolution and SNS development, will impact the traditional theories of public administration and public policy in the governance studies? What are the focal issues to be discussed in e-Government and e-Policy in this era of the comprehensive paradigm shift? What should be the new theoretical principle and philosophy to break-away the so-called criticism of the 'impoverished professionalism' facing the science of public administration and philosophy?

How could we academically link the theoretical principles of the knowledge-created e-Government with the traditional administrative, policy, and network governance theories? Could the e-Government be the most effective, transparent, and accountable democratic governance model facing the turbulence of the upcoming Smart knowledge revolutions, especially in the developing countries? What would then be the effective strategies and policy tasks to face and solve the related, presumably enormous challenges and thereby realizing a democratic e-Governance?

This book is written as an attempt to answer these kinds of academic as well as practical questions, searching for a new paradigm of e-Government and e-Strategy facing the Smart revolution and knowledge society in this 21st century. The author uses the theories from the field of public policy, new public management, and new governance to link the gap between the new theories of e-Governance and the traditional model of public administration.

Since the conception of Management Information System, many focal points as well as academic changes have been brought in the field of e-Government and Public Administration. At the outset, administrative and policy theories gave emphasis on the introduction of theories of Information society and technical structure of information systems.

Since mid-90s, the introduction of the information superhighway as part of national policy, research emphasis was centered on administration of data-processing theory, information society and information policy. The introduction of the e-Government law since 2001 has paved full-scale application of e-Government and e-Policy. In addition, academic interest in the field of e-Government, Knowledge Government (Knowledge Management System), and e-Policy as a research area has been tremendously increased. Furthermore, for the sake of the New Public Management (NPM) and the Network Goverance(NG) thoery, e-Government and e-policy are required to have a governance perspective. Also, in the new cyberspace, e-Governance and Cyber-governance are needed to have an integrated perspective. Finally, the contemporary development of new social network (SNS) and the advancement of the Green revolution are caused by the amalgamation of ICT revolution, such as u-Technology, m-Technology, and other SMART technologies.

The motivation for the writing of this book is to crystallize the focus and locus of new emerging theories of e-Government and e-Policy facing the swirling turbulence of ICT and SMART information technologies.

The first focusing audience group for this book is the government officials and students of the developing countries. The lessons and implications, casting for the advanced countries from the comparative perspective, may not be overlooked; but they already have their own model of e-Government. Korea was evaluated as the world best in the UN e-Government assessment of 2010, 2012 consecutively. Therefore, it might be logical to infer that Korean model would be the most applicable model to the developing countries. This is especially true when we consider the fact that Korea could have achieved its success within a short time of period of a few decades, about only 60 years since the Korean War destruction of 1953.

Every year a large number of government officials in the developing countries apply for the Global MPA e-Government Program, the Graduate School of Governance, SKKU, the graduate institution the author is associated, indicates that Korean e-Government model has a real reputation to be benchmarked from the perspective of developing countries.

The Korean model is really attractive for them, as mentioned because this country has developed its model up to the world best within a few decades, especially from the Korean War-torn ashes of 1953. The country, then receiving ODAs from the then advanced nations, now accomplished the world best model and become one of the OECD nation to offer the ODAs to many developing countries. Hence, the lessons from this country, who developed with her own will and strategy, would be more plausible and appropriate for other fellow developing countries who also ardently want to become upgrade to the world-best nation at this moment.

This book consists of six parts.

The first part presents topics that will give a clear and broad understanding of the Information Society. Discussion will start on the environmental factors that surround e-Government and e-Policy by looking and examining information technologies. It will attempt to explore the relationship between information technology with the standpoint of the history of civilization. Succeeding chapters will lay the fundamental foundation and theoretical perspectives of information technology, driving forces of information society, and an emphasis on the important theoretical views on information society.

The second part presents the essentials of the theory of Governance in Information Society. In this part, it will review the position of e-Government in the whole body of Public Administration and Public Policy theories.While reviewing a variety of concepts and models of new governance and cyber-governance recently emerged as the theories of governance in information society, this section will shed light on the relationship of e-Government and Governance models. What kinds of a new governance paradigm and the administrative model are needed to build a smaller but more efficient knowledge-based e-government? What kinds of sub-systems are to be included in the model? In public administration of information society, how could we theoretically color and position the theories of e-government based on the Smart revolution? These academic inquiries will be addressed in this chapter.

The third part presents the e-Government theories. Based on the theoretical discussion of the concept and vision of e-government, this book will examine the trends and strategies of Korea and other countries in the adoption and development of e-Government. In addition, it will look into the external and internal components as well as strategies of e-Government. Also, it will provide a profound discussion of the core elements of the Smart e-government based on the emerging trends of e-Government, such as m-Government and u-Government. Finally, this section will examine some strategic methodologiecal techniques to realized an effective innovation, such as BPR(Business Process Reengineering), ERP(Enterprise Resource Planning) and IRM(Information Resource Management) among others.

The fourth part of this book presents the theory of knowledge government. It will start on examining the recently growing concepts and components of knowledge government in the academe, while exploring its relationship to the traditional e-Government. In addition, while examining the governance issues of knowledge governance and government innovation, it will discuss knowledge government's technical components and strategies.

In short, while introducing the various discussions on the emerging e-Government and knowledge government in Part I and II, it will present the diverse government innovations and policy instruments to set up an effective foundation of the new e-government operating system.

In the theorical perspective of Policy Science, e-Government and Knowledge Government are placed in the policy system's new decision-making mechanism. And this specific output of policy system is called 'e-Policy.'

The part five and six present an elaborate discussion of e-Policy. In Part 5, e-Policy I, Policy Science of Information Society is discussed. And the relationship between e-government and policy theory, and the logics of e-policy will be reviewed.

In Part 6, e-Policy II, the particulars of the specific policy are discussed. E-Policy is classified according to the unit of governance, state(government), market(enterprise), and civil society(NGO). The efficiency, democracy, and reflexivity dimensions of e-Policy will be examined with the relevant policy cases. According to the specific policy cases, the related concepts, issues, and strategies will be reviewed.

Finally, the final chapter will wrap up the overall summaries and findings discussed in this book. The executive summary along with policy implications and recommendations will also be discussed in this chapter.

September 2014

Gi-Heon Kwon, Ph.D
Professor of Public Policy & E-Government
Director of Global e-Policy & e-Government Institutue,
Graduate School of Governance,
SKKU-Samsung Foundation

Table of Contents

PART 5 THEORY & STRATEGY OF E-POLICY I: OVERALL REVIEW

PART 6 THEORY & STRATEGY OF E-POLICY II: PARTICULARS OF SPECIFIC E-POLICY

OVERVIEW

When paradigm changes, the world itself changes.

- Thomas Kuhn

1. Question (Background)

As the 21st century unfolds, we are living in a chaotic and turbulent society, characterized by time, speed, and uncertainty. Speed of thought becomes very important as knowledge is the most critical factor of national competitiveness. As new information technology combines broadcasting, telecommunications and mobile images, the new space, called cyber-space has been created by using the SMART technological innovations such as Smartphone, PC Tablet, and Internet.

The integration of SMART Information Technology (IT) and Green Revolution lifts up the economic development. The full integration of knowledge and skills stacked in thousands of human history, by dint of digitization and the advancement of Smart information technology (IT), enables the paradigm of e-Government different from the traditional machine of bureaucracy. The concept of time and space was totally obliterated due to the innovation of the Smart revolutions. The current form of governing paradigm is completely changing due to the creation of new social network (SNS) such as Twitter and Face book, so that the relationship between government, market, and civil society is changing.

Such swirl of information revolution requires an unsullied evaluation of existing governance model and its operating system. In particular, up until now, the bureaucratic model has led the modern development and its operating system is largely dependent on the steep, rigid, and hierarchical system based on command and control.

The bureaucratic model is basically monopoly, exclusively governing the society based on the top-down approach. This kind of hierarchical operating system is not working very effectively any more in this knowledge-based society.

Firstly, the policy decision-making process based on the rigid, hierarchical structure is not very effective to aptly respond the modern speedy technological changes in the global market. As a consequence, many scholars have suggested various model of governance, e-governance in specific, reflecting the rapid environmental changes, reflecting diversity, dynamic, and creativity of the modern knowledge activities.

The second reason is related with the phenomenon of power shifting. In this modern knowledge society, power is shifting. Previously, the bureaucratic government kept all the most valuable information and knowledge of the society. But it's not true in this knowledge society any more. The ordinary people can access information and knowledge easily; they sometimes know the important information before the government. The red-zone disappears; there is no secret. Power shifts. As a result, the modern society becomes transparent as an increasing speed. The cooperative or network governance based on e-Governance, in which government consults with its partners, the corporate business and NGOs in the civil society, with the spirit of trust and collaboration, becomes more and more effective form of governance in this modern knowledge society, even in the developing countries.

How these kinds of an enormous change and innovation, swirling from the high-technological environmental changes such as SMART revolution and SNS development, will impact the traditional study of public administration and public policy in the governance studies? What are the focal issues to be discussed in e-Government and e-Policy in this era of the comprehensive paradigm shift? What should be the new theoretical principle and philosophy to break-away the so-called criticism of the '*impoverished professionalism*' facing the science of public administration and philosophy?

How could we academically link the theoretical principles of the knowledge-created e-Government with the traditional administrative, policy, and network governance theories? Could the e-Government be the most effective, transparent, and accountable democratic governance model facing the turbulence of the upcoming Smart knowledge revolutions, especially in the developing countries? What would then be the effective strategies and tasks to face and solve the related, presumably enormous, policy challenges and thereby realizing a democratic e-Governance?

This book is written as an attempt to answer these kinds of academic as well as practical questions, searching for a new paradigm of e-Government and e-Policy facing the Smart revolution and knowledge society in this 21st century. The author uses the theories from the field of public policy, new public management, and new governance to link the gap between the new theories of e-Governance and the traditional model of public administration.

2. Analytical Model: Linkage between E-Government & E-Policy from Governance Model

The author will discuss e-Government and e-Policy based on the framework of public policy process. From the theoretical perspective of policy process, e-Government and the knowledge government is the newly emerging policy decision-making mechanism in the overall governance scheme.

As shown in 〈Figure A-1〉, the policy input which is comprised of demand and support from civil society will be transferred to the policy decision-making models, composed of e-Government and knowledge government. Through a transforming process, e-Policy as a policy output will be produced.

Information technology and information system play roles as the important infrastructures for e-Government and knowledge government(see Figure A-1).

Figure A-1 E-Government(Policy System) and E-Policy(Policy Outcome)

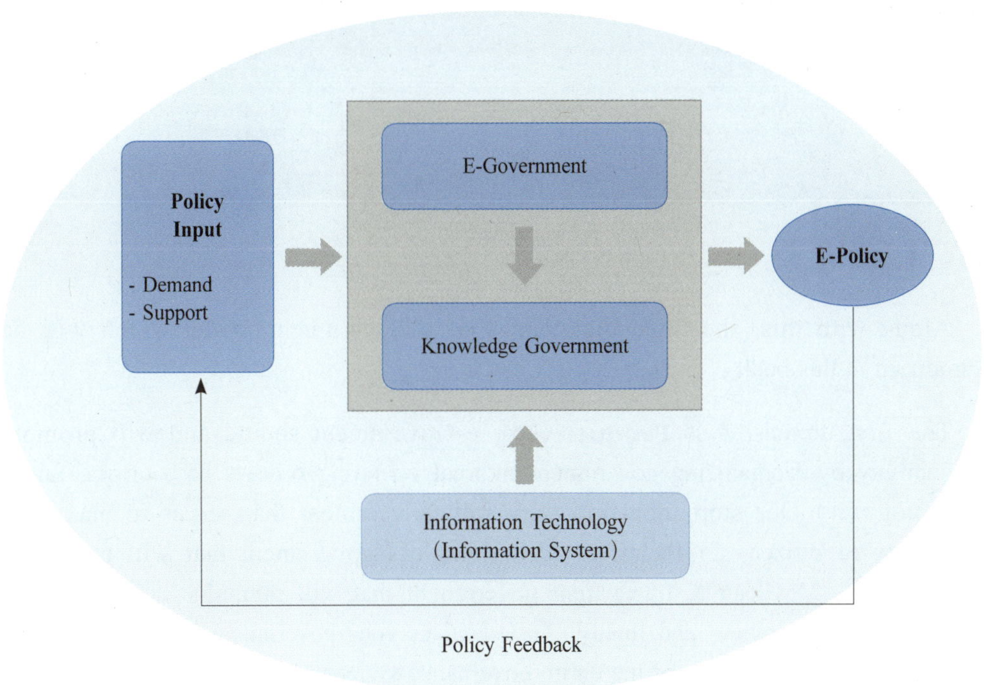

There have been few attempts to categorize information policy. However, in this book the author will discuss the typology of information policy into three distinct dimensions: (1) state(government), (2) market(enterprise), and (3) civil society(NGO).

There are three significant areas and features of e-Governance: 1) *Economic Area*, in which government productivity and national competitiveness are the most critical, 2) *Political Area*, in which civil participation and participatory democracy are the most crucial, 3) Finally, *Social Area*, in which trust building and reflexivity are the most critical for a healthy civic community.

Figure A-2 Analytical Model: E-Governance and E-Government

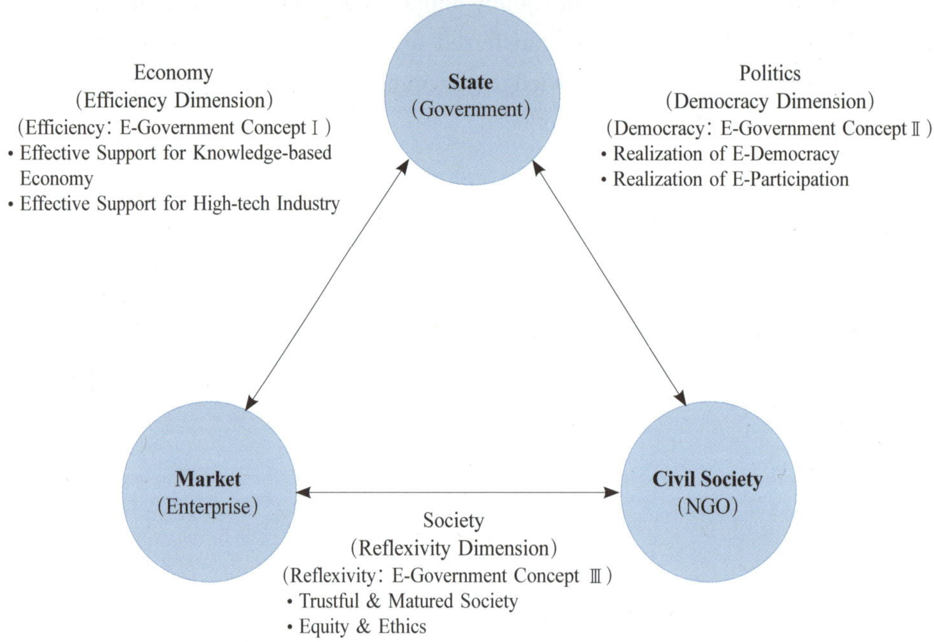

Along with this, the three dimensions of e-Government model which will be introduced in this book.

The first dimension is **Productivity**. e-Government should and will promote productivity by reorganizing government internal operating process base on the Smart technology. 1) One stop, non-stop, any stop government that serves to maximize the utility of citizen, 2) Paperless & buildingless government that will maximize digitalization, 3) Clean & transparent government that will minimize corruption and maximizing transparency, and finally, 4) Digital nervous government that will optimize the decision making process of the entire governance system.

The second dimension is **Democracy**. E-Government is using information technology to promote e-Democracy that is composed of e-Policy and e-Politics. E-policy is possible through transparent and participatory e-Policy process, while e-Politics is possible through e-Voting and e-Legislation. These two components are essential to accomplish a democratic governance.

The third dimension is **Reflexivity**. This is the highest dimension of the policy goals and ideals which leads to the respect of human dignity. Also, it is considered as the highest philosophical domain that is the underlying principle for e-Government. Through information technology, e-Government activates horizontal and vertical communication, through various venue of public spaces within the platforms, to create an open, active, and mature communication, and thereby to achieve trust building of social communities. In consequence, e-Government's supreme goal is to build a trustful and matured, a harmonious and integrated society in which each citizen could have a dream and possibility to realize his/her own self-actualization. In this book, the author refers the function of those features in e-Government as the reflexivity dimension.

3. The Structure of the Book

The analytical framework discussed here is an outline of the following topics which is divided and organized into six parts.

Part I of the book covers the theory of Information Society. In here, it will dissect and review the theoretical foundations of information technology as the basic infrastructure of e-Government. It will further provide a wider perspective by tracing the historical development of civilization; the driving forces of the information society.

Part II focuses on the theory of Governance in Information Society. In this part, it will review the position of e-Government in the whole body of Public Administration and Public Policy theories. While reviewing a variety of concepts and models of new governance and cyber-governance recently emerged as the theories of governance in information society, the relationship of e-Government and governance models will be highlighted.

What kinds of a new governance paradigm and the administrative model are needed to build a smaller but more efficient knowledge-created e-government? What kinds of sub-systems are to be included in the model? In public administration of information society, how could we theoretically color and place the theories of e-government based on the Smart revolution? These scientific inquiries will be addressed in this chapter.

Part III covers the theory of e-government. In here, based on the vision of the Smart e-Government, it will review the recent e-government strategies of Korea. In addition, it will examine the strategic components of e-government divided as internal and external. It will also discuss the key strategic and methodological techniques of the Smart e-government based on emerging trends of e-Government, including the discussion of m-Government and u-Government. BPR(Business Process Reengineering), ERP(Enterprise Resource Planning) and IRM(Information Resource Management) among others, will be examined as those technical strategies of e-Government.

Part IV covers the theory of knowledge government. In this chapter, it will review the relationship between e-government and knowledge government, while discussing the concepts and components of the knowledge government. In addition, the components and strategies of knowledge-government will be discussed, while reviewing the issues of government innovation and national innovation. By introducing various discussions on e-government and knowledge-government, the various plans and strategies of government innovation and governance will be proposed for these systems to play an effective role in the new governance model.

From the perspective of Policy Science Theory, E-government or Knowledge Government can be positioned as a new decision-making model of the policy system. And E-policy is an output of these policy system.

Part V and Part VI cover the theory of e-Policy. In Part V, e-Policy I, Policy Science of Information Society will be discussed. And the relationship between e-government and policy theory, and the logic of information policy[1)] will be reviewed.

In Part VI, e-Policy II, the particulars of the specific policy are discussed. E-Policy is classified according to the unit of governance, state(government), market(enterprise), and civil society(NGO). The efficiency, democracy, and reflexivity dimensions of e-Policy will be examined with the relevant policy cases. According to the specific policy cases, the related concepts, issues, and strategies will be reviewed.

Finally, the final chapter will wrap up the overall summaries and findings discussed in this book. The executive summary along with policy implications and recommendations will also be presented in this chapter.

---

1) In this book, information policy and e-policy will be used in an interchangible way. As e-government is an upgraded form of Management Information System, e-policy is an updated version of information policy. However, this book regards those difference as negligible and uses those two words as the similar meaning.

A final note. The prime motivation of writing this book is to present the theories and strategies of Korean e-Government model for the government officials and students of the *developing countries*. I would emphasize, repeatedly, many *developing countries*.

Korea was evaluated as the world best in the UN e-Government assessment of 2010, 2012 consecutively. Therefore, it is logical to consider that Korean model would be the most applicable model to the developing countries. One of the reason that the Korean model is really attractive for them, is because this country has developed its model up to the world best within a few decades, especially from the Korean War-torn ashes of 1953. The country, then receiving ODAs from the then advanced nations, now accomplished the world best model and become one of the OECD nation to offer the ODAs to many developing countries. Hence, the lessons from this country, who developed with her own will and strategy, would be more plausible and appropriate for other fellow developing countries who also ardently want to become upgrade to the world-best nations at this moment.

PART 1

THEORY & PRAXIS OF INFORMATION SOCIETY

In this 21 century we are witnessing the rapid and swift social change in a global scale. This movement is a fundamental change of civilization caused by the merging impacts of SMART technologies, Biotechnology, and new SNS media, called by the name of Megatrend, Age of Discontinuity, Power Shift, and Knowledge Society. Where are we standing on, to which direction we are facing? To understand the humane dimension of e-government, first, we should theoretically review the history of humanity and civilization, thereby explore and understand the modern contemporary waves of Smart Knowledge Revolution.

Chapter 1

INFORMATIN TECHNOLOGY AND CIVILIZATION

Technology is a double-bladed sword. On the one hand, it surely advances and giving happiness to the mankind, but it demands a cost and sacrifice on the other hand.

- Jacques Ellul

Objectives

The purpose of this chapter is to elucidate the relationship between information technology and civilization. This chapter focuses on information technology and civilization and gives light on the theoretical foundation of Information Society.

The issues of information technology and civilization can be divided into pre-civilization, the origin of civilization, the Dark Ages, the Industrial Revolution, and the Information Society. These historical stages of development are to be revisited to look for the main content of each part of human civilization, and learn its relationship with information technology.

First, it will discuss the pre-civilization era and look further into Earth's birth, biological understanding of human origins, and the Neolithic Revolutions.

Second, it will discuss the origin of civilization and look further into the settlement from ancient agricultural revolution, technological development and life settlement, and the development of letters and alphabets.

Third, it will discuss the Dark Age, a stagnant era of the Medieval age, and look further into the new movements of a new civilization and the industrial society.

Fourth, it will discuss the stage of Industrial Revolution, and look further into the breakthrough on science and technology that brought material affluence but with side-effects such as mental alienation and social dilemmas.

Fifth, it will discuss the period of Information Society, and look further into the transformation of the society due to the Information Revolution and their subsequent effects on the way of life and social well-being.

Pre-Civilization Era

Birth of the Earth

In the mid-20th century, for the first time in history, mankind had an opportunity to see the earth from the outer space. What they had observed from the space was that, 'the earth is at the center of the universe' is incorrect. This finding has deeper insight to the ideas of mankind than the Copernicus' discovery that the earth, not the sun, is circulating around the sun. The thought that the 'earth is the center of the universe' turned out to be only reflection of the human self ego-consciousness. Certainly, the habitat of humankind is like a small ball when seen from the cosmic space, only 1/12000 of the Sun, and 1/130 of the Jupiter (Choue, Young-Sik, 1997:30).

The origin and formation of the earth is still not known exactly. About 46 billion years ago, the solar system was created as a small part of the galaxy, and the earth, in turn, was created from a meteor of the sun. The slow formation of rock layers begun to create the current form of the earth (Cho, Uae-Seul, 1971:25).

Biological Understanding of Human Origins

About 46 billion years ago Earth was an extremely hot that did not allow any life form. Then, about 10 billion years ago, blue-green algae and similar organisms started to thrive. What is the background of the emergence of these organisms? In other words, how did life come into existence? To solve this problem, interesting speculations were attempted as well as ingenious experiments have been carried out. One of the most important milestones in the process of understanding the birth of life was the emergence of self-replicating RNA or ribonucleic acid (Steven Weinberg, 1996:91).

Initial raw material of life was created by the components in the Primordial atmosphere, methane, hydrogen, water, ammonia, and etc, being decomposed by

Ultraviolet rays from the Sun, Cosmic rays, discharge, and the heat energy created from the Meteorite fall, then these decomposed components fell into the ocean, and their interaction created nucleic acid and protein. The first living organism was simply a nucleic acid with a protein shell, a single cell such as primitive viruses (virus); this can be said to be in between living creatures and inanimate objects. The scientist explains that the emergence of human beings started with this primitive single cell which gone through a billion years of evolution and development.

For about 4.2 billion years since the earth was created, no life existed and this planet was full of desert and rocky mountains. In Paleozoic mid-age, 4～500 million years ago, a bony fish with a spine started to appear and these sea animals began to come up onto the land. This was the beginning of the land creatures. Then, plants started to thrive on lands which were followed by insects that ate those plants. Spiders which ate these insects emerged and later Amphibians. The first Amphibians appeared approximately 50 million years after plants emerged, which was speculated to have evolved from a lungfish with four legs and a lung to breath. It is told that the landing of these organisms was as big of an event as the birth of it.

About 60 million years ago, finally, Primates (Dryopithecinae) began to emerge, and human-like appearance animal started to appear in the Tertiary, in geological term, i.e. estimated to be about 3 million years ago (Steven Weinberg, 1996). The oldest fossil which is the first ape, close to human (Hominies-near men), was founded in 1964 in East Africa by British anthropologist L.S.B. Leakey, fossil of the Homo Habilis (Homo Habilis: man with ability).

About 1 million years ago, in mid-Pleistocene, repetitive Ice ages began; this was the time when the once extinct Dinosaurs and Giant animals were alive. The survival period of Homo (Pithecanthropos) found in Central Java in 1871 and Peking man (Sinanthropus Pekinensisin) found in China in 1923 is estimated to be about 500 to 600 thousand years ago, and Neanderthals (Homo Neanderthalensis), discovered in 1856 in the Upper Rhine, were reported to have lived approximately 100 to 150 thousand years ago. They had to survive through the much severe crust, climate, and natural calamity as well as fighting against the Giant animals. Although, they didn't have the power and speed of large animal, they were able to use their brain power to create tools and wisdom to overcome the adversities of Nature.

For a long period of time, according to the principle of the survival of the fittest, humans have genetically adapted and proliferated to this day (Choue, Young-Sik, 1996). Whether it is an organism or an animal, they adapt genetically; the naturally adapting properties of organisms, a Living Will (Gene) should be highly appreciated. Moreover, it is needless to say, the action of the human will and mental consciousness should be highly evaluated.

Neolithic Revolution

Homo sapiens called Cro-Magnons, appeared 43,000 years ago. They live in the caves, prominent and skilled hunters, toolmakers using woods and animal bones, used clothing made from animal skins, and are artists evidenced by the murals painted in the caves where they lived. Cro-Magnons started to live a life walking around the plains in a warmer climate; they have a larger cranial capacity having fairly low skulls than the Anthropus and Homo. The inventions that are attributable to Cro-Magnons, characterized by bones and antler tools, such as stone knives, stone axe, arrowhead, stone sickles are refined and developed by the fast-developing technology of Masonry. As a result, it was now possible to settle down with a better house and the authority and power structure became organized based on the collective society of tribal unity with the same blood and regional affinity.

These developments of transformational change, called 'Neolithic Revolution,' created the foundation of a new civilization. In nearly three million years, no remarkable changes have been recorded; nevertheless within 10,000 years, many historical changes have been occurred. Why this happens? Crane Brinton (1967:9) interpreted it as a 'accumulative movement' of human civilization: The broad sense of culture (including food, clothing, shelter, language, technology, ideas and traditions) are handed down from one generation to the next generation, some core elements of cultural foundation has reached a critical mass; until reaching a critical mass it happens little; but after reaching a crucial mass, the accumulative movement was possible. In this dialectical development of human history, in which coping with the natural calamities, humans were starting to become a critical conscious being having a better condition of their life.

Origin of Civilization: Ancient Agricultural Revolution

Humans first lived a sedentary lifestyle in the Neolithic Period. However, from 6000 years humankind started to abandon the primitive way of life and was able to introduce various technological developments, satisfaction of their own material needs, and established their own life.

The human being has various unique characteristics that animals don't have. It has the ability to stand erect in a standing position, walk on two legs and handle instruments.

This human attributes have shaped the civilization of humanity and has given them the ability to continue and create their own technology. From the invention of ancient tools made up from the stones during the Primitive age to the development of Agricultural technology, the human race was gradually brought closer to the new civilization.

Ancient civilization that occurred around 5,000 years ago in the four major river basins of India and China, and about 6,000 years ago in Egypt and Mesopotamia is a product of the stable development of agricultural technology and opened the foundation of the flourishing human intelligence. In particular, the discovery and development of ancient Alphabet and subsequent writing system have resulted in a major transformation of human civilization in terms of social and cultural settings and accordingly, it opened the door for the new civilized society. These kinds of development succeeded through the cultural civilization of China and India in the Oriental Hemisphere, and the civilization of Greece and Rome in the Western Hemisphere. In other words, the accumulation of the ancient creative cultural activities paved the way to lead a state governance system in the unfolding civilization of Middle Age.

Dark Ages in Medieval Period: Inner Struggle toward Reason and Knowledge

Medieval period was a dark age in a sense, very stagnant in terms of civilization. It was characterized of dominating Catholic power, not allowing any human rational activities such as printing or experimenting. If the religion considered it violated the will of God, the indicted people faced capital punishment on the street without any procedures of law; it was called as witch-hunting.

Nevertheless, in these constant wriggling of internal conflicts and struggles, it surprisingly hastens the preparation and foundation of a new civilized society.

In the 10th century, the revival of Commerce began in the Northern Italy. The commercial people lived and agglomerated in the city and formed a middle class instead of serf and lord life in order to focus on commercial activities. They calculated numbers and developed mathematics in the process of commercial transaction; it is understood as the foundation of scientific development of the 17th century.

The apparent consciousness of the citizens increased the desire for freedom and consequently demanded for the autonomy of the city. In the process of political conflict, they achieved a performance-oriented society that a talent, not blood, was the criterion to be successful.

People began to explore new values that took off Divinitas of the Middle Ages, and this indicated to signal that the Renaissance Age was gradually opened in which human being is a center of civilization based on the spirit of Humanitas. This means that people began to create a human-centered society in which the human personality and achievement, and human dignity was the supreme goal of social community.

Once established the foundation of civil cultural life, the infinite potentiality of humans was unfolding, and the Western civilization was flourished in the multi-dimensional directions.

First, the development of ship technology, compass, and map made it possible such as long-distance voyages; it also helped to develop the east and west routes. Batholomeo Diaz found the Cape of Good Hope; 10 years later Vasco DA Gama do approach to India. In 1492 Columbus landed on the island in Central America and the Dominican Republic. The expansion of scientific knowledge was also remarkable. Heliocentric theory that was claimed in the "Revolutions of the Heavenly Spheres" of Copernicus, published in 1543, has evolved greatly by Galileo and Kepler who studied the heavenly bodies with a telescope. In addition, the development of typography played a major role in order to spread new knowledge widely.

Humanism is directed to a human rational thinking and promotes scientific thinking of the Westerners. The 17th century can be gleaned as the era of "scientific revolution" because it produced prominent and known scientists Like Copernicus and Galileo. Moreover, as argued in the "Discourse on Method" of Descartes, the positivist method of scientific thinking that suspects everything and tries to find logical evidence, was displayed. Descartes argued, "people should suspect everything except to the fact that I suspect myself." In addition, the famous thinkers like Francis Bacon established the fundamental philosophical foundation of scientific development. Mentioning that "Knowledge is power," he argued that the scientific development based on knowledge is beneficial to the improvement of human life.

The scientists in this period adopted a new experimental method. By accepting the philosophy of Descartes and Galileo, they began to pursue the principle of logical positivism which denies the mere ideological notion but to investigate the empirical knowledge based on the scientific analysis. In particular, I. Newton, in "The Principle of the Universal Gravity"(*Principia* of 1687), by breaking the theory of the existing biological viewpoint of Aristotle and proposing the new theory of scientific paradigm, gave a tremendous impact on the thought of the Enlightenment philosophers in the 18th century.

Industrial Revolution: Material Affluence but Spiritual Poverty

The Western civilization against these backdrop of the 17th century entered into another transformational change once again, which is called the Industrial Revolution of the 18th century. With the scientific and technological innovation and economic wealth that has been accumulated in the society ever combined, it made a breakthrough to open a new civilization that called industrial society. The industrial revolution began to take place from the second half of the 18th century, rapidly changed the Western society.

The civilization of industrial society, which started from the Steam engine of James Watt in the UK by the mid-18th century, began to spread all over the world for more than 200 years. When the Steam engine applied to the weave, the revolution of the weave was realized; when it applied to the train, the revolution of land transportation was realized; when it applied to the ship, the revolution of naval transportation was realized. This was to promote fundamental social and economic revolution of the Western society.

To be replaced by a machine, the mass production and mass consumption was possible; the material affluence from the machine revolution cannot be compared with the previous society. Moreover, beyond the technical level, the production structure began to become established as a principle of the industrial society.

However, the development of industrial society has led to another problem. The modernization of industrial society means to dominate the nature with the power of humans and machine. The paradigm of social mass production means to exploit the limited natural resources in an uncontrolled way; to destroy the ecosystem of the earth; and to devastate nature through mass production of industrial wastes.

This indiscriminate expansion of the social structure and the expansion of the market led to the "Crisis of Control." The principle of competition and efficiency, and the division of labor and the bureaucratic paradigm to solve this crisis produces another side effects of the industrial society (Beniger, 1986). In other words, the bureaucracy, designed to control the efficiency of the production process, brought about the side effects of emerging the most-centralized bureaucratic organizations in a political areas, and of emerging the most-standardized bureaucratic employees in economic areas. As a result, human being became more atomized, de-humanized in which self-identity and self-autonomy has been disappeared.

Advent of Information Society: a New Civilization?

If we identify the source of Industrial Revolution from the Steam engine in the 18th century, the new energy source of Information Revolution comes from the Electromagnetic field at the end of the 19th century. If Industrial Revolution was intended to overcome the limitations of power and muscle of human body, Information Revolution is said to extend the capabilities of human intellectual brain.

Developing a fusion of optical fiber and digital technologies, information and broadcasting technologies, and satellite and mobile technologies, it began to develop the new Smart ICT Revolution at the end of 20th century.

At the moment the 21st century has been carried out for more than 10 years, no one doubts that the 21st century will be the century of information and knowledge revolution. The rate of development of the smart information technology is now being revolutionary enough; the impact on the social life of the people, is beyond our imagination. The combination of ICT and Smart Revolution with the various social network services created a new growth engine of national competitiveness.

The optimistic views like D. Bell and N. Negroponte argued that the digital revolution and the information technology, based on diversity and individuality, would overcome the paradigm of standardization and mass production of the industrial society. The wired network society advanced through the spread of digital technology will bring a better quality of life with increased leisure.

However, the critical theorist philosophers like H. Marcuse and J. Habermas predicted that the modern science and technology will constrain human being rather than liberation. The machine, science and technology, institutions and ideologies, created by the human collective intelligence, now constrains and dictates human being in a reverse way.

Would the digital revolution based on the new Smart information technology, be able to overcome the paradigm of material civilization of industrial society? Or, would it rather accelerate the phenomenon of human alienation?

To answer this question, a number of theorist and philosophers, provided a variety of theory and explanations about the paradigms of information society. As an effort to address some of these intriguing questions, in the following chapters, we will investigate the views and perspectives of the theorists of information society.

Key Point!

◎ Pre-Civilization Era

Birth of the Earth

- About 46 billion years ago, Earth was a deserted place without any life form. Then, about 10 billion years ago, blue-green algae and similar organisms started to thrive. What is the background of the emergence of these organisms? One of the most important milestones in the process of understanding the birth of life was the emergence of self-replicating RNA or ribonucleic acid.

Biological Understanding of Human Origins

- About 60 million years ago, finally Primates(Dryopithecinae) began to emerge, and human-like appearance animal started to appear in the Tertiary, in geological term, i.e. estimated to be about 3 million years ago.
- For a long period of time, according to the principle of the survival of the fittest, humans have genetically adapted and proliferated to this day.

Neolithic Revolution

- Homo Sapiens called Cro-Magnons, appeared 43,000 years ago. They lived in the caves, prominent and skilled hunters, toolmakers using woods and animal bones, used clothing made from animal skins, and were artists evidenced by the murals painted in the caves where they lived.
- These developments of transformational change, called 'Neolithic Revolution,' created the foundation of a new civilization. In nearly three million years, no remarkable changes have been recorded; nevertheless within 10,000 years, many historical changes have been occurred.

◎ Origin of Civilization: Ancient Agricultural Revolution

- From the invention of ancient tools made up from the stones during the primitive age to the development of agricultural technology, the human race was gradually brought closer to the new civilization.

- Ancient civilization that occurred around 5,000 years ago in the four major river basins of India and China, and about 6,000 years ago in Egypt and Mesopotamia is a product of the stable development of agricultural technology and opened the foundation of the flourishing human intelligence.

◎ Dark Ages in Medieval Period: Inner Struggle toward Reason and Knowledge

- Medieval period was a dark age in a sense, very stagnant in terms of civilization. However, in the constant wriggling of internal conflicts and struggles, it hastens the preparation and foundation of a new civilized society.

◎ Industrial Revolution: Material Affluence but Spiritual poverty

- Western civilization against these backdrop of the 17th century entered into another transformational change once again, which is called the Industrial Revolution of the 18th century. With the scientific and technological innovation and economic wealth that has been accumulated in the society ever combined, it made a breakthrough to open a new civilization that called industrial society. The industrial revolution began to take place from the second half of the 18th century, rapidly changed the Western society.

- The development of industrial society would stir up the phenomenon devastation of nature. This indiscriminate expansion of the social structure and the expansion of the market lead to the "Crisis of Control." The principle of competition and efficiency, and the division of labor and the bureaucratic paradigm to solve this crisis produces another side effects of the industrial society.

◎ The Advent of Information Society: a New Civilization?

- If we identify the source of Industrial Revolution from the Steam engine in the 18th century, the new energy source of Information Revolution comes from the Electromagnetic field at the end of the 19th century. If Industrial Revolution was intended to overcome the limitations of power and muscle of human body, Information Revolution is said to extend the capabilities of human intellectual brain.

■ Developing a fusion of optical fiber the computer chip technologies, new materials, a microprocessor of communication technology skills and the electromagnetic field of satellite, and digital that began to develop by leaps and bounds since the mid-20th century in particular, woken up Smart IT Revolution.

Key Question!

◎ In Pre-Civilization Era, we looked about Birth of the Earth, Biological Understanding of Human Origins, Neolithic Revolution. In Origin of Civilization, we looked about settled life through ancient agricultural revolution, the beginning of civilization through skills development and settled life and development of a character. Let's clean up for the main content of each.

◎ Medieval period was a very stagnant in terms of civilization. However, it hastens the preparation and foundation of a new civilized society. Let's clean up scientists and achievements in this era.

◎ The advent of the industrial revolution and the information society has brought material prosperity and improving the quality of life through due to scientific and technological innovation. But that has led to the threat of human survival and social exclusion phenomenon according to the degradation of the nature. Let's thinking about the positive and negative aspects of development of science and technology.

◎ Developing a fusion of optical fiber the computer chip technologies, new materials, a microprocessor of communication technology skills and the electromagnetic field of satellite, and digital that began to develop by leaps and bounds since the mid-20th century in particular, woken up Smart IT Revolution. Let's clean up about future prospects and problems according to the advent of the information society and the development of information technology.

Chapter 2

THEORETICAL PERSPECTIVES OF INFORMATION TECHNOLOGY

In this modern high-tech age, knowledge is separated from its philosophy. As a result, science of reflecting itself is rare, but there is only the science of moving its forward without any reflection.

- Albert Schweitzer

››› Objectives

The purpose of this chapter is to elucidate the theoretical perspectives of information technology. Traditional logical positivists think that science and ideology can be clearly distinguished such as science and religion, science and politics, and science and art do. They consider science as a means or tools to dominate or control human nature and believe that all scientific knowledge is a 'good thing' which can be utilized to benefit the entire human community.

However, there is a strong criticism to this approach. The critical theorists like Marcuse or Habermas argues that scientific knowledge is not neutral(cannot be seperated from an ideology) and knowledge itself is an ideology playing a role for the ruling classes. This line of thoughts corresponds to the philosophical discussions concerning a continuous tensional relationship between 'human' and 'science'. Theorists have discussed whether the scientific advancement let human beings free in its own inner space since Marx raised the matter of trust between 'science' and 'scientific ideology'. These philosophical discussions on 'human' and 'science' carried over to the Neo-Marxists.

Thus this chapter will take a theoretical review of human and science. It will consider Marx, J. D. Bernal as a Neo-Marxist, H. Marcuse and J. Habermas as the representative thinkers of Frankfurt school of criticism, and finally D. Bell and A. Toffler as major debaters of Information Society.

Marx's View of Technology

According to K. Marx, the technology means an extension of human capabilities and a starting point of society reform. Marx defined the production as the origin of human history; human history is the history of the productivity (means of labor, capital and instrument, and technologies) and production relations. He argued that technology affects the elements of productivity, and the change of elements leads to the change of production relations.

According to this perspective, the biggest impact on the form of social existence is the relations of the production, along with the tools and instruments of production. And the Stone Age, Bronze Age, Iron Age, and the progress of the agricultural, industrial and information revolutions are depending on the mode of production. Marx considered history as a process of transition from one economic era to another economic era, and in this progress, technology can transform the relations of production we have, and aggravate the contradictions between the capital class and the labor class. Furthermore, Marx believed that the changes in the relations of production could even affect a metaphysical condition of human consciousness. In short, technology has been one of the most important driving forces of the history development in Marxist's theory.

Marx criticizes the capitalist's scientific technology advancement combined with division of labor. In his ideal society, there was no division of labor and all human beings live their holistic life. He describes his utopia in 'German ideology,' stated as follows:

> Until now, in all forms of society, human is just a hunter, a fisherman, a shepherd, or a critic. In addition, human ought to be the one of them in order not to lose his means of livelihoods. But in a communist society, anyone does not have special exclusive field of activities. Universal production is controlled by the society. He could hunt in the Morning, fishing in the afternoon, and drive a flock of sheep in the evening; after dinner, he could have a time for discussion. He don't have to be a critique as a profession, hunter, fisherman or

shepherd, but if he wants, he can do all of them.

Marx put in his German ideology that slavery, feudal, and capitalism are three different forms of division of labor. By tolerating wage disparity and professional specialization, division of labor causes the gap between rich and poor and class conflict.

Bernal's View of Technology

J. D. Bernal is Marxist historians and reviewed science and technology from a slightly different angle. Bernal considers the nature of science to understand the impact of science and technology on the human history. According to him, the progress of science and technology is the product of the socio-economic needs.

Bernal maintains his position as opposed to Marx about the role of science and technology to human happiness. Marx criticized the role of science and technology combining with capitalism, specialization, and division of labor, whereas Bernal, that if science and technology could be used in a proper way, it could improve the standard of living of the entire human being.

If we recognize scientific research and its application made the improvement of mankind both physically and mentally, disturbing science development could be sinful. Reducing the cost of scientific research and education hampers development of science and causes tons of people went into poverty and deprivation without any reason. The lack of medical and agricultural research will insinuate illness, death and hunger (Bernal, 1985:13).

Hence, Bernal thought the ideal way of the use of science technology, not the maximal profits of multinational enterprises or military purpose, should be for the welfare of the public and the improvement in the living conditions. He focused his critical eye on science and technology in the structure of capitalist mode of production. In other words, the increase of productivity and the accumulation of wealth through the development of science in the capitalist countries would serve the interests of a particular group, nor increase living conditions of the population. Nowadays, in capitalist world the intensive scientific research and development is caused mainly by the motives of either high-tech defense industries or multilateral corporate profits. The time when the scientific development is from their personal achievement is virtually disappeared. Without the research support of large corporations or government agencies, scientific development is almost impossible in these days. Thus, according to him, depending on the capitalist society or socialist society, the results of the science and technology application could be differentiated. Eventually, Bernal also interprets the result of the science and technology from an ideological perspective.

Bernal's argument can be evaluated to point out and analyze the structural problems of the modern capitalist society and provide much civic awareness of our society. However, his claim could not cast insight into the essential of the science and technology itself. If science and technology developed for improving the welfare and living conditions of the people, would that be enough for civilized society? Many critical authors have casted this fundamental philosophical question. For these kinds of fundamental criticism, it needs to pay attention to the theory of Marcuse and Habermas of the Frankfurt School of Criticism.

Marcuse's Critique of Technical Rationality

'One Dimensional Man' of H. Marcuse, the Frankfurt School, in the criticism of science technology, is regarded as a representative writing criticizing the inherent problems of the science and technological progress in advanced society. Marcuse is a scholar, influenced immensely by the works of Hegel, Marx, and Freud; he nevertheless formulated his unique theory. Borrowing the thought of Hegel's dialectic law, he established his unique theory of dialectic movement of 'self-realization' and 'self-alienation.' 'Negation' and 'spirit of negation' is required for a complete fulfillment of self-realization in the process of dialectic tension of 'self-realization' and 'self-alienation.'

Marcuse argued that science and technology are ideologies. And, he criticized the opinion of Bernal that science and technology are tools of value-neutral production. He argued that science and technology are not value-neutral; but tools for the ruling class.

> Technical rationality itself is an ideology. The application of technology as well as the technology is already a tool for dominating nature and human. In other words, technology is a methodological, calculated, and calculating domination. A technology with the specific interest relationship is not 'accidental.' Rather, it is inherently embedded in the modern mechanism of production (Marcuse, 1968:223).

Science and technology, a result of technical rationality, contain ideological elements. The results of science and technology are used ideologically and furthermore it is an ideology itself. Advancement of science and technology can conceal the purpose of the ruling class and the limitation of capitalism; serve to the benefit of those who are taking advantage of it (Sin, Jung-Seop, 1992:302).

> The scientific method to control the nature provides an effective tool for human being to dominate other human being. Moreover, in the modern age, the controlling mechanism of dominating the nature and human is being perpetuated itself. And, technology gives the legitimacy to the political power which controls the entire human life (Marcuse, 1964:223).

Marcuse thought the meaning of 'technology neutrality' is already disappeared in the modern capitalist state, and technology is being used by political forces, under the name of 'technical rationality.' The ruling class of the advanced countries has been utilizing the development of science technology as a cause of the development of society as a whole. They also use the technical rationality to make the ordinary citizen believe their origin of the "happy consciousness" and creating a new 'conformism.'

Also, Marcuse analyzed the superficial prosperity of modern industrial society as the target of his criticism, and the possibility of radical social movements is diminished by the development of technology as the technological development is offering material abundance to the general public and workers to some extent. The ideology which would lead to the low-class struggle is disappearing and so is the spirit of 'negation.' As mentioned from D. Bell's "The End of ideology," in the highly industrialized society, the absence of the spirit of 'negation' is pointing to the problem of the 'one- or uni-dimensionality' of the modern 'mass.'

Marcuse's philosophy is also indicating the absence of spiritual philosophy in the modern age. With the spirit of the 'negation,' he claimed to regain the natural human life from the domination of ideology of the modern science and technology. Depriving the autonomous subjectivity of the human being, he advocated the spirits to adhere to the 'two-dimensional' tensions of the ideal and the reality.

Theory of Marcuse has been appreciated as the theory of criticism that pointed out unleashed development of science and technology in an advanced society. Nevertheless, he underestimated the positive contributions of science and technology such as overcoming the absolute poverty, the social benefits from the leisure, and so on, by weighing science and technology too much from the ideological standpoint.

Habermas's Legitimacy Crisis

J. Habermas also criticized the ideological attributes of Science and Technology and agreed with Marcuse's views that the modern science and technology is dominated by politics (government) and economic (corporate) interests in modern advanced society.

J. Habermas, nevertheless, criticized that Marcuse could not propose an alternative scheme about science and technology only by highlighting a pure 'negation' spirit. Habermas regarded the reality of the technological development of modernity as a process of institutionalization of ideology. If rationalization of technology is reinforced by the ruling power, the general public will be deprived of their opportunity to participate in a public debate, which will tend to diminish the area of 'public space.' This, a 'depoliticized' phenomenon, will lead to the situation of 'welfare' without liberty, which might be called a legitimacy crisis of modern society.

Theoretical and practical goal of J. Habermas's work was to establish a 'critical social theory,' pursuit of human emancipation. He asserted that science, even a certain aspect of the philosophy, cannot take the critical role to judge the value of "Social Vision and Dream" anymore and became fall to the slave of 'instrumental-rationality.' Thus, science and technology in the capitalist era is destroying the cultural life of human and do harm to the human existence and human fulfillment (John Dordrecht, 1996).

Instead, J. Habermas argued, science and technology, with the aid of civic awareness, should be served for restoration of public space by revitalizing network and communication disjointed and separated in this post-modern age. By doing so, he maintained, the civil society should realize the value of "Social Vision and Dream."

As seen from above, the criticism such as Habermas or Marcuse, under capitalism, emphasized that science does not lead the human to the ultimate 'inner freedom' because it, as an ideology, supports the interests of the ruling class. Therefore, we might need to pay attention to the critical theory which can help to constantly monitor with a civic awareness and critically participate in the modern e-Governance. The spirit of e-Government should also pay attention to these critical theories and strive for the restoration of public space to realize a genuinely democratic governance in the modern knowledge era.

Bell's Knowledge Society

D. Bell, in his legendary work, 'The End of Ideology,' it is meaningless to distinguish the capitalist society and socialist society because political ideology itself will demise. As the revolution of science and technology affects the mode of production, industrial society transforms into a post-industrial society. Bell described the concept of post-industrial society as follows:

> The term, feudal society, capitalist society, socialist society, is a series of conceptual scheme fitted to the Marxist framework of the mode of production. Pre-industrial society, industrial society, post-industrial society is a concept categorized from the mode of knowledge. By taking the axis of knowledge, the United States and the Soviet Union are, in fact, the similar industrial society (Daniel Bell, 1969:24).

Bell emphasized that the information and computer technology is the representative technology in the post-industrial society. As intellectual knowledge replaces the traditional mode of technology, he predicted that information society will be coming in which information and knowledge play a key role. In addition, this information society is predicted to be an efficient and economizing society that is structured by the principle of functional efficiency.

In this post-industrial society, theoretical knowledge or methods of decision-making relating with computer technology is critical. The capacity of knowledge accumulation in the development of science technology, the function of university and research center, will play a pivotal role for promoting its national competitiveness.

Toffler's Perspectives on the Flowing and Transient Technology

Toffler, in his first work, "Future Shock"(1970) depicted technology as the booster engine to mobilize the modern society, comparing the fuel to the knowledge. It gave a huge impact to the intellectual society at the time, as it was the first work to think that human can become shocked by the future. The concept "The Future Shock" created by Toffler immediately added in the "Dictionary of Modern Thought."

The central theme, discussed in his book, was that the speed of technical and social changes become accelerated in the future, it is really hard to be accustomed to the changes. It is expected that the relationship between human beings, humans and objects, human and organization, is going to be fluid in extraordinarily fast way.

> The people in the past and present tend to live relatively 'low transience' of life, and their relationships tend to persist for a long time. However, in the future people live in 'high transience' condition, that is, the short duration with an extremely fast transaction. Place, human, ideology and organizational structure are quickly 'consumed.' This compressed time will enormously enhance the complexity of the society that is constraining the ability to adapt to the future environment; and it will increase the risk of future shock (Alvin Toffler,

1989:60).

According to Toffler, the relationship between humans and things, a pattern of lifestyle, is like a paper cup, once used it and thrown away consecutively. The relationship between humans and place is going to be changed in a transient way, as people will not stay in one place in a permanent way.

The bureaucracy, the suitable organization for the mass production in the industrial age, is no longer proper for the changing society. Rather, an adhocracy is predicted to be suitable for fast decision-making or working style in the future society. As a result, it is meaningless to distinguish capitalism from socialist society, so does the ideology itself.

It has been passed over 40 years since Toffler's book published. As Toffler has predicted, from 1970s through the 90s our society, especially in the development of the computer, internet, or smart information technology has undergone drastic changes, also in the tremendous changes and still in the vortex of turbulent changes.

In a nutshell, Toffler's futuristic insights gave a huge impact to the society. It is criticized, nevertheless, that he mostly focused on the bright sides so that he might overlook the whole picture of information society. To understand information society in a fundamental way, we may need to critically explore the historical contexts as well as socio-economic structures derived from the development of science and technology. To figure out the implications of information technology in a systematic way, we may need to pay more attention to analyze the dynamic relationship among the various driving forces and elements of information society.

Summary and Conclusion

So far, we have reviewed the perspective of science and technology from the critical as well as positive viewpoints.

Science as seen from the epistemology can be distinguished from the relations of power. The epistemological position of the knowledge is independent of action of power. Power cannot actively participate in the acquisition of knowledge. In this regard, the logical positivists, viewing science as a value neutral and see the science separate from the work of power, are right to a certain extent. However, we cannot overlook the fact that the power or the capital maneuvers science and technology in a deeper ground in this modern capitalist society, as the critical theorists pointed out (Sin, Jung-Seop,

1992:309).

In modern society, it cannot be ignored that most of the important u-technology or Smart technology projects is carried out and controlled by the large conglomerate (Schiller, 1989). Smart industry such as Smart Phone, Tablet PC, and SMART TV integrating broadcast technology, imaging, and a portable media is quickly becoming a large-capitalized, and commercialized. It could be irresponsible or even hypocritical to assume the logical positivist's position and saying that science is a value neutral in a modern society.

If the modern information technology is serving for 'goal-oriented' for something, the goal should be derived from social consensus and carried out on the basis of the public agreements (Sin, Jung-Seop, 1992:310). Citizens have their own right to see and monitor the large scale ICT or e-Government projects and they should have their own rights to participate in their policy-making process in a transparent way.

What kinds of impact and consequences are occurred from the current Smart technologies or other large-scale IT projects? Are they consistent with the ideals of information society that the citizens are really aspiring for? How about mega-projects about genome or biotechnologies? Don't the results of such studies contain some social and ethical issues?

All members of human society need to know and has right to know these issues in a transparent manner as it could change our mode of human identity in a fundamental way. Information openness, privacy issues, and citizen participation are so crucial and critical. And the public officials in their decision making process should have open and humble attitudes than ever before. The role of e-Government is also important than ever before.

Now, in this regard, in the following chapters, let's discuss more about the essence and fundamental realities of information society. Those inquires include: What are the substances and what are the driving forces of information society?

Key Point!

◎ Marx's View of Technology

- According to K. Marx, the technology and human capabilities are a starting point of social transformation.
- According to K. Marx, the technology is a starting point of and human capabilities and social transformation. Marx defined the production as the origin of human history; human history is the history of relations of the production(means of labor, capital and instrument, and technologies). Technology affects the elements of production, the relations of the production, and eventually law and political ideologies of the society.

◎ Bernal's View of Technology

- J. D. Bernal is Marxist historians and reviewed science and technology from a slightly different angle. Bernal maintained his position as opposed to Marx about the role of science and technology to human happiness. He argued that if science and technology could be used in a proper way, it could improve the standard of living of the entire human being.

◎ Marcuse's Critique of Technical Rationality

- 'One Dimensional Man' of H. Marcuse, the Frankfurt School, in the criticism of science technology, is regarded as a representative writing criticizing the inherent problems of the science and technological progress in advanced society.
- Marcuse argued that science and technology is an ideology. He argued that science and technology is just a tool for the ruling class.

◎ Habermas's Legitimacy Crisis

- J. Habermas regarded the reality of the technological development of modernity as a process of institutionalization of ideology.

- If rationalization of technology is reinforced by the ruling power, the general public will be deprived of their opportunity to participate in a public debate, which will tend to diminish the area of public sphere and end in a 'depoliticized' phenomenon as a result. This will lead to the situation in which a 'welfare' without liberty, which might be called a legitimacy crisis of modern society.

◎ Bell's Knowledge Society

- Bell emphasized that the information and computer technology is the representative technology in the post-industrial society.
- In this post-industrial society, theoretical knowledge or methods of decision-making relating with computer technology will play a pivotal role for promoting its national competitiveness.

◎ Toffler's Perspectives on the Flowing and Transient Technology

- Toffler argued that the speed of technical and social changes become accelerated in the future; it is really hard to be accustomed to the changes.
- It is expected, Toffler maintained, that the relationship between human beings, humans and objects, human and organization, is going to become fluidified in an extraordinary way.

Key Question!

◎ This chapter is taking a theoretical review of Marx's and Neo-Marxists,' J. D. Bernal's, representative thinkers of the Frankfurt school of criticism, including H. Marcuse's and J. Habermas,' and the positivist theorists of Information Society, including D. Bell's and A. Toffler. Once again, let's clean up their claims.

◎ Let's organize our thoughts about the relationship with modern information technology and human based on the claims of many scholars for science and technology view's. Especially, let's try to think about what is needed for the e-Government to develop in the direction of promoting the benefit of the entire citizen.

Chapter 3

THE DRIVING FORCES OF INFORMATION SOCIETY

Being complexly interactive, maintaining its self-identity however, the issues of information society are intertwined interdependently. This is the reality, real substances of the information society.

Objectives

The purpose of this chapter is to explore the driving forces of information society.

Did the Information society come as a coincidence? Or was it comes from a systematic preparation of human consciousness?

The revolution of C&C (Computer and Communication) leads to a various types of Smart Revolution combined with Big Data, sensor/chips, RFID, Algorism, and Knowledge Government. Information technology has caused the revolutionary changes in P2P (person-to-person) relationship and even cultural lifestyle in the society.

Then, is the only information technology the main driving force of the information society? What about the social demand factor? This chapter, centering around these questions, will discuss the driving forces of the information society to derive its real implications.

Driving Forces of Information Society

When we discuss the driving forces of the Information society, there is an inescapable question coming arouse: supply or demand, which comes the first?

It is like a circular reasoning, which came the first, like the question of the chicken or the egg. Beniger(1986) stands in the view which consider social need more important than technology. He insisted that deployment of information society started from "necessity" of information, which was caused by social organization's changes from the end of 19th to the early 20th century. But, he explained, from the middle 20th century when computer and electronic engineering technology appeared, information technology has caused the new demand of social organizations. Thus, this problem in some extent is related to how we cover the range of time to be analyzed.

The advent of the Information society can be interpreted as a phenomenon of social-structural deployment based on human intelligence and technological innovation. It is rather a mutually complex process of technical factors and social conditions.

Technical Drivers

If the mechanical technology is a foundation of Industrial society, the base of the Information society is computer and communication technology. The information technology revolution started from the first signal burst at Bell Lab of AT&T Corporation in the late 1940'. As a group of this company invented the transistor, microprocessor, memory cell, and the integrated circuit which was the physical support of all information technologies. Then the memory of computer chip has tendency to increase twice every 18 months, as the Moore's law indicates (Seo, Sam-Young, 1996: 27-28).

The most important discovery was the digital technology which enables us to convert from all information of text, sound, graphic and mobile picture images to the form of digital numbers of one or zero. Once information is converted to digital number it can be inputted and stored in long bits, list of ones and zeros. Therefore it can be said that all information is comprised of interval bits regardless of its types or contents.

Though the atom, the smallest part of a particle or a material, is tiny it can be seen and touchable. But, the bits, the basic unit of information, comprised of ones and zeros, cannot be seen or touched. These two paradigms, the atom of industrial/material society and the bit of information/digital society, are sharply different in terms of delivering and distributing its information.

The best example is to compare the existing library and e-library. In the existing library if someone borrowed a book others cannot use it. But in e-library everyone can use the e-book at the same time with no limit. In addition, digital technology transmits information more clearly and accurately compared to the previous analogue style (Negroponte, 1995: 18-20).

Another innovation was the invention of fiber-optical cable and satellite communication. The telephone coaxial line has 64Kbps processing speed and cannot receive or transmit multimedia information including sounds, data and mobile videos. Invention of fiber-optical cable could provide a 1.7 billion bps processing speed which is equivalent to the same speed of 25 thousand telephone connections at the same time. And the development of Satellite communication makes the age of global village realized.

Other efforts of communication technology were the transmitting capability. Even without using fiber-optical cable, the transmission technologies are rapidly developing. One of them is the digital compression techniques, the other is technical improvement of transmission facilities; both of them made the existing transmission network more powerful and efficient.

Since the ENIAC (Electronic Numerical Integrator and Calculator) which is known to us the earliest modern electronic computer in the world appeared in 1946, the weight and price of Computer have been lower at least 1/10000. Even the first-tier experts in the world cannot predict the future of the computer or internet industry. Bill Gates himself, in his book, "The Road Ahead," confessed this reality. To show clearly width and size of the changes PC(Personnel Computer) has driven, frequently auto industry is cited as comparison target. If technical changes of the auto industry was as dramatic as PC industry, the cost per unit of Rolls-Royce, the epitome of a deluxe car, will be down at 2.75$ and the fuel efficiency per gasoline 1 liter will attain to 2 million km.

In conclusion, the information society was triggered by improvement of electronic technology, digital technology, high-speed communication network, development of compression technique, and the transmission of digital technology. The technical combination of e-technology of computer, associated with digital and high-speed transmission communication technology, made it possible the new information network society.

Social Demands

If the development of information technology played its role of supply aspect, the increase of social needs about information communication played a role of accelerating the progress of information society at the demand side.

As society has been increasingly industrialized and material affluence has satisfied people's basic needs, modern people have turned to satisfy more high-level desires like social needs or self-realization needs which lays beyond physiological needs.

People want to escape from flood of massive, monolithic information which was provided by mass media like television, radio etc. in industrialized society and they tend to choice more diverse information which they think more suit for their tastes. These kinds of social needs and demands have necessities the advent of new Smart media like Internet, Smart phones, Tablet PC, SMART TV and etc. which makes mutual, interactive communication possible.

In addition, in the choice of products they are demanding more individualized ones to satisfy their unique needs. The production mode of 'mass production/mass consumption' based on standardization could not possibly gratify their desires which was more diversified and more individualized; they need more 'customized production' suitable to their unique fashion and trend.

In brief, innovative revolution of information technology such as computer, digital, and transfer technology provided the basic driving power of the information society and the increasing desire of communications and new smart media of the individual members of the society played roles as a social factor that accelerated the formation of the more advanced information society.

The Essence of Information Society: Industrial Society vs. Information Society

Today, all over the world many countries willy-nilly are facing to the transition period of social changes entering into the information society. Although different styles with different logic from the society, it is commonly accepted that in the future deployment of information society is inevitable. However, there is still much debate and uncertain about what is the real essence of information society.

About the relation between the information society and industrial society, the theoretical perspectives are largely divided into three schools: Transformists, Continuists, and Structuralist.

The transformists are like D. Bell and A. Toffler who insist that information society is clearly distinguished from industrial society. While in industrial revolution age mechanical techniques enlarged the muscle of human, electronic techniques in information age, bring a quantum leap for the expansion of human intelligence. Furthermore, this perspective maintains that electronic techniques basically can change thoughts, creativity, innovation, brain power and eventually the human consciousness.

Otherwise, the continuists are like J. Schement and H. Schiller who insist that information society is not clearly distinguished from industrial society. Information technology, albeit with their physical appearances, is not fundamentally different from industrial technology (Simon, 1987; Giddens, 1989). Development of information technology is nothing but one case of changes of social techniques which is continuously developed in the capitalization process of human history and it is nothing more than pigment to expect the new revolution from information technology.

The third view, as a neutral position for the above-mentioned both perspectives. The structuralists insist that they acknowledge the innovative nature of information technology but it does not incur fundamental disconnection from the previous society in the social acceptance process. In other words, the function and effect of modern high information technology are innovative; however, they think it cannot bring the overall structural changes of our society as what the transformists argued (Jeon, Seok-Ho, 1995:32-34).

It is important to grasp the reality of a complex multi-layered structure of the information society. Characteristics and evaluation of the information society is bound to vary depending on the issue such as a structure of ego, identity, ethical & social structures, and cultural contexts. Even though in sectors like education, medical treatment, environment and culture, the social benefits that new media technologies bring to us are tremendous, we must not ignore the defects and flaws inherent in information society.

If we regard information society as the multi-layered structure, it is not appropriate to compare the industrial society and information society in a linear dimension. The core of information society is not just meaning of industrial structure or economic foundation. Rather, it is to be understood as social networking that information and network is playing an increasing role in all sectors of social relationship and civil life such as politics, economy, society, education, and culture. Being complexly interactive, maintaining its self-identity however, the issues of information society are intertwined interdependently. This is the reality, real substances of the information society.

The Paradigm of Information Society

Information society has following different natures from industrial society in terms of social efficiency, equity and ethical context.

Firstly, information society is the society in which temporal and spatial boundary disappear. As the central axis of production mode is moving from industry to information, time and space is meaningless. Integration of the new smart information technologies and social network services makes social organizations more intelligent.

Secondly, information society is the society in which industrial boundary disappear. Introduction and application of information techniques such as BPR(Business Process Reengineering) and e-Commerce has broken the boundaries of inter-sections, inter-organizations and inter-industries. Convergence phenomenon between visual media is now possible by digital technology and in developing nations the movement to institutionally support the convergence is rapidly proceeding.

Thirdly, Information society is an open society and competitive society. The information society enables free communication at the speed of light by global integration as well as locals and individuals. These mechanisms undermine a secretive society and/or closed society which has anachronous secrets, corruption, and authoritarianism. Informatization, however, has the possibility to accelerate elements of competitive society at the same time that will cause more problem of digital divide. Information gap between the countries will be expected to be more serious, and it will be one of the important issues of the international community.

Finally, information society is a society that raises ethical issues more seriously. And the severity or impact of these ethical problems will be more dangerous. Cyber terrorism, hacking, with the other cyber crimes will continuously threaten human peace.

Summary and Conclusion

The history is made with a blend of necessity and coincidence. The invention of personal computers came into existence because of the discovery of semiconductor chip microprocessor (or the so called MPU: Micro Processor Unit). These great creations have brought the internet and information society a topic in human civilization.

Microprocessor, the No. 1 supplier of Japanese electronic calculators was invented from the 'stresses' or Japanese economic hardships (Tomomi, 1994:28). In fact, Intel's '8080' that is denoted as the world's first PC microcomputer kit was introduced on April 1975. It was at this time that a full and operational PC era started.

Jacques Ellul, a Nobel Peace laureate, have pointed some important issues on technological innovations. First, while technological advancement provides immeasurable contribution for the society, there are compromises equated in it. Second, technical innovation essentially brings negative effects as well as positive effects. Third, all the technological advances also brings about problems associated with it (Ellul, 1962:394).

The new Smart technology is rapidly changing in every field of our social life; it includes the ways of government, business relations, and even our thinking patterns. Undergoing such a revolutionary change and/or a 'transition period' in our society requires wise choices and responding mechanism. The government as the main caretaker of the affairs of the state has to engage into strategic policy choices that will effectively address the issues of the emerging society. The information technology as a tool in the government has to be manifested through policy strategies. Hence, e-Government and e-Strategy has to be given emphasis. The ensuing discussion of this book focuses on these two aspects and how they are interconnected with each other.

Key Point!

◎ Driving Forces of Information Society

Technical Drivers

- The information society is triggered by improvement of electronic technology, digital technology, high-speed communication network, development of compression technique and the conversion of this technology.

Social Demands

- The increase of social needs about information communication played a role of accelerating the progress of information society.

◎ The Essence of Information Society: Industrial Society vs. Information Society

The relation between the information society and industrial society existing views of scholars are largely divided into three such as Continues, Transforms and Structuralist.

- Transformist: Information society clearly is distinguished from industrial society(D. Bell and A. Toffler)
- Continuist: Information society is not clearly distinguished from industrial society(J. Schement and H. Schiller).
- Structuralist: A neutral position for the above-mentioned both perspectives. The function and effect of modern high information technology are innovative; however, it cannot bring the overall structural changes of our society as the Transformists argued.

◎ The Paradigm of Information Society

- Information society is the society in which temporal and spatial boundary disappear.
- Information society is the society in which industrial boundary disappear.
- Information society is an open society and competitive society.
- Information society is a society that raises ethical issues more seriously.

Key Question!

◎ The driving forces of the information society can be divided into technological drivers and social demands. Let's explain the contents of each viewpoint.

◎ In the realities of the information society, we looked into Transformist, Continuist, Structuralist according to the relationship of information society and industrial society. Let's explain the contents of each viewpoint.

◎ In the paradigm of information society, we look into the relative social efficiency, equity and ethical contexts that information society especially has different natures from industrial society. Organizing for this contents and Let's think what some other features that can distinguish information society and industrial society.

Chapter 4

THEORETICAL VIEW OF INFORMATION TECHNOLOGY

The first rule of any technology used in a business is that automation applied to an efficient operation will magnify the efficiency.
The second is that automation applied to an inefficient operation will magnify the inefficiency.

- Bill Gates

Objectives

The 21st century is characterized by the advancement of information technology that has big effects in modern society. Information and communication technology (ICT) and social network services (SNS) tremendously broadens the scope of human intellectual capacity.

This chapter will explore the theoretical aspect of information technology in modern society. It will cover various perspectives from eminent scholars in the past to understand the context and development of information technology in modern society, including optimistic view, negative view and multi-dimensional view.

First, it will examine the optimistic view. Optimistic view argues that the development of information and communication technology will create improvement of productivity, advancement of people's welfare and cultural enrichment. Some of the great scholars that share the optimistic view are J. Martin, W. P. Dizard, A. Toffler, J. Naisbitt and N. Negroponte.

Second, it will also examine the negative view. Negative view see the development of information and communication technology will only accelerates human alienation more and more, because of the imbalance of social structure. Some of the great scholars that share Negative view are Jorge R. Schement, Smythe and Herbert I.Schiller.

Third, it will finally discuss the multidimensional view. This view emphasizes that there is a need for an analysis of the total social phenomenon besetting information society to compare with industrial society. Some of the major scholars that support multidimensional view are D. Bell, Masuda, and Benjamin J. Bates.

Optimistic View

Optimist's view of information technology in society believes that the development of information and communication network is capable of promoting international mutual understanding, peaceful human life and culturally rich society.

They emphasize the merits that the characteristics of information technology which is based on individuality and diversity will be able to overcome the paradigms of standardization and mass-production of industrial society. Furthermore, they insist that a highly wired society through the network of digital technology will promote people's quality of life.

Even at this time communication satellite is transmitting and receiving a great deal of information such as texts, images, and mobile broadcasting programs ranging from Seoul to Bangkok, from London to New York in a short period of time. The increasing demand of international data communications as well as international calls and also the realization of teleconference using high-capacity satellite leads to a more sophisticated and diversified information interactions.

The development of information and communication technology (ICT) has exceeded time and spatial limitations and it also hastened political, economic, social and cultural assimilation amongst countries. Such phenomenon is similar to the so-called the realization of "global village" which M. McLuhan (1964) has foreseen.

Another scholar, J. Martin (1977; 1981; 1984) pointed out that the spread of digital technology is the core element of a high network society. Furthermore, he argued that it will result in the improvement of the quality of life, and enhancement of leisure as well as reduction of time and cost.

In a more practical point of view, W. P. Dizard (1984) analyzed the political, economic and social impacts of information technology, and predicted that when it reaches a high network society, which is the complete phase of informatization, the access costs to information and services will almost be eliminated.

Toffler (1980) stated that new civilization made by information revolution, the third wave which follows after agricultural and industrial revolution, is based on highly scientific technologies. It will be new information civilization that overcomes the limits of industrial society such as standardization and mechanized processes. He also foresaw this high-network society will promote more understanding amongst countries and bring enhancement of human's welfare globally.

J. Naisbitt has proposed 10 mega-trends in the 21st century gateway in his book (Megatrends 2000). The main stream he proposed was the following:

a) From industrial society to information society
b) From hard technology to high-tech, high-touch technology
c) From centralization to decentralization
d) From parliamentary democracy to participatory democracy
e) From organizational dependency to network relationship
f) From the industries to rural & leisure life
g) From all or nothing to multiple-selection era

The argument proposed by Naisbitt (1990) as a new mainstream for the 21st century was more optimistic. He insisted that as we can witness the successful EU(European Union) unification case, global economy will be integrated, peace will be everlasting and economic growth will keep on going based on free-market competition. In addition, he also argued that information technology will contribute to the diverse aspects of people's artistic and cultural life.

Negroponte stated in his book, "Being Digital", predicted that a 'bit' in information society will replace 'atom' in industrial society, and pointed out the attributes of future society as decentralizing, globalizing, harmonizing and empowering. Negroponte insisted that the attributes of digital technology will influence accessibility and portability. It is important to note that his ground is based on the possibility of humanity and the importance of education using the Smart ICT devices. Such perspective is same point-of-view as Bill Gates (1996).

It is important that this futurological insight has enlightened transitional realization about new social changes are bringing to us. But these discussions were overly optimistic outlook of the whole phenomenon of information society and separated the problems of information technology from political and socio-cultural contexts. That is, the discussion was ruled out about the results of information which interlinked with cultural, social, political-structural contradictions, especially domestic and international imbalance and digital inequality that are inherent to our society.

Negative View

The pessimists raised a question on the argument that the paradigm of information technology in society is basically different from that of industrial society. They insist that information technology in society is a line of industrial capitalist paradigm which is based on efficiency and competition and will only accelerate human alienation by specialization and maximizing efficiency.

Posing the fundamental question that information technology in society really exists as a distinctive characteristic from the industrial society, Jorge R. Schement (1989) insisted that information society is another industrial society based on capitalism. Smythe (1985: 14), in particular, pointed out that information society are basically nothing more than flowery words for advanced countries to strengthen their national hegemony in the world political economy.

Also, the social benefit from the information society has been questioned by various groups of pessimists. They contended that there is a wide disparity of different countries in terms of economic and social conditions. In this noticeable gap of information technology, the information-forming process will go along disproportionately which may bring further problems such as 1) regional inequality of information resources; and 2) imbalance in international information distribution. In short, the pessimists argued that, since information technology is a political and cultural product, technological development will eventually bring the most benefits to advanced countries or to a few multinational or transnational corporations (Salvaggio, 1983; Schiller, 1981 & 1989; Smythe, 1985).

As a serious critic, Herbert I. Schiller also influentially criticized information technology in society in the context of socio-economic structure. Pointing the structural imbalance between countries and corporations, he insisted that under the current international political and economic unbalance system, ICT revolution is nothing more than a new type of ruling strategy to maintain the profits of the world ruling class.

He argued that in the corporate world, Multi National Corporations (MNCs) such as IBM, Chase-Manhattan, Citicorp, etc were pushing, if could not be called as stimulating, the establishment of global info-communications infrastructure in order to maintain international business network and maximize their corporate profits (Schiller, 1989:107~110).

Consequently, he emphasized that in this condition a critical thinking about information should start on how we correct or reform the structural contradictions inherent in information and communication system. He further argued that the imbalance and contradiction in present military, industrial and class structure have to be eliminated, and from only then, one can say that the new information technology will give much benefit to human beings.

Negative view has some valid points in the way that information society is not basically different from industrial society in industrial and class structure matter. Nonetheless, this negative view is overly disregarding the potential facet of information technology in society. If we follow their arguments on the new service sectors, all possiblc social benefits come from the new smart technology that associated with better education, medical service, environment and culture, will be excluded.

Multi-Dimensional Approach

Daniel Bell's multi-dimensional approach on post-industrial society aroused a lot of sensations. In his sensational book, 《The Coming of Post-Industrial Society》, he predicted that the new information technology will be the new impetus of post-industrial society. He also predicted this intellectual technology will replace the existing mechanical technology.

He adopted the approach of "axial principles and structures" which means that social change takes place according to the changes of the axial structures. He classified those three contents of the axial structures as:

a) Social structures pursuing maximizing efficiency of resources in economical and technological areas;

b) Political structures pursuing increasing democratic participation in political areas;
c) Cultural structures pursuing realizing self-realization and self-development in cultural areas.

The aforementioned principles and structures suggested that the post-industrial society has the following characteristics:

a) Creation of service economy
b) Emergence of specialized job and professional expert's class
c) Central role of theoretical knowledge as the imperatives of social innovation and policy making in society,
d) Possibility of future-oriented technological growth,
e) Creation of new intellectual technology, such as management science and system analysis in the organizational decision making.

In particular, putting emphasis on the importance of intellectual and information technology, he argued that the knowledge of information society is qualitatively different from any other societies. For example, 19th century represented by steam engine, steel manufacturing and auto industry. Key drivers leading the industrial society at the time was not systematic knowledge based on scientific principles or thoughts. The society was dependent on individual inventions such as a lamp, electric phonograph and projector by Thomas A Edison, generator by Siemens, phone by Alexander G Bell, and wireless radio by Marconi, etc.

On the other hand, Daniel Bell predicted that in the 20th century characterized by information industry or post industry, the core drivers leading the information society is a systematic invention, not individual invention, represented by the state or industrial research centers based on the theoretical knowledge such as quantum physics or molecular biology.

Therefore, one has to pay a special attention to the fact that after the mid 20th century scientific technological industry such as computer, genetic engineering, AI, robotic and bio industry is based on the firm foundation of theoretical sciences. That's why Bell's arguments are valid in many parts. He argued that in information society management sciences utilizing theoretical knowledge such as system analysis, decision methodology, linear programming, and probability theory are more important than the hardware information technologies such as computer itself or communication network. Its importantly indicates that the structure of theoretical knowledge is one of the most critical drivers of national competitiveness. In the other hand, national competitiveness also depends on the capacity of human capital and HRD issues in this modern smart age.

In a more analytical dimension, emphasizing necessity of multidimensional approach to analyze general social phenomenon of information society, Benjamin J. Bates (1984; 1988; 1989) argued that information society should be categorized by some of its own characteristics. He pointed out that the difference on social structure or diversity of value system among countries, the development of information society will be also different. In addition, casting a warning on a potential risk that computer and communication network fall into a new type of physical commercial capital, he emphasized that there is a need to analyze and study how citizens can cultivate their civic virtues and at the same time how citizens can freely access information to make a genuinely civilized information society.

Summary and Conclusion

Would information technology in society qualitatively different from the industrial society? Could the new paradigm of information technology help to overcome the defects of material civilization of the industrial society? And, what are the essential substances of the information technology in society? Various theories of information technology in society have been explained to answer those questions and proposed various theories and explanations.

The optimists suggested that the characteristics of information technology and digital revolution based on individuality and diversity could help overcome paradigms of standardization and materialism of industrial society.

Some scholars have raised questions about the paradigm of information technology in society whether it is really different from the industrial society. Suggesting a fundamental question about the essential substances of the information society, Jeorge R. Shement (1989) proposed that information technology in society is just another industrial society which is based on products of information and had the fundamental nature of capitalism and industrialization. A group of scholars like H. Schiller (1989) questioned about 'social benefits' which information society bring to us under the current existing capitalistic structures of inequality.

However, these critical theorists, by focusing on the socio-structural aspects they criticized, underestimated the potential social benefits driven by new information technologies. In other words, information technology in society has interaction with all components of society such as social organizations, company's production, consumer preferences and behavioral changes of people. Also, it has constantly aroused many social changes in human consciousness, better life, cultural diversity, modes of fashion, green city, health and life styles, and so on.

Therefore, the multidimensional approach is required to understand exactly the information technology in society. The reason being is that, information technology in society cannot be defined simply by the new information technology or its underlying industrial infrastructures. The perspective that the impact of social benefits will be fantastic or optimistic by technological determinism is nothing more than simple logic.

Similarly, we need to be careful about the perspective of the theory given to understand information technology in society only in the logic of classes or capitalistic economic structures. The reason is that the information society, as Bates (1984) aptly pointed out, is not only technical infrastructure, economic structure, or industrial organization. Rather, information society is a complex composition of multidimensional structures of life style, social relationships, social organization and management patterns, and even its spiritual or ideological elements.

Key Point!

◎ Theoretical View of Information Society

Optimistic View

- The optimists of information society believe that the development of information and communication network is capable of promoting international mutual understanding, peaceful human life, and culturally rich society.
- Optimists emphasize the merits that the characteristics of information technology which is based on individuality and diversity will be able to overcome the paradigms of standardization and mass production that accelerated human alienation in industrial society.

  - J. Martin(1977;1981;1984) pointed out that the spread of digital technology is the core element of highly wired society.
  - A. Toffler(1980) stated that new civilization made by information revolution, the third wave which is following after agricultural, industrial revolution, is based on highly scientific technologies and will be new information civilization that jumps the limits of natures of industrial society such as standardization and mechanized processes.
  - N. Negroponte is predicting that 'bit' in information society will replace 'atom' in industrial society, and pointed out the attributes of future society as decentralizing, globalizing, harmonizing and empowering.

Negative View

- The pessimists insist that information society is a line of industrial paradigm which is based on efficiency and competition and will accelerate human alienation by specialization and maximizing efficiency.

  - Jorge R. Schement(1989) is posing the fundamental question that information society really exists as a distinctive characteristic from the industrial society.
  - Herbert I. Schiller(1989) criticized information society in the context of socio-economic structure. Pointing the structural imbalance between countries and corporations, he insisted that under the current international political and economic unbalance system, ICT revolution is nothing more than a new type of ruling strategy to maintain the profits of the world ruling class.

Multi-Dimensional Approach

- D. Bell(1973;1989) emphasized information technology is represented by electronic computer as a new impetus of post-industrial society. Adopting the approach of "axial principles and structures," he classified the three contents of the axial principle as: (1) Social structures pursuing maximizing efficiency of resources in economical and technological areas; (2) Political systems pursuing increasing political participation in political areas; and (3) Cultural pattern pursuing realizing self-satisfaction and self-development in cultural areas.

Key Question!

◎ Let's organize the main arguments of scholars that have an optimistic view for the information society and think about what are the present evidence. Also, let's find the difference between scholar's arguments and thinking about the limitations of these claims.

◎ Let's organize the main arguments of scholars that have a negative view for the information society and think about what evidence and opinions they have about the limitations of these claims.

◎ Let's organize the main arguments of scholars that have an multi-dimensional approach for the information society and think about what evidence and opinions they have about the limitations of these claims.

PART 2

THE THEORY & PRAXIS OF GOVERNANCE

In Part II, the Theory and Strategy of Governance, we will review the linkage point between the theory of public administration and information society. Governance is very important framework to analyze the various aspects of information society. In this part, we will examine the governance models including new governance and cyber governance in order to strategically trace the historical development of the public administrative theory.

Chapter 5

PUBLIC ADMINISTRATION OF INFORMATION SOCIETY

Future Government is more than willing to discard the old way of business process and program repertoires. Imaginative and creative. Willing to take a risk-taking project. The innovative government says, " let's make it accomplished!" and "never afraid of dreaming a great vision".

- *"David Osborne & Ted Gaebler"*

>>> Objectives

The purpose of this chapter is to explain the public administrative theory in information society. It will trace the historical development of the administrative theory and derive the public administration theory in information society.

First, it will cover the historical patterns of administrative theory to identify the governance model that is relevant in information society.

Second, it will discuss the paradigms of the information society to derive the role of government that is appropriate for information society. Part two consist of two sections, the first section will discuss the knowledge society and the state governance, and the second section, will cover governance philosophy of the knowledge society.

Dialectic Trajectory of Administrative Theory

As the fate of the modern society, countries becoming more complex, the importance of governance began to be recognized more serious. To understand the concept of governance, we need to investigate the theory of modern public administration. The first modern article of public administration theory was, "The Study of Administration," written by W. Wilson of 1887. Since then, the theory of public administration has shown real dialectical progress.

> After Wilson defined the uniqueness of public administration from politics standpoint, in regard to understand the fundamental theme of public administration is always turn out to be the source of debate: Is it the matter of management or should it be approached differently as it is the domain of public area(so that public value or democratic governance is more important)?; Is it the matter of management or should it be approached differently as it is the domain of politics(so that political conflicts based on its power relations are more prominent)?

The dialectical progress and debate centering are elaborated on the following patterns:

First, there was a traditional approach of public administration. Scholars include W. Wilson himself who argued that public administration is unique different from the area of politics so that we should set up the unique principle of public adminstration as the theory of the modern public administration. Later on, L. Urwick and L. Gulick set up the seven principles of public administration as POSDCoRB, the selection of scientific principles that the modern government should follow as a priciple of public management. These line of thought is called, 'Politico-Administrative Dichotomy,' the traditional approach of public administration.

Second, is the challenge to dogma. If we call the traditional approach as a dogma, we term this as 'Politico-Administrative Uniformity.' Scholars include P. Appleby and F. Dimock. P. Appleby, the scholar and practitioner who had gone through the experience of the New Deal, wrote the book, 《Policy and Administration》(1945). He argued that public administration cannot be seperated from the area of politics. As to policy making, the political nature of government is something far more important than the scientific analysis of public administration.

The third pattern, is the establishment of administrative science. The prominent scholar in this era is H. Simon, the Nobel Laureate. He wrote the famous book, 《Administrative Behaviour》(1947). He confronted the traditional administrative theory, by saying that the priciples of public administration such as POSDCoRB was just a matter of 'proverb' which had not gone through a rigorous scientific empirical tests.

Based on logical positivism, to set up a genuine science of public administration, there is a need to seperate value from facts. This kind of approach is called 'Politico-Administrative New Dichotomy.'

The fourth pattern, is the challenge to the science of public administration. The prominent scholar, in this line of thought, is D. Waldo. The narrow mindedness of logical positivism resulted to solve the poor problems of the modern society. In the modern society government should deal with a diverse problems, naming a few, poverty issue, social welfare, racial discrimination, justice and human right, anti-corruption, traffic issue and urban planning. To deal with these all kind of social problems, public administration theory should face with the issue of value squarely. The issue of social equity, participation, proactive attitude of public officials are more important than staying at the laboratory to build up an empirical theory in a narrow sense. This line of thought is called 'New Public Administration.' This was developed in the late 1960s and early 1970s, when the scholars faced the vortex of turbulence, such as the defeat of Vietnam War, racial discrimination and human right issue, student demonstration, social welfare issues, and so on.

> The field of policy analysis and evaluation was also progressed at the time. Policy Science, proposed by the legendary scholar, H. Lasswell, from the famous article, "the policy orientation"(1951), also argued that, to solve social fundamental problems is the most important to achieve human dignity of our society; to do that, we need to move beyond a narrow-approach of logical positivism, we need a problem orientation based on contextuality and interdesciplinary approach. New Policy Scicne should be a theory based on a normative foundation, not avoiding the ethical issues, social equity, and value so that government search for an innovation and customer-focus along the line of NPM(New Public Management), and search for participation and trust along the line of PVM(Public Value Management) such as e-Governance or New Governance. The bottom line is to achieve a human dignity in our community, personal growth of every citizen and their self-realization should be guaranteed.

In the process of dialectical trajectory, the historical development of administrative theories has been structured(see Figures 5-1 for the summary). Also noticed along the development the role of environmental, exogenous schock was very critical. For example, The Great Depression and the New Deal was driving background force to develop the theory of 'Politico-administrative Uniformity.' The Social turbulence of the late 1960s centering on the defeats from the Vietnam War and racial issues was also the background to search for a new theory of public administration, called 'New Public Administration.'

My academic question, then, is what about the information revolutions? A new exogenous shock called revolutionary information technology, how will it affect the theory of public administration? The issues of how government should be restructured and what would be appropriate value of government facing these challenges of Smart IT environment, this should be a critical puzzle for the student of e-Governance. These are also the key issues of so-called e-Government and policy science. And these are one of the main themes addressed in this book.

Figure 5-1 Historical Patterns of the Public Administration Theory

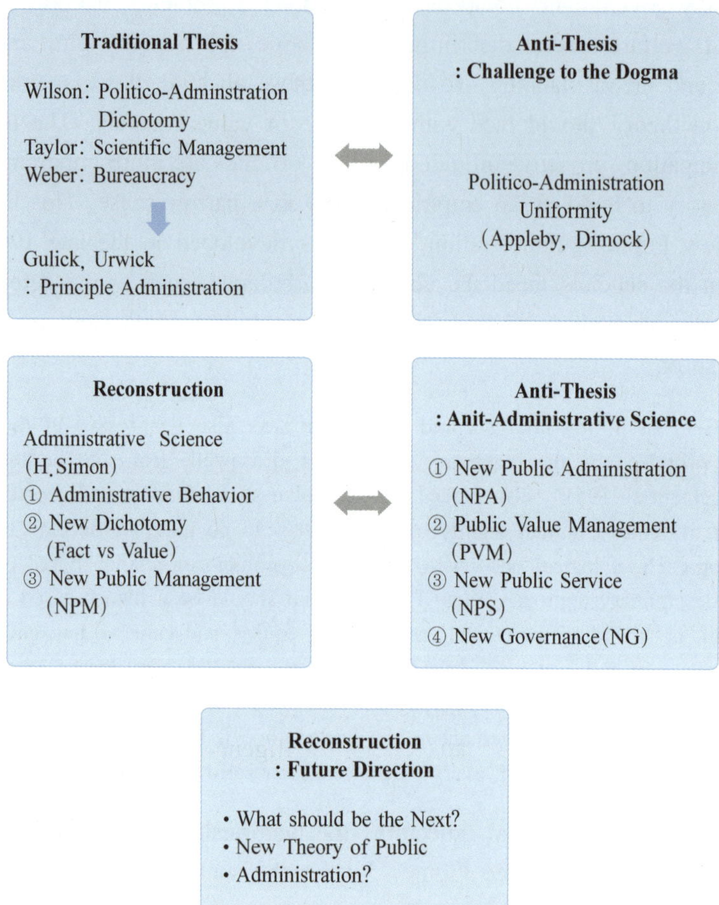

Governance Paradigm of Knowledge Society

Knowledge Society and the State Governance

The rapid development in Information communication technology, and social media, has achieved a wide area of the information space and it has increased even more the importance of knowledge as a nationlal resource. To understand the social implications of technological development, we should investigate its historical and social contexts, thereby we could derive the lessons of governance reform of the modern society. Three key socio-structral changes of information technology are as follows:

First, knowledge work based on mental capital, is the key driving force to run the knowledge-based society. Human beings, therefore, tend to engage more in mental work associated with the creation of information knowledge and they will search for self-actualization through the intelligent work.

Second, change in the principle of social organization. The organizing principle of industrial society is a bureaucratic, centralized, authoritarian, and uniformity. On the other hand, the principle of information society is a governance, decentralized, horizontal, and diversity. Information and knowledge society is the creativity of information and knowledge, which are the driving forces of the society. This kind of creativity will enhance the autonomy of human being which will lead to the evolution of human community itself.

Third is the change in the economic field. In the economic sector, the software industry will be more important than the hardward industry. Human service industry based on human being's intelligence or professional expertises, for example, education, HRD issues, health and medicial services, which serve to the diverse human needs, is much more critical and value-creation than manufacture-based industry.

The challenges relating from informational technology, on the other hand, are also tremendous. To name a few, they include information monopoly, information gap, international dependency problem, unemployment, human alienation, and the privacy issues.

The traditional organizational structure, such as bureaucracy has a limitation to solve these kinds of the modern problems as these problems need a quick decision-making and more network based problem solving among policy actors. Rather, a network based e-governance in which the free discussion among the related policy actors seems to be more plausible for this information society. It will enhance policy capacity of this modern knowledge-based society

Governance Philosophy of the Knowledge Society

The governance philosophy of the knowledge society, should be directed to the value-oriented humanism based on the value, such as democracy and justice, not just to the technical-oriented bureaucracy based on the narrow-minded efficiency. The key point is to enhance people's quality of life, a subjective autonomy of people's life.

For this end, government should be reformed to allow and enlarge the public space in which people can freely discuss the public agenda and social problems. This is not to say that efficiency is not important any more at this stage, but to say that myopic view of efficiency might often cause to the bigger problems. Government regulation and direct-control management is too risky in this modern age, because technological change is too fast in this modern knowledge-based society. Government failures to predict complicated market situations are huge. Therefore, in this high-tech age, government should closely consult with market(business) and civil society to solve the social problems. The role of government is evident from this kind of logic and thought:

> Government should show the bule print of social development based on not merely by the government officials but by the broad consensus of the people. Therefore, the e-government should aim for a more humanism-based governance which can share people's sadness and joy together under cause of democracy and justice. The core of humanism is to guarantee people's quality of life and that could be further strengthened from the free discussin in the public space in e-government.

More specifically, in the dimension of e-policy, the role of the e-government should be redefined as follows:

> The core spirit of e-policy is to achieve information democracy which allows free and open access and equal distribution(based on universal service) so that the problem of digital divide should be softened and alleviated.

In a nutshell, the roles of e-government can be summarized as: 1) government as Facilitator of Civic Spirit; 2) government as a Network Manager; 3) government as a New Builder of New Information Infrastructures; 4) government as a Social Change Manager.

Figure 5-2 **The Human-centered e-Policy Paradigm**

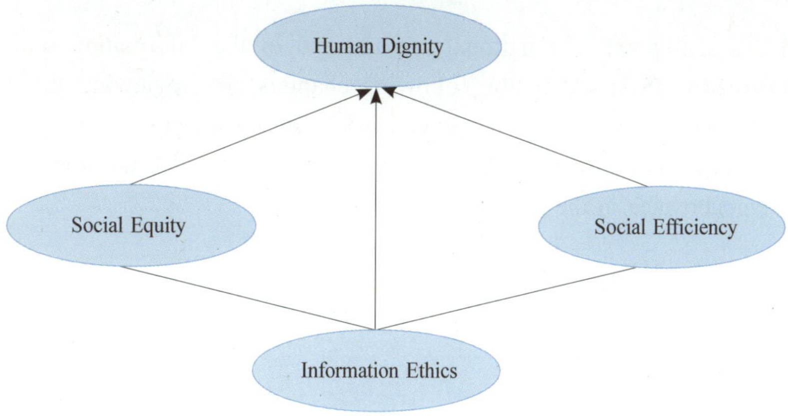

- ▶ *Procedure Equity*
  - ▷ *Open Access*
  - ▷ *Participation*
    - • *Information Education*
    - • *Democratic Procedures*
  - ▷ *Universal Service*
- ▶ *Substantial Equity*

- ▶ *Government Productivity*
  - ▷ *E-government*
  - ▷ *Knowledge Network (SNS, Smart Grid)*
- ▶ *Revitalizing Private Sector*
  - ▷ *Law & Deregulation*
  - ▷ *Minimizing Investment Risk & Uncertainty*

In other words, the proper roles of e-government are to promote democratic procedure and information education while enhancing social efficiency by not suffocating the vitality of the private sector; to solve the problem of human alienation and keep the important traditional values. Efficiency, democracy, and ethical values are the three key elements of e-policy(see the Figure 5-2).

Summary and Conclusions

Beyond the Industrial Age of the 20th century, a new chapter of the history of the information age of the 21st century has been unfolded. Industrial age based on mass-production and mass-consumption simply lowered the curtain, knowledge age with a smart information technology has been progressing.

Under the turbulent changes of rapid development of information technology, we are facing a new task of establishing the new paradigm of e-government. It is very crucial to build an e-governance system that could effectively implement humanistic ideal through promoting social communication in the public space and e-domain.

From this standpoint, the national management of the information society will be more specifically discussed in the following chapters. By reviewing the concepts of governance, new governance, cyber governance, we will examine the issue of how to integrate the governance theory with e-government, thereby redefining the new analytical model of e-governance in the knowledge society.

Key Point!

◎ Dialectic Trajectory of Administrative Theory

Historical Patterns of Development in Public Administration

▸ Traditional Approach of Public Administration

- W. Wilson argued that public administration is a uniquely different from the area of politics which calls for the setting up of unique principle of public administration as the theory of the modern public administration.
- L. Urwick and L. Gulick set up the seven principles of public administration as POSDCoRB.
- 'Politico-Administrative Dichotomy' was the traditional approach of public administration.

▸ The Challenge to Dogma

- P. Appleby and F. Dimock
- Politico-Administrative Uniformity
- Public administration cannot be separated from the area of politics.
- As to policy making, the political nature of government is something far more important than the scientific analysis of public administration.

▸ The Establishment of Administrative Science

- H. Simon, the Nobel Laureate
- Politico-Administrative New Dichotomy
- Based on logical positivism, to set up a genuine science of public administration, there is a need to separate value from facts.

▸ The Challenge to the Science of Public Administration

- D. Waldo
- New Public Administration
- Public administration theory should face the issue of value squarely. The issue of social equity, participation, proactive attitude of public officials are more important than staying at the laboratory to build up an empirical theory in a narrow sense. This line of thought is called 'New Public Administration.' This was developed in the late 1960s and early 1970s, when the scholars faced the vortex of turbulence,

such as the defeat of Vietnam War, racial discrimination and human right issue, student demonstration, social welfare issues, and so on.

◎ Governance Paradigm of Knowledge Society

Knowledge Society and the State Governance

- Knowledge work based on mental capital is the key driving force to run the knowledge-based society.
- The change in the principle of social organization. The organizing principle of industrial society is a bureaucratic, centralized, authoritarian, and uniformity. On the other hand, the principle of information society is a governance, decentralized, horizontal, and diversity.
- The change in the economic and manufacturing fields. In the economic sector, the software industry will be more important in an increasing way.

Governance Philosophy of the Knowledge Society

- The governance philosophy of the knowledge society should be directed to the value-oriented humanism based on the value such as democracy and justice, not just to the technical-oriented bureaucracy based on the just narrow-minded efficiency.
- The key point is to enhance people's quality of life, a subjective autonomy of people's life, that is to say human dignity.
- Human-centered e-Policy:
  - Social Equity: Procedure Equity(Open Access, Participation: Information Education & Democratic Procedures, Universal Service), Substantial Equity
  - Social Efficiency: Government Productivity(E-government, Knowledge Network(SNS, Smart Grid), Revitalizing Private Sector, Law & Deregulation, and Minimizing Investment Risk & Uncertainty.
  - Social Ethics

Roles of E-Government:

- Government as facilitator of Civic Spirit
- Government as a Network Manager
- Government as a New Builder of New Information Infrastructures
- Government as a Social Change Manager

Key Question!

◎ Arrange academic structure of Public Administration with the historical development patterns.

◎ Discuss a human-centered e-Policy model to realize humanism in information society.

◎ Discuss a human-centered governance model for the desirable future-oriented governance network for information society.

Chapter 6

GOVERNANCE MODEL OF INFORMATION SOCIETY

Smart IT revolution changes the meaning of power, pattern of management, and its governance system.

Objectives

The purpose of this chapter is to elucidate the governance model of information society. It will explore the various concepts of governance and discuss the relationship between the cyber-Governance and e-Government.

First, it will explore the concept of Governance, new governance, and cyber-Governance. It will further explore the multi-dimensionality of governance theory. It depends on the pattern of relationship among state (government), market (enterprise), and civil society (NGO).

Second, it will examine the concept of cyber governance model. It will further examine the role of e-government in its actualization of cyber-governance.

Third, it will discuss the governance model of information society. It will further discuss how the new Smart information technologies could change the governance of information society.

Governance, New Governance and Cyber Governance

The Concept of Governance

Governance is a new form of governing system emerged from the rapid progress of globalization and informatization. The government bureaucracy was the main governing model in industrialization era, but since 1990s, starting with the United States and the Britain, under the slogan of 'governance without government; smaller government and more governance,' each countries felt the need to redefine the relationship among state actors such as government, market, civil society in the progress of embarking to innovate the states and its public agencies. In the 1990s under the rapid progress of globalization and informatization, the many countries faced a sharp decrease of government's financial capacity, while the demands of public services were continuously increasing. Decreased governing capacity and increased governing demand were the backgrounds that caused the paradigms of governance (were) emerged.

Under these paradigms of governance model, government could not only solve the public problems in the society but also should provide public services with the cooperative partnership of market and civil sectors. In other words, the role and function of government is changing as the relationship among state (government), market (enterprise), and civil society (NGO) has been changed.

In the changing process, there has been a new spirit that resulted in the relationship between these three actors that should be more horizontal and network-oriented based on trust and cooperation, rather than vertical and top-down based command and control. These new type of governing models is comprehensively called as governance.

The Concept of New Governance and Cyber Governance

New Governance, called 'New management of state' or 'New governance of state,' has recently emerged with Governance, though it is not fundamentally different from the theory of Governance.

There are three types of governance: 1) the old state-oriented governance, 2) market-oriented NPM governance, 3) network-oriented new governance. The old state-oriented governance is the governance operated by the bureaucratic form of government; it is a top-down, hierarchical governance run by command and control of a few political elites. The market-oriented governance is the governance operated by the market mechanism or NPM (new public management); it is market-oriented managerial governance that emphasizes efficiency, effectivity, and competition of 'invisible hands.' While the network-oriented new governance is the governance operated by the network mechanism or PVM (public value model of governance); It is network-oriented, participatory, cooperative governance characterized by trust and cooperation between the public and private partnership. It, nevertheless, emphasizes a self-steering, self-formative, and self-organizing social civic network.

New Governance emphasizes trust and cooperation among the main actors of the society whether it is online based or offline based. e-Government or Cyber Governance is an online form of New Governance; utilizing the Internet based Cyberspace or the Mobile based Smart technologies.

E-Governance or Cyber-governance can be understood as a form of new governance. E-Governance or Cyber-governance (or Cybernance) is the core component of the new governance. Whether it is the old or new, it cannot escape the recent developments of smart information technologies in the governance under the modern society. It can be understood that the terminology being considered by "new" highlighted on the need for creating the new form of the governance model which is more suitable to the modern states of art or the Korean situation.

The Concept of Cyber-Governance

Cyber-governance is a form of governance formed in the virtual space, compared to that governance in reality. In other words, it is a new type of governance as if, in

Figure 6-1 The Concept of Cyber Governance

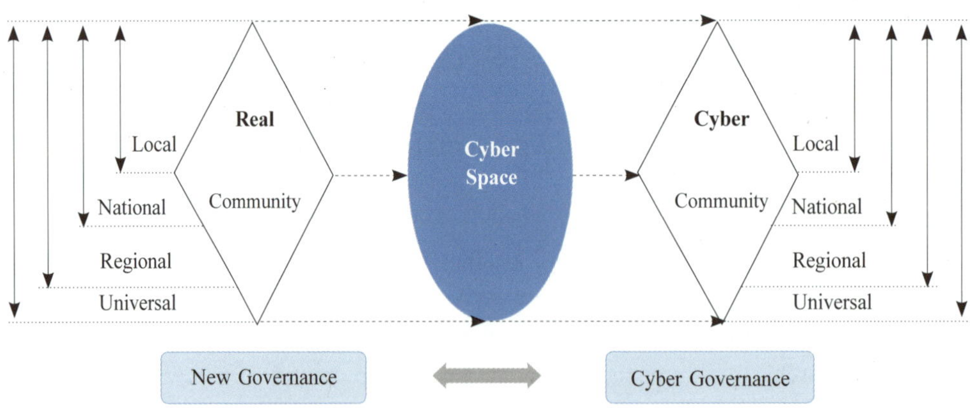

* Source: Revised from Kim, Suk-Joon et. al (2000: 278).

the opposite symmetrical world, reflecting level of governance in reality. As shown in 〈Figure 6-1〉, it is possible by connecting the virtual spaces as the thirds axis to world of governance consisted of second-dimension, with X-axis of policy issues and Y-axis of physical ranges which includes global, regional, national, and local ranges.

Multi-Dimensionality of Governance Theory

The Multi-dimensionality of Governance Concept

With respect to governance, the concept is variously interpreted depending on the characteristics of the individual academic fields and areas of interest. In the field of the Public Administration, it can be interpreted as a means of new national governing (Jung, Jeong-Gil, 2000: 433-546; Korean Association for Public Administration, 2000), and in the field of political science is seen as network governance, collaborative governance were defined as the way of governing cooperation between the plural subjects (Cho, Myung-Rae, 1999: 39), in the area of institutional economics, it is defined as autonomous system or institution of autonomy (E. Ostrom, 1990), and in the sociology, it is defined as the social adjustment patterns(Jessop, 1998: 31), or self-steering, self-formative, and self-organized networks (Rhodes, 1996).

Governance Concepts based on the Centrality of the State, Market and Civil Society

The concept of governance is defined differently from the standpoints of the operating system and its main actors, the state, market and civil society.

The governance theories, according to its principal actors, are classified as State-centered governance (State Governance), Market-oriented governance (Market Governance), Civil society-centered governance(Civil Society Governance or NGO governance), and Cyber-oriented governance (Cyber governance or E-governance).

Governance Network Model

1) Stand-alone Type

Stand-alone type is a governance system independent of each other; the state, market, and civil society are operating according to their own principles. The state is performing the governing activities based on bureaucracy and management; the market is operating in accordance with the principles of competition and market mechanism; and civil society is operating with the principles of democracy, participation, and civic community.

2) Alliance side-by-side type

Alliance type is more like governance style than the traditional hierarchical model. Although more merged and allied than the stand-alone type, State, market, and civil society is still sticking to their working principles.

3) Network Type

Network type is a connected, integrated governance system as a ONE entity sharing a common goal and value. While maintaining their autonomy based on their own operating mechanisms and principles, they organically connected as a unique ONE system to actively respond to the new world order or the external environment.

The Direction of the New Governance

National innovation means the comprehensive national reinvention redesigning the fundamental nature and relationship of government, civil society, and market (Kim, Suk-Joon et. al, 2000). It is important to establish the new framework of national governance with the principle of co-existence and co-prosperity of the three actors, while ensuring competition and cooperation within the system in a balanced way. It is also desirable to evolve and develop its system from its independent stand-alone type, through alliance type, and to the more integrated network type.

Cyber-Governance and E-Government

Cyber Governance Models: Concept and Significance

Cyber-governance is formed in the virtual community which is another form of governance, unlike the physical type of governance such as global, regional, national, and local governance. Virtual community is a community where a group of people exchange their ideas and visions through internet and computer networks (Rheingold, 1993).

Cyber-governance will and should contribute to the development of democracy by promoting active and transparent government, democratic values for citizens and

NGO, and efficient and fair market competition for business. And in the future, with an increasing role of the young generation in the state governance, the importance of e-government and virtual community, and cyber-governance will be hugely increased.

Cyber-Governance and E-Government: The Visionary Relationship and Its Strategy

Cyber-governance is a new form of governance with the rapid and widespread diffusion of Smart ICT and Internet devices. E-Government places as a focal mechanism of the Cyber-governance.

Governance theories, as mentioned, posed as an alternative governing mechanism which could overcome the limitations of the previous hierarchical-oriented bureaucratic model. It highlights a horizontal and cooperative relationship, based on trust and cooperation, among the three actors, government, market enterprises, and civil society. In other words, the basic idea of governance is trying to overcome the narrow mindedness of state convenience or bureaucratic-centrism and redefine the relationship between the state(government)-market(business enterprises)-civil society(NOGs) on a more democratic, balanced way. Therefore, the policy idea of governance are the democracy, transparency, accountability, and reflexivity, move beyond of the narrow interpretation of political control or market efficiency. The ideology of Cyber-governance, as it is a new form of governance, should be based on this network spirit of mutual trust and cooperation.

The vision of e-Government, in this regard, should be the one of democracy and reflexivity move beyond of internal inefficiency and productivity. E-Government is improving all the process of the administrative business process by utilizing smart information communication technologies. However, it should be more than that. E-Government should provide high quality services to citizens and realize the participatory democracy emphasizing citizen participation in the policy process. E-Government should also realize the trust and mature civic community by revitalizing the public space function of the smart ICT devices.

Successful realization of e-Government is depending on that what is highlighted between the vision and objectives which are ultimately pursued, and on how they are willing to improve the government. Thus, with endeavor of modifying the traditional role of government and to switch over the idea, it is essential that a new way of governance need to be explored that the two major crises of failures, i.e. government failure and market failure, can be overcome. In addition, dynamical relationship between the government and market, government and civil society must be reviewed and reestablished. That is the core spirit that the cyber-governance and e-government is aim to realize.

Information Society and Governance: Analytical Model

Information, Governance System, and Governance Outcomes

The advanced form of informatization or information society will be accomplished when the people's consciousness or mindset are ready to accept the information technologies, as the Technology Acceptance Model aptly indicated. Technological invention, innovation, diffusion, and acceptance are the process of informatization. The smart technological revolutions, cu1rrently, are acting as a powerful administrative environment and give a tremendous pressure to the existing governance system.

〈Figure 6-2〉 shows the relationship between information technology, governance model and governance outcomes. Information technology and innovation, as an exogenous variable, give impacts to the governance system. The governance system is composed of Political-Administrative Structures & Legal Framework, Policy Strategy & Government Organization Models, Strong Leadership & HRM/HRD (Human Resources Management/Human Resources Development), Budget Resources & Performance Management, and National Ideology & Organizational Culture.

Figure 6-2 Information Technology, Governance System and Governance Outcomes

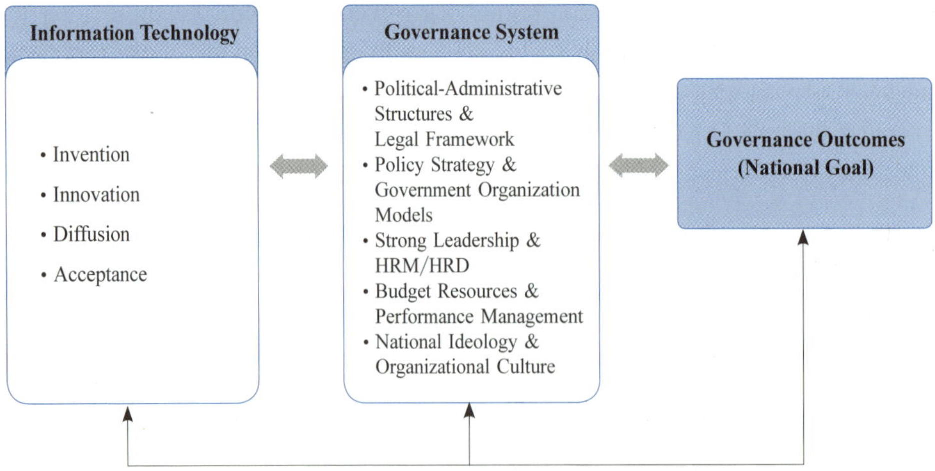

These governance factors act as a contextual variable affecting the governance outcomes. The effect of information technology is different to the different region and nation. It is because of the difference of contextual factors of the region. Especially, the Political-Administrative Structures & Legal Framework(Anglo-American Style vs. European-Continental Style), Policy Strategy & Government Organization Models(Bureaucracy, NPM, or Network Governance), Strong Leadership & HRM/HRD(Human Resources Management as Competent & Dedicated Human Resources), Budget Resources & Performance Management(Budget Resources Management as Fair & Effective Performance Management), National Ideology(National Spirit & Confidence), and Organizational Culture(Open & Sharing Culture) are the important components of the Governance system that serve as a mediating factors(Dutton and Blumer, 1989).

In short, governance management system surrounding the informatization or Smart information technologies can be identified as the process of a series of complex interaction among information technology, governance system and governance outcomes or the national goal. The national goal will be expressed similar to national competitiveness or people's quality of life which eventually leads to the "construction of civilized human-centered knowledge society." What we explore in this book is also trying to find out the best policy mix of e-Government that could achieve the goal of the best knowledge society under the premise that the Smart information technology can actively interact with the national governance system and its people.

Open System as a Governance Strategy

The striking development of information technologies forces government to open its governance model. 〈Figure 6-3〉 shows the Open System as a governance strategy. System is a set of elements organically connected by its sub-elements to effectively achieve the purpose of the system(Ahn, Mun-Seok, 1991). When governance is conceived as a living organism, it is interacting with its external as well as internal elements. Globalization and Informatization especially emerged as the new spirit of the times; the status of the government cannot help but has to be changed in accordance with the external world system.

The governance system reacting with its components, such as organizational structures and technologies, human and budgetary resources, and law and regulations. Especially leadership and policy strategies are considered as the most crucial independent variable affecting the performance of the governance system. With this in mind, in the following chapters, we will highlight the new types of governance system, including e-Government, knowledge Government, mobile Government, ubiquitous Government, or Smart

Government. These are the most important policy-making mechanism and are deemed as one of the most critical policy strategic instruments to achieve national goals such as national competitiveness and people's quality of life.

Figure 6–3 Governance as Open System

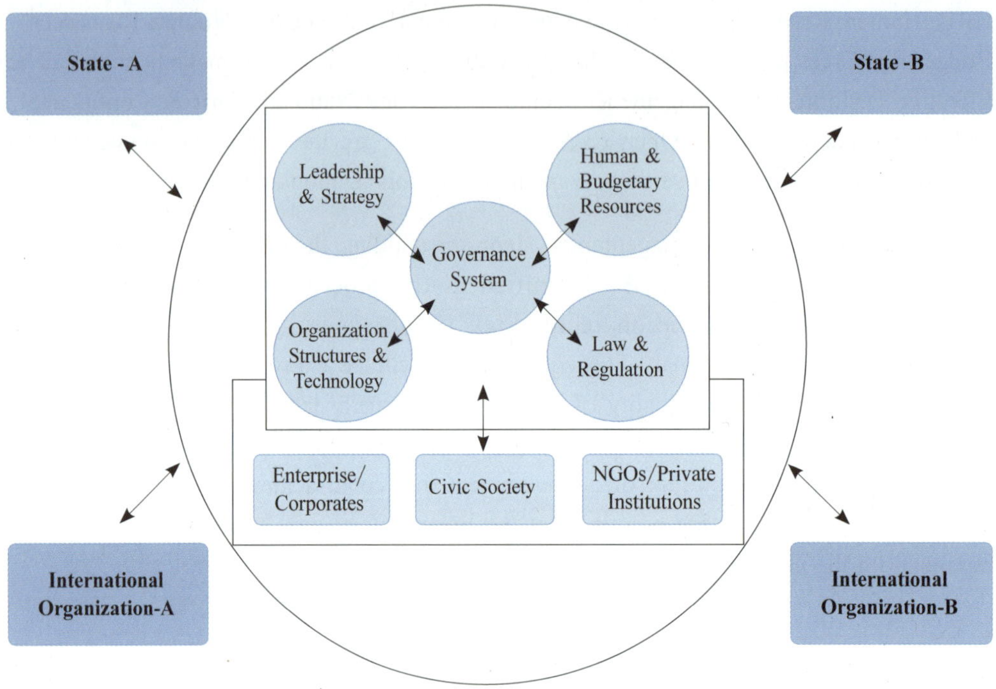

Key Point!

◎ Governance, New Governance and Cyber Governance

▸ Governance model reflects the spirit of the times where there is a harmonious relationship among the three actors of State(Government), markets(enterprise), and civil society (NGO).

▸ Governance is a new form of governing system emerged from the rapid progress of globalization and informatization.

▸ Under the slogan of 'governance without government; smaller government but effective governance,' each countries felt the need to redefine the relationship among state actors such as government, market, and civil society in the progress of embarking to innovate the states and its public agencies.

▸ Cyber-governance is a form of e-Government governance in the virtual space.

◎ Multi-Dimensionality of Governance Theory

▸ Governance Concepts based on the Centrality of the State, Market and Civil Society

- The governance theories, according to its principal actors, are classified as State-centered governance(State Governance), Market-oriented governance(Market Governance), Civil society-centered governance(Civil Society Governance or NGO governance), and Cyber-oriented governance(Cyber governance or E-governance).

▸ Governance Network Model

- Stand-alone Type
- Alliance or side-by-side type
- Network Type

◎ Cyber-governance and E-Government

▸ Cyber Governance Models: Concept and Significance

- Cyber-governance is formed in the virtual society which is another form of governance, unlike the physical type of governance such as global, regional, national, and local governance.
- Cyber governance will and should contribute to the development of democracy by promoting active and transparent government, democratic values for citizens and NGO, and efficient and fair market competition for business.

◎ Information Society and Governance: Analytical Model

▸ Information, Governance System, and Governance Outcomes

- Governance management system surrounding the informatization or Smart information technologies can be identified as the process of a series of complex interaction among information technology, governance system and governance outcomes or the national goal.
- Information technology and innovation, as an exogenous variable, give impacts to the governance system.

▸ Open System as a Governance Strategy

- System is a set of elements organically connected by its sub-elements to effectively achieve the purpose of the system. When governance is conceived as a living organism, it is interacting with its external as well as internal elements.

Key Question!

◎ What is the concept of governance?

◎ What is the concept of new governance?

◎ Governance theory is classified with reference to various entities, such as government-centered governance, civil society-centered governance, market-centered governance, NGO governance, Cyber-governance. Arrange various forms of governance models.

◎ Think about the relationship between Cyber-governance and e-Government.

◎ Discuss the effective governance model for the future-trend of information society.

PART 3

THEORY & STRATEGY OF E-GOVERNMENT

In Part III, Theory and Strategy of E-Government, the various aspects of e-Government theory will be explored.

First, the concept and vision of e-Government based the three dimensional approaches will be reviewed.

Second, the operational strategies of e-Government from the both sides, back-office as well as front-office, will be examined.

Third, the next generation model of e-Government by reviewing the theoretical relationship between e-Government and information technology, will be discussed.

National innovation system is a critical concept in knowledge society. It indicates the national knowledge governance system to upgrade the problem-solving intelligence by reorganizing and reconnecting knowledge and resources scattering all around the nation and by accelerating knowledge cycle of creation, accumulation, sharing, utilization and learning.

E-Government and Knowledge Government are the key institutional decision-making mechanism of National Innovation System. In PART III, we will first discuss the paradigm of E-Government. Knowledge Government will be discussed in the next PART.

Chapter 7

E-GOVERNMENT THEORY I: THE E-GOVERNMENT PARADIGM

E-Government must be able to realize a society that emphasizes humanity rather than technology, a life rather than a material, the goal rather than the means, and the process rather than the mere result.

Objectives

This chapter will focus on the discussion of the paradigm of e-Government. Generally, it will explore the foundational theories of e-Government and highlight its three important dimensions. It will also explore the important issues to consider in promoting e-Government in a more balanced approach.

First, it will highlight to give a holistic understanding of e-Government, different e-Government definitions and conceptualization of the previous scholars' approaches.

Second, it will highlight the three dimensions of e-Government (i.e., productivity, democracy and reflexivity).

Third, it will highlight the important issues to consider in promoting e-Government in a more balanced way. In specific, the three dimensions of e-Government exemplify distinct characteristics that need to be satisfied in order to achieve a successful e-Government framework. In the productivity dimension of e-Government, it will discuss the critical factors such as 1) Strong Leadership and Commitment, 2) Business Process Reengineering (BPR), 3) Linkage of Information Technology and Government Innovation, 4) The Mindset of

Information Sharing, and 5) The Linkage of Learning. Also, in the democracy dimension, it will discuss the critical factors of Policy Participation (e-Policy) and Political Participation (e-Politics). It will critically review two concepts of the Public Space that can be traced from H. Arendt's Republicanism and J. Habermas' Discursive Democracy Model. Lastly, in the reflexivity dimension, it will discuss the critical factors of Reflexive Policy as a means for realizing trustful and matured civic community.

Problem Definition

Since 1990s, there has been an increasing demand for government to innovate. The call for innovation was fueled by the continuous influence and growing capacity of private enterprises and the inefficiency of government to address the needs of the citizens. In addition, the government is required to help meet the diverse needs of the civil society and innovate to break the pattern of low efficiency and high expenditure. Citizen wants to directly participate on various decision making of their community and has been demanding the government to increase their governance capacity- building.

Looking into the evolution of public administration, the traditional bureaucratic paradigm could no longer addressing the tremendous demands of the stakeholders, thus resulted in the emergence of New Public Management or NPM. Basically, in NPM, it advanced numerous radical changes and transformation in public governance and management which curtailed the hierarchical layers of decision making and other cumbersome bureaucratic processes. The managerial and technological reforms in the NPM era highlighted the role of ICT in improving the overall performance of the public sector. This gargantuan goal of "reinventing government" requires a mechanism that is capable of delivering effective measures for meaningful reforms. Various scholars and practitioners in the field of public management have seen the consequential convergence (or we might put a term of 'marriage') of the NPM and e-Government values – e-Government as a means or tool while NPM as the concept and idea for reform. The emerging role of e-Government in the modern society continuously being carried out as the thrust of public governance is moving towards public value model or network governance.

The paradigm of e-Government needs to adapt with the inevitable waves of unexpected tweaks or environmental shifts in information society. E-Government is a new concept and means of directing customer satisfaction and citizen participation in the public domain of the government, thereby creating a trustful and matured civic community. To achieve this vision, e-Government should promote its internal productivity, democracy, and reflexivity.

However, in the existing literature, there are preconceived notions that building e-Government is focused primarily on internal productivity such as cutting expenditures and restructuring business processes. The fundamental vision and hope of e-Government such as increasing e-Democracy and e-Reflexivity appears to be the least priority, which is obviously inappropriate as we discuss later.

Thus, in this chapter we will critically review the concept and initiatives of e-Government including those inevitable conclusions. For this purpose, we will review the theoretical and practical background of e-Government, comprehensively considering the concept and ideas of e-Government based on domestic and foreign literature, and derive conceptual elements as the central focus for the promotion of the Smart e-Government.

Some Background Issues

The Environment around the Government

According to Lenk (1998), the environmental factors that necessitate the e-Government paradigm may be characterized as:

① Relative weakening of state power and increase of the need to cope with more complex and new problems.
② Reduction in the ability to influence the social relationships and policy instruments and increase of cost on public services provided by government intervention.
③ Nation's tax burden evasion, people's demand and increasing desire for participation in the decision-making process.

Here, we will discuss the environmental factors surrounding e-Government in three folds - internal, external, and technology.

1) Internal Environment: Inefficient Government Agencies

The efficiency of the government is far behind the level of the private sectors. While the private enterprises pursue the continued efficiency of the organization as a matter of survival, government agencies tend to disregard the importance of internal efficiency because they are not threatened of facing any risk face of bankruptcy. Government agencies do not have many incentives to cut costs because they operate the organization with the tax revenues which are always levied at a certain level anyway.

However, this story is no longer true. The inefficiency within the government has been increasingly challenged by the private sectors, especially civil societies and NGOs in particular. The development of internet and Smart SNS media like Twitter or Facebook fueled these challenges more effective. These kinds of challenges boosted the need searching for a new paradigm of government, which may be called e-Government.

2) External Environment: Interface between Government and People

Factors affecting the introduction of e-Government are more external than internal factors. Notable examples of these external stimuli are the needs of the customer satisfaction, the needs of the participation of civil society, and the rapid environmental change of international political economy. The notable environmental changes includes the rapid development of Internet, the growth of civil society, the heightened world trade competition as the introduction of WTO and the movement of New Liberalism.

3) Development of Information Technology

Rapid development of information technology and speed of knowledge economy does not allow the slow decision making of the traditional steep and hierarchical pyramid structure of bureaucracy. Quick response and fast decision making based on accurate information necessitated the development of e-Government based on Smart technologies.

Literature Review

Technical and social factors associated with the e-Government should be comprehensively studied in order to define the concept of e-Government. Particularly, we should consider the relevance and influence of these two factors in the implementation of e-Government.

1) Technological Determinism and Social Construction

(1) Technological Determinism

This theory argues that e-Government is largely a reflection of e-Technology and makes much importance of the technical aspects of e-Government. It puts theoretical emphasis on the digitization and network of e-Government that is based on information technology. But this descriptive definition has limits that cannot escape from the categories of technological determinism and involves defects that are reducing the concept of e-Government by limiting the discussion only to the aspects of information technology.

(2) Social Construction

This theory argues that e-Government is not just the result of e-Technology. The development of e-technology can cause many changes in the organization, but by itself can't transform social relations or management of the organization.

The new information technology can bring many changes in the administrative organization such as job, staffing, and organizational structure. Nevertheless, the relationship between the administrative organization and information technology is not a one-sided relationship that always brings change to the administrative organization.

Thus, this perspective claims that the concept of e-Government should be defined not just from the standpoint of information technology, but from the broader social management contexts, including the role of leadership and management.

2) The Origin of E-Government

The origin of e-Government can be traced from the policy efforts during the administration of President Clinton and Vice President Al Gore of the United States. Vice President Al Gore initiated the National Performance Review (NPR) in 1993 in order to implement President Clinton's commitment to improve public service as well as reduce the budget deficit.

The NPR analyzed the business processes of the federal government for half a year and focused on how the government should work, and not on what the government should do. These efforts soon led to the development of e-Government.

Al Gore's NPR for the federal government's reform adopted private management techniques such as TQM (Total Quality Management) and BPR (Business Process Reengineering). Also, the NPR suggested that citizens are to be regarded as customers and set the highest value on the customer satisfaction, and must pursue entrepreneurial government and new public management that are responsible for performance, rather than the adherence to the administrative rules and procedures. These TQM or BPR was accompanied by the widespread utilization of information technology and e-Government has emerged as a key means of government innovation.

3) Definition of E-Government

A practical and academic definition of e-Government is still not clear. Therefore, not to our surprise, e-Government is defined differently by scholars and practitioners.

(1) Jeong Chung-Sik: Highlighting Electronic Democracy Elements

Jeong, Chung-Sik (1997) defined e-Government as an innovative administrative model that redesigns administrative works using information technology, improve the quality of life by promoting public service, and realize the idea of democracy.

New result in his study was to be added 'e-Democracy' elements in the concept of e-Government. This concept of e-democracy is becoming more evident in the literature of foreign scholars. With the prominent development of information and communication technology that can interact with multiple users, the emergence of the new information society empowers directly the citizens, business enterprises, and politicians (Castells, 1996; Bangemann, 1994).

Loader (1998) proposed that the concept of e-Democracy means strengthening the creativity and participation of the citizens in the democratic process of civic community. He claimed that citizen should be treated as a subjective agent, not object possessing responsibility to express, deliberate, and participative in the civic issues in the society.

(2) Kim Kyung-Sub & Han Se-Eok: Intelligent Government

Kim Kyung-Sub and Han Se-Eok defined e-Government as an "intelligent government that is possible to work anywhere, anytime, through an enhanced process that is capable of overcoming obstacles of time and space. Also, it can handle all kinds of administrative processes by using information technology."

(3) Lee Yun-Sik: Enhancement of National Competitiveness

Lee Yun-Sik stated that, "e-Government is an innovation based on information and communications infrastructure in order to create and provide efficient and effective government services for the convenience of the general public." It means that e-Government should address the needs and demands of citizens by improving national competitiveness. Therefore, he argued that e-Government will strengthen government and national competitiveness as e-Government is the 1) Future-oriented government based on the information and communication technology, 2) Small and productive government, 3) Customer-oriented government, and 4) Open government that takes responsibility for the outcome.

Table 7-1 Typology of e-Government

Object / Content	Government (Internal)	Between Government Agencies	Government (External)
Business Process	Internal Affairs Computerized, Business Processing Efficiency (Personnel DB)	Business Processing Efficiency Among Many Related Inter-Agencies (National Comprehensive Land Computerization Network)	Civil Service Computerization, Civil Petitioner Satisfaction (Issuance of Passport Computerization Network)
Information Production	Policy DB, Support of Decision-Making (Policy DB of Diplomatic Activities)	Information Sharing, Policy Coordination Among Many Related Inter-Agencies (Policy DB of International Trade)	Open Government , Administrative Transparency, Increase of Right to Know, Collect of Public Opinion (Open Government Services)

(4) Kim Dong-Uk's Types of E-Government

Kim Dong-Uk (1996) defined e-Government as "government that works by putting citizen in the first priority with the use information technology and the network and digital information strategically and efficiently." He further argued that informatization of public administration is a process worthy to explore in order to realize e-Government's ideal. In this context, e-Government can be classified by the content and object. For the content, it can be divided by administrative business process and the production of information output; for the object, it can be divided by government (internal), between government agencies, and government (external). (See Table 7-1)

Kim divided the types of e-Government as business process and information production. The first thing means to increase productivity by reinventing business process, while the second thing highlights the flow of knowledge for better policy decision-making and transparent government. Kim's research emphasized that e-Government should improve efficiency in government through smart information technology and sharing information first, open information to the public, and then improve public services to the people.

(5) Summary and Discussion

E-Government does not only improve productivity but also enhance the quality of service delivered to the citizens. Although many scholars have different definitions about e-Government, e-Government in the information society is expected to provide public services responding to the changes of creative and customer oriented environment. Thus, e-Government should include four elements: (1) government innovation through information technology, (2) customer-oriented government through interface with the public, (3) implementation of e-Democracy, (4) and enhancing e-Reflexivity.

However, the previous literature, as noted, mainly highlighted the dimension of productivity and competitiveness, or the dimension of a customer-oriented government; while the aspects of democracy or reflexivity have been relatively neglected.

One of the key points of this book is to highlight the democracy and reflexivity dimensions of e-Government and the subsequent discussions will emphasize the three essential dimensions of e-Government: the issues of why they are important and how they could be accomplished.

The Three Dimensions of E-Government

The concept of e-Government can be summarized as: 1) productivity, 2) democracy, and 3) reflexivity dimensions. First of all, the first dimension of e-Government can be considered in terms of the government's internal productivity or efficiency. This is the dimension that involves the issues of government reform and innovation, thus enhancing productivity. This productivity dimension is composed of the following four sub-elements:

First, One-Stop, Non-Stop, and Any-Stop government. This is the government to maximize the convenience of the people. It builds a comprehensive administrative service system and settles civil complaints by batch-process through the joint use of inter-agency information. In other words, it makes it possible for people to handle various administrative civil petitions from a single window.

Second, Paperless & Buildingless government. It is characterized by the reduction of document through information technology, maximization of administrative efficiency through e-Approval, e-Policy DB, information opening, BPR (business process reengineering) and cost savings.

Third, Clean and Transparent government. This is the concept of clean & transparent government to root out corruption, and to establish a transparent policy process.

Fourth, Digital Nervous Knowledge government. This is the concept of government that supports scientific and systematic policy decision-making through a knowledge management system. This is the neutral network government to accelerate cycle of knowledge such as knowledge creation, accumulation, sharing, utilization and learning. Furthermore, this is the concept of government to strengthen policy decision-making capacity.

These four sub-elements (i.e., government to maximize people's convenience, paperless office, clean and transparent government, reinforcement of policy decision-making capability through digital nervous system of knowledge management) makes up the concept of e-Government that maximizes internal productivity within government.

However, the concept of e-Government does not simply mean to increase government's productivity. It is linked with democracy and reflexivity, the second and third dimensions of e-Government respectively.

Democracy dimension denotes that government has to realize e-Democracy. From the perspective of government external interface, it fundamentally means that the traditional relationship between government and people is democratically restored. Reflexivity dimension means a more philosophical viewpoint and has a close association with democracy. This highest dimension of e-Government enables our society to revitalize open and strong dialogue and public space to realize the trustful and matured civic community.

To summarize, the concept of e-Government falls into three categories: productivity, democracy and reflexivity.

1) The first dimension of e-Government is **PRODUCTIVITY** (i.e., maximization of efficiency within the government)

(1) One-stop, Non-stop, and Any-stop Government
(2) Paperless & Buildingless Government
(3) Clean and Transparent Government
(4) Digital Nervous Knowledge Government

2) The second dimension of e-Government is **DEMOCRACY** (i.e., the interface with external of government, revitalization of e-democracy)

(1) Policy Participation (e-Policy)

(2) Electronic Democracy (e-Politics)

3) The third dimension of e-Government is **REFLEXIVITY** (i.e., interface with external social community as the means to realize trustful and matured civic community)

(1) Human Dignity (at Individual Level)
(2) Trustful and Matured Community (at Community Level)

Key Elements to Promote E-Government

As discussed above, according to the three dimensions of e-Government, productivity, democracy, and reflexivity, the key elements to consider when promoting e-Government can be summarized as follows.

The First Dimension of e-Government: Productivity
Maximizing Internal Government Efficiency

Through the introduction of SMART information technology in the government, the traditional and out-dated procedures of doing government business were abrogated and replaced by technology-aided mechanisms. Though, maximizing information technology as a tool for increasing government efficiency cannot be accomplished only through the introduction of high-tech or state-of-the-art equipment. These SMART technologies should be used as a means to transform and simplify cumbersome government processes through administrative reforms such as BPR, standardization of work process, and information sharing and collaboration. However, these issues of administrative reforms are part and parcel of a more essential requisite in enhancing government efficiency which is strong leadership and commitment on e-Government.

1) Strong Leadership and Commitment

Strong leadership and commitment on e-Government is very important. In many cases of the developing countries, the weak implementation of e-Government comes from the lack of the strong and consistent leadership. As it will be discussed in Chapter 10 of this book, one of the successful factors of Korean e-Government was the strong leadership and commitment, a combined strategy of top-down and bottom-up approaches. Presidential committee (or sometimes Prime minister), with a high authority of political coordination, provided the clear policy blueprint and implemented it in a consistent manner.

2) Business Process Reengineering (BPR)

One of the key techniques to accomplish a successful e-Government is the adoption of Business Process Reengineering (BPR) which has its roots from the private sector practices. It simplifies unwieldy administrative processes and claims to be capable of reducing cost. However, the introduction of information technology in an organization that is embedded on traditional and classical administration practices (that is, without introducing change management techniques) can only infuse confusion and inefficiency. The detailed strategies of BPR will be discussed in Chapter 9 of this book.

3) Linkage of Information Technology and Government Innovation

Government innovation will not be accomplished only by the hardware-oriented infrastructure. It should be supported by the software-oriented management. And this management should include human elements like the education and training from e-HRD. The other management factors should be considered such as (1) document reduction and administrative cost reduction, (2) BPR using information technology, (3) the re-design of work process and business flow, and (4) increasing information sharing and collaboration based on the standardization of interagency work.

4) The Mindset of Information Sharing

The smart e-Government means open government that facilitates people's access to government information regardless of time and space. Therefore, the realization of e-Government must not simply depend on the technical aspect of administrative business processes, but on the inter-agency coordination and changes in civil servants' consciousness and mindset. Department sectionalism and authoritarian bureaucratic behaviors, the chronic problems of bureaucracy, make it difficult to realize open government which promotes information sharing and collaboration. Therefore, to have an effective e-Government, the strategies to change public officials' consciousness and mindset should be seriously considered. The detailed strategies of changing mindset will be discussed in Chapter 13 of this book.

5) The Linkage of Learning

Learning is a new form of labor in this knowledge society. Learning is the core of the productivity as it creates, share, and utilize knowledge. It makes competent organization by infusing the new knowledge and insights into the organization. E-Government should therefore encourage the learning activities of its organizational members from knowledge creation, accumulation, sharing, utilization, and diffusion.

The Second Dimension of E-Government (Democracy): E-Policy & E-Democracy

The basic premise of e-Government is network. Electronic network transcends time and space. It aims connections within the government and between the government and the people. Utilizing the establishment of e-Government and expanding the interface (contact points) of government and the people, the government should make efforts to realize a more democratic governance providing people more opportunities to participate in government's decision-making processes, thereby achieving a more transparent and accountable governance. For this purpose, we will discuss the two aspects of democracy: 1) policy participation, and 2) political participation.

1) Policy Participation: e-Policy

E-government has a lot of policy instruments to quickly respond to the needs of the people. To do this, e-Government should provide what the citizen wants based on the urgency and importance of policy. This means that e-Government should promote the e-Policies that reflect the needs of the people.

In the past, based on the centralized economic development or the authoritative top-down approach, the policy did not consider and reflect the needs of citizen. Government officials determined the needs of the people from the paternalist viewpoint of eliticism. People simply had to follow the instruction or the orders of the government.

This story no longer holds truth. If competition is being introduced in order to increase the efficiency of the public sector, people could turn their back to the public sector which is behind in the competition, and organizations could be even disappeared. People are not the passive objects only to react inactively to the government policies in this knowledge era. They are the owners of the democratic government. E-Government, by utilizing various platforms of websites, should encourage an active policy participation of citizen.

2) Political Participation: e-Democracy

The role of citizen is very important in e-Government. Citizen plays an important role in the realization of democratic form of governance, not government. Thorson(1998) identifies governance as the trustful network relationship between government and citizen.

In modern capitalist society, government-citizen relationships are characterized by wrong dissension between efficiency and participation. The market-oriented paradigm like the NPM (New Public Management) misinterpreted the fundamental nature of public services as the concept of the economic transactions or the market mechanism.

Policy making and the provision of public services was considered wrongly as a politico-administration dichotomy

The democratic citizenship and network relationship should be the central concept in the democratic governance of e-Government. The public space should be defined as "the space of democratic relationship to make decision for the common good rather than personal gain or private transactions" (Thorson, 1998).

(1) Two Concepts of the Public Space

(A) H. Arendt's Republicanism: Emphasis on Civic Virtue

H. Arendt looks for the original form of the public space from the ancient Greek city-states. Arendt argues that public space is the "the expression and exchange of the moral and political idea to the others." H. Arendt further argues that the public space has been reduced through narrow interpretation of the public space and expanding the concept of market mechanism; as a result, the economic and commercial issues gradually penetrate the public space. She expects information technology, e-Government in particular (if the author might add), to contribute to the recovery of public space in the modern age.

(B) J. Habermas's Discursive Democracy Model: Expanding Public Space

J. Habermas argues that conversation and participation should not be only limited to the political realm, but also extended to the social and cultural realm. He argues that the only way to ensure legitimacy in a democratic society cannot be achieved under the constraints on the technical neutrality or dichotomy of logical positivism, but through an active and open debate in the public space.

Thorson (1998) argues that Habermas model is the most appropriate in the information society. As J. Habermas said, "In a democratic society, democracy is achieved by the formation and development of the voluntary 'public space' among participants." 'Universal morality' and 'altruistic reciprocity' could be considered as the general principle of the information society. Ensuring open and equal access to ICT infrastructure should be another important principle as well. Ensuring openness and diversity of information contents should also be added.

Through this, e-Government should be able to overcome the passive government-citizen relationships of the past industrial society and develop the more trust and network based government-citizen governance relationship that is appropriate to the information society.

The Third Dimension of E-Government (Reflexivity): E-Government as a Means for Realizing Trustful & Matured Civic Community

As we have discussed above, there have been divergent views on the concepts of the 'public space.' However, these concepts altogether seem to remind a 'reflection' on the development trajectory that 'modernity' and 'modern information technology' have brought. Discussion of these concepts directly provides many lessons in the e-Government discourse.

Above all, there is a need to reflect on the fact that our society has been too much focused on the technological aspects and we are already accustomed to this pattern of thought. Superficial progress without deep reflection is not so desirable.

Before defining what the fundamental meaning of information technology is, if we give all the praises and expectations about information technology and its application, it would not be also advisable. Since modern times of the late 18th century, many enlightenment philosophers have dreamed of the realization of 'Social Vision & Dream' including liberty, equality, philanthropy, and peace (or, wisdom, liberty, and tranquility). Habermas argues the fundamental possibility of expanding social communication and the public space, emphasizing ongoing pursuit of Unfinished 'Modernity Project,' the then project of the enlightenment thinks like J. Rousseau and J. Locke.

These philosophical discussions will come to fruition of the realization of open society living personal freedom and identity, and the possibility of self-realization based on genuine trust among the members of the society. For the realization of such a society, e-Government should be deemed to be a 'government for reflexivity.' That is, e-Government should ensure participation of the citizens and the members of the organization with the use of smart information technology. Through this, it should be the citizen-oriented one that opens the real possibility of achieving Social Vision and Dream. By this process and efforts, e-Government should realize the 'open government' that encourages 'creativity' and 'self-realization' of individuals in our social community. These efforts require the government's sincere efforts and reflection attitudes.

The realization of e-Government needs to redefine the role of government and citizen. Such as the introduction of smart information technology in government, expansion of the interface with the public, and the realization of the e-Democracy should be given a clear role to play in this redefining process. It notifies that the relationships between government and society, and between government and citizen is changing. Under the current vortex of these changes, we need a 'careful change management'. This kind of change management based on reflection will play a role as 'antibiotics' to the diseases and maladies of the superficial high-tech, commercialism-oriented civilization of the modern times, the results of mechanical path dependency without any reflection of the fundamental thoughts. This way of fundamental reflection is required when discussing the paradigm of the genuinely civilized e-Government.

Summary and Conclusion

The core starting point of e-Government is to improve administrative efficiency through the introduction of information technology. However, discussion of e-Government simply does not only dwell on the technical characteristics but also other factors within and outside the government realms. We should not merely interpret 'e-' as the word 'electronic,' with a implication of technical system.

As our lifestyles continue to change with the introduction of smart information technology, the function and concept of e-government also be changed with the progress of e-technologies. The citizen-oriented e-Government and e-Democracy has been greatly expanding the inter-space between the government and citizen. With the introduction of Smart SNS and media, this kind of network society will be more enlarged, which can contribute to the civil participation in the democratic governance processes.

But we cannot easily predict as we are not so sure that ICT and e-Government paradigm would get over to the numerous pathologies that emerged from the industrial and capitalist society. More so, a serious reflection should be made constantly on e-Governance, especially on the relations among the key stakeholders, such as government, business, and civil society, in order to fully realize the new era of open, trustful, and matured e-Government. Thus, every citizen could realize wisdom, freedom, and tranquility in the process of their search for a self-esteem and self-realization in their pursuit of life journey.

Key Point!

◎ Exploratory Study on the Concepts of E-Government

- Background of e-Government: it is affected by the spatial concept of government's internal and external environment on the basis of information technology which promotes Government Innovation.

  - Government internal environment: inefficient government organizations
  - Government external environment: government faces the demands for strengthening the interface between the government and the people, and rapidly changing world environment.

- **Aspects in defining the concept of e-government**

  - Technology determinism: This is the theory that the serial development of technology lead to changes in the organizational structure, and these flow induces changes in business itself.
  - Social Construction: Although the development of technology can cause changes in the society, technology by itself cannot transform social relations and management.

- **Various definition of e-government**

  - All administrative processes are handled electronically by the use of information technology, overcoming the constraints in time and space independent on local to handles real-time business that is called intelligent government.
  - The government works focusing on residents effectively using information technology (network and digital information) strategically.
  - The government can provide public service that utilize common ICT-based as the medium for communication between people and government more easily and quickly, and networked with various administrative services provided in the most appropriate way anytime, anywhere.

◎ The Three Dimensions of E-Government

▸ Productivity: Maximize the efficiency of internal government

- One-stop, Non-stop, and Any-stop Government
- Paperless & Buildingless Government
- Clean and Transparent Government
- Digital Nervous Knowledge Government

▸ Democracy: Interface with the outside of government-the activation of e-democracy

- Policy Participation (e-Policy)
- Electronic Democracy (e-Politics)

▸ Reflexivity: Interface with the outside of e-government as a means of implementing a trust society and mature civil community

- Human Dignity (at Individual Level)
- Trustful and Matured Community (at Community Level)

◎ Key Elements to Promote E-Government

▸ The First Dimension of E-Government(Productivity): Maximizing Internal Government Efficiency

- Strong Leadership and Commitment
- Business Process Reengineering (BPR)
- Linkage of Information Technology and Government Innovation
- The Mindset of Information Sharing
- The Linkage of Learning

▸ The Second Dimension of E-Government(Democracy): E-Policy & E-Democracy

- Policy Participation: e-Policy
- Political Participation: e-Democracy

▸ The Third Dimension of E-Government(Reflexivity): E-Government as a Means for Realizing Trustful & Matured Civic Community

- Human Dignity (at Individual Level)
- Trustful and Matured Community (at Community Level)

Key Question!

◎ E-Government is affected by development of the information technology, internal and external environment of the government. Let's straight out the main content of each.

◎ For the definition of e-government, the two important perspectives are the technological determinism and social construction. What are the main contents of these?

◎ The concepts of e-government are differentiated from scholars. Figure out how they define them and discuss the concepts to define e-government.

◎ What are the three dimensions of e-government and what kinds of strategic policy should be considered to promote a successful e-government?

Chapter 8

THE THEORY OF E-GOVERNMENT II: THE VISION AND STRATEGY OF E-GOVERNMENT

E-Government aims to realize a customer-oriented,
Open government through smart information technology.

››› Objectives

The purpose of this chapter is to explain the vision and strategy of the "smart" e-Government. Smart e-Government means "the advanced e-government model in which people receive the most updated services utilizing the new smart ICT devices and interacts with each other regardless of time, space and device."

First, it will review the visions of Smart e-Government that includes: 1) Seamless: the seamless service linkage and integration within each government MDAs(Ministry, Department, and Agencies) so that seamless services are possible to the people, 2) Mobile: the mobile e-Government so that more convenient services are possible at anywhere, 3) Any time: the anytime services that are available to the people anytime, 4) Real time: the real time services that respond to people's demands quick in real time, 5) Collaboration: the collaborative and cooperative governance that gives win-win situation of the stakeholders. For example, win-win cooperation between large and small & medium enterprises, consideration to the less advantageous classes, and citizen participation and two-way communication with policy target group.

Second, it will review the four driving strategies of Smart e-Government, that is, "Open", "Integration", "Collaboration", and "Green e-Government."

The Vision of E-Government

The vision of e-Government, from the perspective of government innovation, should be: 1) Maximizing convenience of the people through One-Stop, Non-Stop, Any-Stop Government, 2) Minimizing paper documents as the Paperless & Buildingless Government indicates, 3) Non-corrupted and pellucid government as the Clean & Transparent Government implies, and 4) Sharing and learning knowledge by knowledge management system as the Digital Nervous Knowledge Government implies. These are shown in 〈Figure 8-1〉.

In this figure, big dots are the contact point between government and people where one- stop, non-stop, any-stop services takes place, while the connected lines between A-H are the digital neural network connecting the central governments and the local governments, showing the flow of information within the government neural network, Digital Nervous Knowledge Government.

At the point that the government meets people, One/Non/Any Stop government is realized. Such mechanism provides an unparalleled convenience for the people through filing of civil petitions and complaintes. Furthermore, the government agents should continuously endeavor to strengthen their policy knowledge and capacities through

Figure 8-1 Vision of E-Government

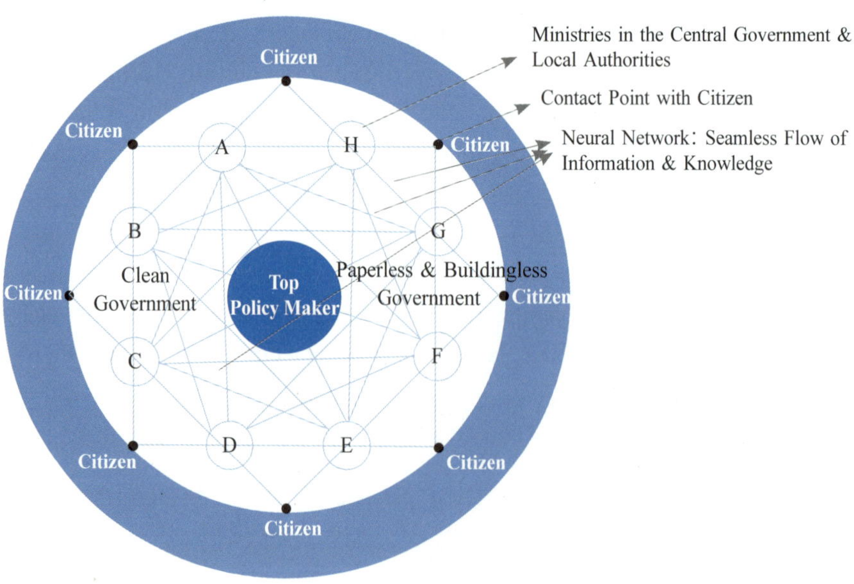

knowledge sharing and learning of the digital neural network system. Such government must totally eradicate red tape, move away from the snail-pace bureaucratic formalities, corruption free, and clean, transparent and accountable government.

① Shows the Contacts between Government and the People Happens - One.Non.Any Stop Government

② Ⓐ-Ⓗ Shows the Government Bodies enhancing the Government Productivity - Paperless & Buildingless Government

③ Connected Lines between Ⓐ-Ⓗ Shows Flow of Information within the Government Neural Network - Digital Nervous Government

④ All Subjects in a Circle and the Connector should be - Clean & Transparent Government

Vision and Strategies of Smart E-Government

Definition of Smart Government

Smart Government means "the advanced government that people use adapted service and interact with each other freely regardless of time, place and media". In Korea, after winning the world best award of the UN e-Government evaluation in 2010, the Ministry

Table 8-1 Comparison between the Previous E-Government and Smart E-Government

Item	Pattern	Previous E-Government (to 2010)	Smart e-Government (2011 and beyond)
People	Accessibility	Only PC	• Various Media (Smart phone, Tablet PC, Smart TV, etc.)
	Service Approach	• Standardized Service from Government Perspective	• Individualized Integration Service • People Develop Directly What They Want through an Open Government
	Civil Complaint Application	• Individual Application • Voluminous Submission even if Documents are the Same	• Batch Processing by only One Application(One Stop)
	Benefit Method	• People Apply Personally	• Government Identifies and Support the Qualification
Public Officials	Work Place	• Office (PC)	• Location is Irrelevant (Smart Work Center/Mobile Office)
	Working Method	• Recovery-oriented	• Proactive and Predictive

* Source: Revised from the Document, Ministry of Public Administration and Security(2011).

of Public Administration and Security announced "the operating diving strategies of Smart Government" for holding the first position of e-Government in the world and showing the global leadership in the field of e-Government.

The previous e-Government services were focusing on the administrative services based on internet. But new Smart Government policies reflect the rapid developing smart technologies including smart and mobile ICT environments. In other words, the smart e-Government services focus on providing various services anywhere and anytime to the people through mobile and ubiquitous network regardless of time, place, and devices.

Vision and Strategies of Smart Government

As discussed previously the four vision of e-Government were: 1) The government maximizing people's convenience, 2) Paperless & buildingless government, 3) Clean & transparent government, 4) Digital nervous knowledge government.

These items are developed to the vision of Smart Government by the evolution and diversification of the smart media. The fundamental principles are maintained but these principles have evolved into five visions which can apply to the various smart devices and mobile media.

- **S**eamless: Service linkage and integration among the various government MDAs
- **M**obile: Mobile e-Gov, convenient service at Anywhere
- **A**ny time: Available service that people want Anytime
- **R**eal time: Service reaction system that respond to people's demand in Real time
- **T**ogether: Win-win strategy to enterprises, consideration for a neglected class of people, advancement of service by people's participation and two-way communication

Smart Government's driving strategies are "Open", "Integration", "Collaboration", and "Green" (Ministry of Public Administration and Security, 2011)

First is "Open". By the "open" of a public information service, a public information and service must be opened to the private sector as well as the public sector in the various phases. Furthermore the main policies and services of government are opened to a public placidly for people's participation and activating communication.

Second is "Integration". The integration through demand-side, need-based service

Figure 8-2 Vision of Smart E-Government

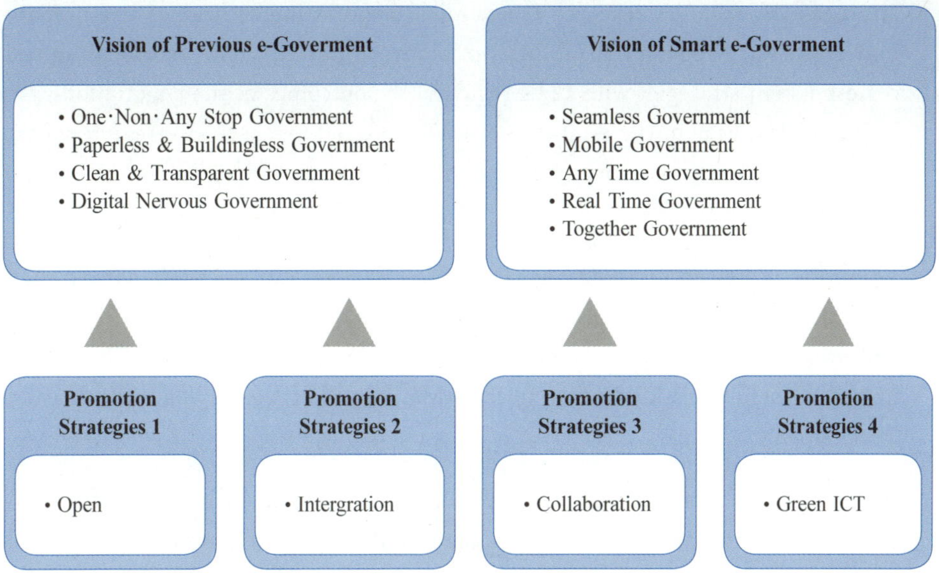

integration and multi-channel promotes to liaise and integrate the government's service/data and multi-channel like Smart phone, Tablet PC, Smart TV, etc. to provide the personalized integrated service to people.

Third is "Collaboration". The collaboration means a cooperation and information sharing between MDAs(Ministry, Department, and Agencies). For the realization of an advanced administration and customized services, interdepartmental cooperation and sharing system (technological level), and culture/system (policy level) must be established.

Fourth is "Green". The "green" means to construct eco-friendly and low-cost system to establish low-carbon green growth foundation in all social field of the nation by utilizing the smart ICT devices and Cloud-computing system.

1) Seamless Government

- Vision: The Seamless Government can provide an integrated service in a seamless way through connecting interdepartmental barrier-less network of MDAs.

K who is the secretary of the Ministry of Maritime Affairs and Fisheries (MOMAF) waiting a fisheries agreement with country C is very busy nowadays. He should check the strategies for the negotiation of C, establish the correspondent strategies of MOMAF, research the detailed negotiating technique and prepare materials. But K doesn't think his works are so difficult. For establishing the correspondent strategies with C, he reviewed the outcomes of the negotiation with country J last year in the e-Library of MOMAF. And he checked research papers about negotiating major strategies of C in the database of the Ministry of Foreign Affairs and Trade(MOFAT).

And then he accessed *the Knowledge Management System* (KMS) for detailed negotiating techniques. In this KMS, there are many research papers that colleagues had written in the meantime. Because MOMAF offers the incentives to officers who upload outstanding information in the KMS, lots of officers upload information competitively.

He used databases associated with the negotiation in the departmental information database and the National Statistical Office (NSO). Another theoretical content are obtained through the e-Library used by all government ministries jointly. As all works are possible over a network, K could work at his home without working all night at the office. On the day of negotiation, K isn't embarrassed at all. Because K could get the needed information through the internet by accessing the intranet of MOMAF.

(1) Knowledge Government

Smart government should be the knowledge government which is the core component of the creative knowledge-based nation in the 21st century. It is the government that accelerates knowledge cycle, from knowledge creation, accumulation, sharing, utilizing, and learning, through digital neutral network. This knowledge government will greatly enhance the policy-making capacities of the government.

To make knowledge government fully realized, there are some of the prerequisite elements: 1) The incentive system as it promotes knowledge creation and utilization; 2) The smart information technology as it should be the physical base of knowledge accumulation; 3) The organizational open culture as it really encourages knowledge sharing and learning within the organization.

(2) Knowledge Government and E-Government

Smart government should be the knowledge government that encourages the

Figure 8-3 Knowledge Government

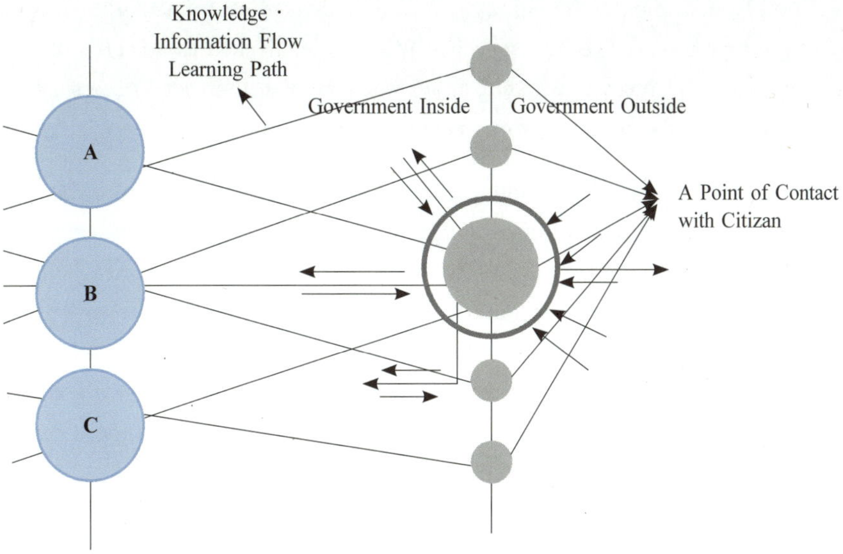

knowledge activities to promote the genuine productivity. Information technology alone, even though how smart it is, could not achieve government efficiency. HRD and management or learning issue should back up the e-Government system. These comprehensive paradigms, emphasizing not only information technology but the HRD and management factors, are called knowledge government. Knowledge government highlights the competent HRD issues and management factors like incentives to encourage knowledge creativity and learning, while the previous e-Government emphasizing only the information technology and information infrastructure.

The failure of learning leads to the policy failures. For example, in Korea, the inappropriate policy response to the foreign-exchange IMF crisis in 1998 was considered as a learning failure. E-Government should prevent this kind of learning failure if it is embedded with knowledge and learning capacities.

2) Mobile Government

- Vision: The Mobile Government can provide mobile service anytime and anywhere by introducing high-tech information technology like Smart mobile devices

One day morning with heavy snow, C who works at the Ministry of Patriots and Veterans Affairs (MPVA) decided to work at his home and mailed to his boss. 'Because of heavy snow, I cannot go to my office, so I would better work at home and finish it as soon as possible, I will help my son to do his vacation homework. He opened his laptop and accessed central server of MPVA. He checked the records of career, number, degree of injury in war, etc. about war veterans, then set a necessary social welfare budget and pay wages through electronic banking.

In the past, it took a long time to check documents because it was paper and if he made some mistakes, a lot of complains were expressed and to solve this, he had to check these documents out again. But now, because all documents are digitalized, he can deal with lots of information with less time and efforts and can work at home through internet. He can work at home with a coffee on rainy (snowy) day. When the meeting was hold, the skype conference using mobile or smart work center is used. The building less government is already becoming more and more common among all branches of the government.

(1) Smart Network of Policy-Making Process

Smart government should construct the comprehensive policy-making network to integrate the separated and disjointed public information. By integrating all MDAs (Ministries, Departments, and Agencies) information into a single comprehensive KMS (Knowledge Management System) system, the effective cycling of the information and knowledge will be realized.

(2) Learning Government

Smart government should be the learning government because learning is the key to solve the problems in the organization. Learning enables to forecast dynamic environment thereby adapting to the upcoming turbulent environment. In the 21st century, digital is characterized as time, speed and uncertainty. Because the policy environment is change rapidly and unsurely, the stereotyped policy approaches cannot solve the organizational problems. The smart government should play a leading role to enhance the learning capacities of the organizational members, thereby setting the example to give the direction and support the private sector.

(3) Knowledge Sharing

Smart government should encourage knowledge sharing and collaboration as these activities are the core foundation for the smart policy decision making. If government agents could use public information jointly with each other, they can collect and produce the key information that is helpful to the intelligent policy-making with less staff and budget. By using the policy information jointly, one department can use the information that other departments have collected and stored. In this way, government inefficiencies will be removed. Therefore, the central government agencies should make valuable public information as a government DB and should store as the government information integrated system.

3) Any Time Government

- Vision: Any Time Government can maximize the customer happiness beyond satisfaction by providing service to the people at any time

> A who live in Seoul had a lovely daughter in August. A had to stay in the hospital for a few days because of her health problem, but she also had to register her daughter's birth office. She couldn't walk to the office from the heat, and her husband worked all day long (he went to work before the office is open and leave work after the office is close). But that was not a problem for her at all in the anytime e-Government. The computerization system was connected with the server of the Ministry of Security and Public Administration and the birth registration was already completed as soon as her daughter was born. Besides, the congratulatory card of her birth arrived next day. A experienced the 'customer happiness' or 'customer impression' service, beyond 'customer satisfaction.'

Smart People can connect government networks easily through the internet and therefore the productivity of the government will be greatly enhanced. Also, improving the accessibility to the public service through network promotes regional development and national competitiveness. Because of realization of One/Non/Any Stop Service, the immediate process of civil complaint and customer impression are possible by the improvement of administrative business process in the government.

(1) Government Innovation Using Digitalization

Smart government should digitalize government document, the fundamental foundation for realization of smart e-Government. The digitalization of documents leads to facilitate writing, storage, search and sharing. So it is very helpful to reduce the cost and improve governance productivities. The governance system should be reformed by using smart information technology like electronic approval, EDMS(electronic documents management system), electronic DB, and TQM & BPR. Therefore, e-Government

Figure 8-4 E-Government with Citizen Satisfaction

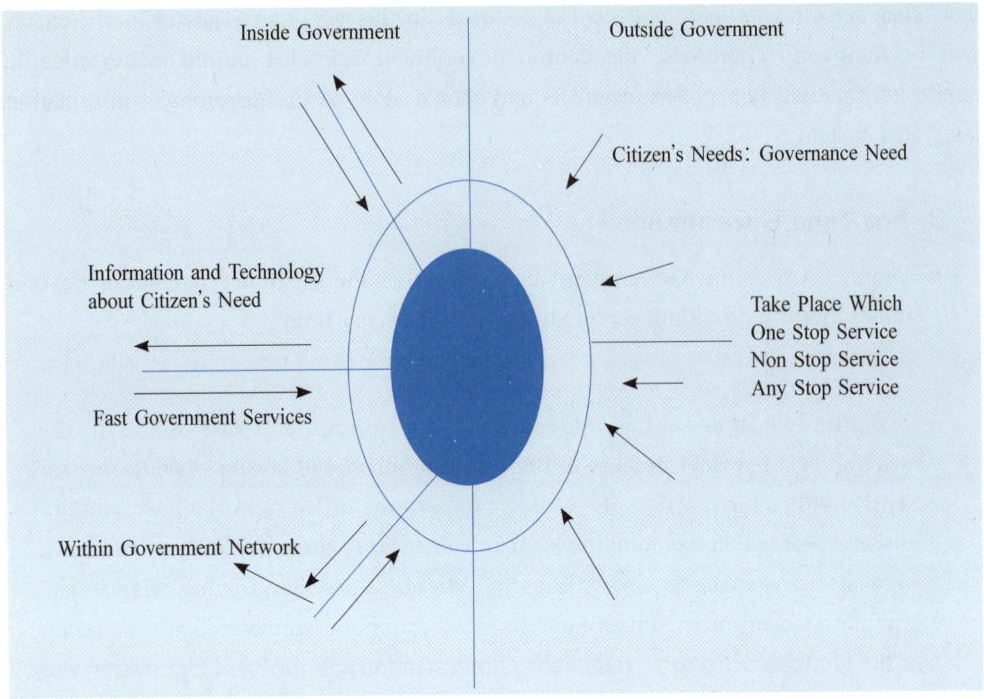

should support the smart technologies to innovate the existing document system.

(2) Government Reinvention Using BPR

Smart government should reinvent the administrative business processes by using BPR. BPR (Business Process Reengineering) is the methodology that makes diagnosis of the existing administrative processes, thereby reducing unnecessary approval stages and improving internal productivities. It upgrades the administrative business process by reducing unnecessary works, reducing waste papers, and simplifying approval procedure through smart information technology.

(3) The Best Cases of Business Management

Some examples of the best government performance utilizing information technology:

- Teleconference: Saving the meeting time and cost if actively introduced
- Smart Electronic Approval System: Saving time and cost of policy decision-making

- Systemic Building of the Policy Database: Preparing and using the system that classify, arrange and research the policy DB is helpful to accumulate the data in the KMS. Also by introduce the searching technique like data-mining, it offers help to create entirely new knowledge and to establish and implement policies effectively.

- Electronic Document Management System (EDMS): EDMS is the system that sort and manage all documents during the work process. EDMS is used to be the core tool of BPR to ultimately change the existing task performance method. And it is the system that save time to analyze the business process by sharing the data and information among departments. It also helps to mobilize lots of information widely and efficiently. Furthermore it enables to promote the data supply through the information opening, to reduce discretion, and to hold each other in check through sharing information.

4) Real time Government

- Vision: Real time Government reacts in real time to the demands of people through a neural government network that are stored electronically

Most works in the local taxes department of A city are handles through the internet. In the internet environment, the taxation data is researched, the tax is imposed in each house and the bill is metered automatically. Because these all processes are computerized by a small manpower, practitioners' subjectivity precludes all doubt and possibility of embezzlement is almost zero. A person who has a objection connect the homepage of the local taxes department, check processes of computation and put in a demurrer. But these objections are decreased rapidly in comparison with the past. The possibility of cozy relations between revenue officers and stakeholders is closed basically because all tax accounting are checked electronically.

C department must deal the purchase and procurement of supplying goods through in electronic commerce. For the regularly upgrade PCs in the end of the month, P who manages all personal PCs of C department researched the stock of ram status through the self-stock DB. A few days ago, the stock fell short of their stock standard, DB recognized that itself and asked the Public Procurement Service for supplement, and then today, enough stock of ram was secured.

But because hard disks were not obtained the latest, C department decided to buy the newest hard disks itself and researched the homepages of hard disk enterprise, finally it found a appropriate enterprise that sales at prices below their regular price (price was 20% cheaper than the regular price). P decided to buy hard disks here, ordered at this homepage, did an account transfer and obtained it by a door-to-door delivery in a few hours.

Because these all processes are recorded in main server, a special qualification procedure is not needed; the inspection was going along electronically. Since all these processes were operated by the government neural network, it is much faster than the existing method and the possibilities of corruption are blocked essentially.

Smart government should establish the real time, digital neural government, by **1) Real Time, Transparent Opening of Public Information, 2) Real Time Digitalization of the Budget and Accounting Process, 3) Real Time Digitalization of the E-Procurement Process, and 4) Real Time E-Audit & Inspection.**

(1) Real Time and Transparent Opening of Public Information

Smart government should promote the opening of public information which is the core element of e-Democracy. So with the only opening of information, e-Democracy will be realized successfully. Through the information opening policy, the administrative

Figure 8-5 Real-time, Transparent E-Government

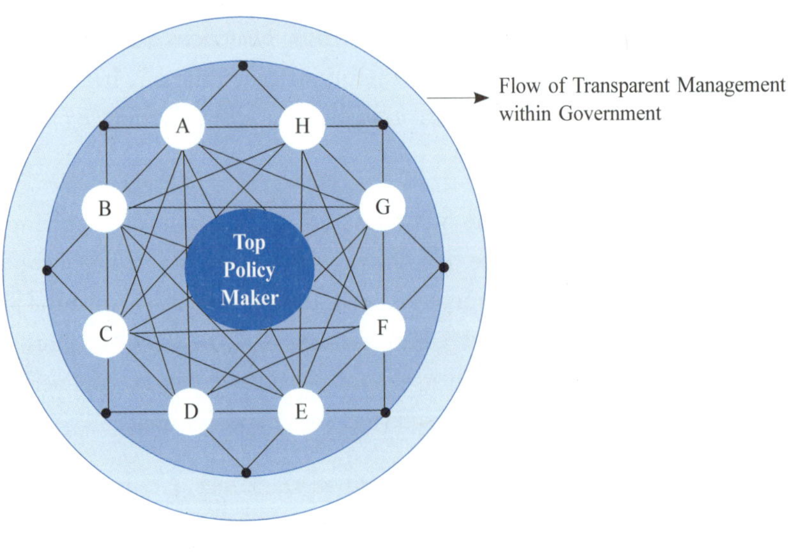

transparency will be improved, and the quality of policy will be dramatically enhanced.

(2) Real Time Digitalization of the Budget and Accounting Process

Smart government should digitalize all the budget and accounting processes in the government, the financial flow will become transparent. The application of information system to the budget and accounting process will also improve the effectiveness and accountability of governance.

(3) Real Time Digitalization of the Electronic Procurement Process

Smart government should digitalize all the government procurement processes which will enhance transparency and accountability of government. If each governmental supply and purchase contract will be performed by e-Commerce and each dealing process is digitalized, as Korean government did, the information about government procurement will be clear and transparent and the government corruption will be removed.

(4) Real Time E-Audit & Inspection

Smart government should digitalize all the government audit and inspection process. The efficiency of e-Audit & Inspection will be greatly improved, if all budget and accounting information is digitalized in the government. If the budget and accounting information are linked with the smart network, the inspection can be operated on a real time basis.

Tons of paperwork and data relating with the audit and inspection process are not necessary, the electronic information and data will be analyzed through standardized e-Audit & Inspection system. As a result, and the efficiency and transparency of the audit and inspection will be transformed innovatively.

5) Together/Collaborative Government

- Vision: Together Government, with a spirit of togetherness with enterprises and neglected class of people, provides service and information based on the participation and communication

C who are salaried worker must pass the way that are in dark because of the broken streetlamp on every his way home. Since there are few people in this street, when C had to pass the way tensely.

C always thought that the ward office fix this streetlamp, but for this he should find the public officer and report the civil complaint though the computer and this was very tiresome. He thought that somebody would report that... but week after week, the broken streetlamp was still here.

But this problem will be solved easily in the smart e-government. First, have the broken streetlamp's picture taken and forward this by App. Especially, by GPS location information service of Smart phone, he didn't need to report auxiliary information such as locations, time, etc.

The public officer who was dispatched to the site upon a citizen's report move and take action immediately, and register the outcome with pictures. These all processes can take by One-Stop, it is quick and efficient. The outcome of this process is forwarded to C's Smart mobile phone; C can check the outcome with picture at anytime and anywhere.

Smart government should establish the together, collaborative government, by 1) The expansion the participation/communication channel based on the smart SNS media such as e-People, and 2) Personalized and customized Services.

(1) The expansion the participation and communication based on SNS

Smart government should be the together government, by promoting the participation and communication of the people using the smart media such as SNS. The dynamic expansion of smart phone and diversification of communication channels provide the solution to improve participation and communication with people which the existing one-way service with no feedback could not solve.

The smart government should build the online communication system connected with social media, the sharing information and opinion interactively with the citizen. Especially, in Korea, "e-People" and "e-Oasis" receives and analyzes various civil complaints or policy ideas and reflects them to the policy making in a systematic way.

(2) Personalized Service

Smart government should be the together government, by promoting the personalized, customized service to people. To make personalized service, the services that are diffuse by the various MDAs are required to be integrated. Korean government approaches this by stages. For example, "People Living Information Integrated Notifying Service (e-Notice)" notifies tax and utility bill by online and provides the payment and breakdown based on wire-wireless integration in one lump.

Key Point!

◎ Vision of E-Government

☐ The vision of e-Government from the perspective of government innovation, e-Government should be:

1) Maximizin g convenience of the people as the One-Stop, Non-Stop, Any-Stop Government,
2) Minimizing paper document as the Paperless & Buildingless Government,
3) Non-corrupted and pellucid government as the Clean & Transparent Government,
4) Knowledge management system as the Digital Neural Knowledge Government.

◎ Smart E-Government (Smart Gov) Vision

☐ Smart e-Government(Smart Gov) means "as convergence/complex between evolving ICT and government services, people want to freely use the personalized services and participate/communicate in the advanced government regardless of the time, space, and medium."

☐ Vision of Smart e-Government

- **S**eamless: Service linkage and integration each government MDAs
- **M**obile: Mobile e-Gov, convenient service at Anywhere
- **A**ny time: Available service that people want Anytime
- **R**eal time: Service reaction system that respond to people's demand in Real time
- **T**ogether: Win-win strategy to enterprises, consideration for a neglected class of people, advancement of service by people's participation and two-way communication

☐ Strategies of Smart e-Government
- Open
- Integration
- Collaboration
- Green

First is "Open". By the "open" of a public information service, a public information and service must be opened to the private sector as well as the public sector in the various phases.

Second is "Integration". The integration through demand-side, need-based service integration and multi-channel promotes to liaise and integrate the government's service/data and multi-channel like Smart phone, Tablet PC, SMART TV, etc. to provide the personalized integrated service to people.

Third is "Collaboration". The collaboration means a cooperation and information sharing between MDAs.

Fourth is "Green". The "green" means to construct eco-friendly and low-cost system to establish low-carbon green growth foundation in all social field of the nation by utilizing the smart ICT products and Clouding computing system.

Key Question!

◎ Concept and characteristics of Smart Government in the advent of smart society was examined. Arrange the main features of Smart government compared to existing e-government.

◎ Smart e-Government have four strategies, open, integration, collaboration, and green. Explain each strategy.

◎ Vision of Smart government is divided into five, Seamless Government, Mobile Government, Any time Government, Real time Government, Together Government. Explain in brief the description of each vision, and state related policy strategies.

Chapter 9

OPERATIONAL STRATEGY OF E-GOVERNMENT(I): BACK-OFFICE STRATEGY

Without a proper set up of the back-office foundation, e-Government could not achieve effectiveness and accountability of the government work processes.

Objectives

The purpose of this chapter is to explain the operational strategy of e-Government from its back-office standpoints. It will examine how back-office building strategy can be employed to improve effectiveness and efficiency of government. To improve productivity of the government work processes, it will highlight the e-Government's Back Office building strategy by discussing the following concepts: electronic document, government information common utilization, public officials digital literacy, collaboration and e-Government 3.0, TQM, BPR, ERP, and IRM.

This chapter will further discuss about Government e-Document Distribution Center, CIO, Government Information Common Utilization Center, Smart Work, and Integrated EA as a successful recent trend of Korean e-Government.

Electronic Document

Electronic document is all the electronic records of the document expressed in characters and symbols to communicate public ideas or opinions. This includes all official documents, email records and contents of conversations that are shared by computer networks or internet.

Necessity and Importance

The complexity of hierarchical bureaucracy led to time wastage for business operations and approval of documents. The need to prevent waste of time and money necessitates an electronic document. Therefore, in order to improve business process by reducing time spent on document processing, e-document must be in place.

Advantages and Disadvantages

Management of electronic documents could reduce the clerical works required for paper management. This also reduces the labor costs. The personnel resources displaced from any department or agency can be redeployed to other functions. These will in-turn save the agency money that would otherwise have been used to hire additional personnel. Electronic documents also facilitate knowledge cycle, from creation to utilization.

However, electronic documents have their own shortcomings. The storage devices for electronic documents (i.e. tapes or disks) are likely to be damaged due to time, external environment factors, heat or humidity, such as exposure to magnetic fields. Damage to the storage devices will result to information lost at once, as compared to the paper documents which might damage pieces of papers in a file. The problems are also discovered with the digital system that may cast doubts on the integrity, authenticity, and newness of the document.

Policy Issues

To encourage the use of e-Document, three major policy challenges had to be addressed.

First, it is required to have a government-wide infrastructure management system. Efficient e-Government infrastructure (document drafting, processing, and distribution) depends on the government-wide common infrastructure management system. This management system includes the measures and standards relating with the government-wide information infrastructure.

Second, it is required to have an Inter-Agency consultation for such document processing, and distribution system. Inter-Agency consultation should involve agreement on infrastructure related planning, standards, and maintenance. This calls for a continued cooperation and consultation between ministries and agencies to ensure the quality of the operational management system, especially in terms of rights and responsibilities.

Third, it is required to improve the documentation system. Documentation system has made innovative improvements over the past; however, challenges still exist in terms of effective electronic document processing and management. Also, the need for a continuous research to improve the document system-related procedures in response to development of smart information technologies.

Recent Trends: Government e-Document Distribution System

Government electronic document distribution system means the electronic distribution services to send and receive documents between government ministries and public agencies according to the life cycle of entire government document process. As of 2013, e-Document had been used in Korea, a total of 1,292 institutions, including 45 central government agencies, 248 municipalities, 636 public and private schools/universities, and 346 public agencies.

Figure 9-1 Recent Trends: Government Electronic Document Distribution System

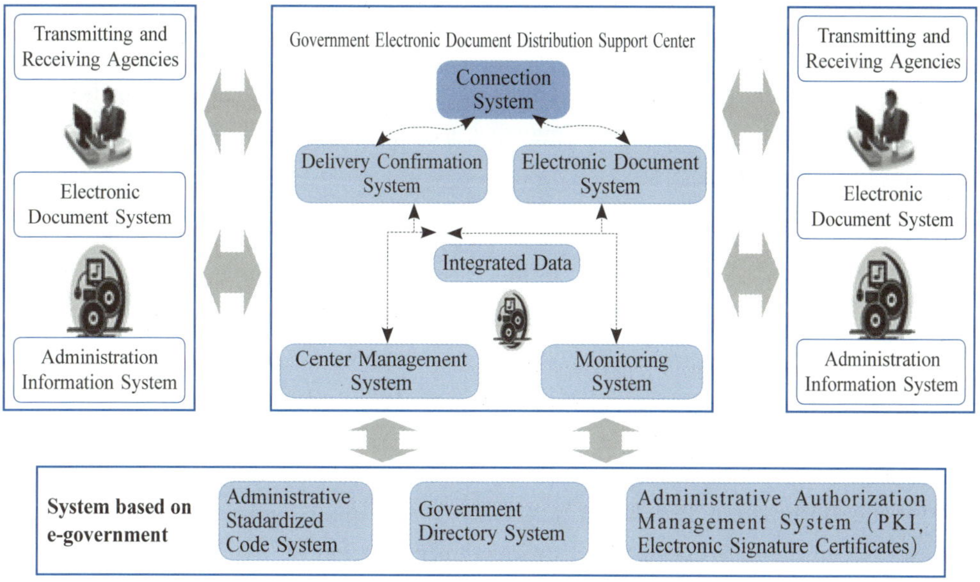

* Source: Ministry of Security and Public Administration(2013).

Government electronic document distribution system provides the services including,
1) Incoming and outgoing electronic documents between systems
2) Link between electronic documents and administrative information systems, and
3) Electronic documents that support the agency's electronic document distribution.

Digital Literacy of Government Officials

Concept

In the information and knowledge society, literacy is determined by the ability to solve their immediate problems by utilizing information technology. Advanced IT equipment and infrastructure will be useless unless members have the competencies to utilize them.

Necessity

Government officials play a very important role in the implementation of e-government. Public official's digital literacy is an important factor in determining the speed and breadth of e-government implementation. This is because they should be the change agent in the process of the e-Government implementation.

Strategy

This is a user-centric strategy that emphasizes on the users, comparing to the initial focus on infrastructure. At the same time, this is a demand-centric strategy comparing to the initial focus on supply.

It is required to have the effective strategy considering the different duties and responsibilities of the individual staff. In this regard, one important strategy is to appoint an effective CIO to enhance digital literacy and competence of government staff.

Recent Trends: Chief Information Officer (CIO)

Korean e-Government has been strikingly developed based on the e-Government law (2001) and Information Promotion Act (1996) and implementing the strategies and policies to open the new era of Smart e-Government version of 3.0. One of the effective strategies to achieve this goal is the genuine utilization of CIO concept.

Chief Information Officer (CIO) is a concept that refers to the high-ranking management position responsible for the overall information-related policy making and implementation. They direct and control the utilization of information technology and information resource management in order to enhance the organizational performance.

As far as Information technology and business process reengineering is concerned, they play the key role of integrating the organization's business strategy and the entire enterprise resource planning. In other words, CIO oversees purchase of information technology, a variety of information services of the information systems department; but most importantly he plays a key role of improving the organizational performance by formulating the strategic plan relating with information resource management. Rockart(1982) defined, in this regard, the CIO as a thinker, planner, and coordinator rather than the person who enforces and performs.

Public Information Common Utilization

Concept and Significance

Public information common utilization is to share and utilize information in a collaborative way between departments within the government agency, agency and citizen, or agency and enterprise to achieve the common value of government that is the happiness of the people. The transaction of citizens and business enterprise with the government necessitates information common utilization among government agencies. The rationale behind this is simple; it reduces cost, save time, and efficiently facilitates communication among line agencies and thereby results to customer and citizen satisfaction and organizational performance.

Typology

Public Information Common Utilization is classified depending on the type of administrative information and management information system. Thus, the following classifications are possible:

1) **Common Internal Administrative Functions of Government Agencies.** Public information joint utilization of common administrative tasks requires administrative processing that is in accordance with the public organization's standard operating procedures or SOPs. Each government agencies has their own internal procedures

that are deemed necessary and in consonance with legally accepted principles of public management. The examples are e-document management, e-finance management, and e-Procurement.

2) **Common Use of Information for Decision Support.** Government agencies that have international economic and trade transactions may take advantage of the co-Database information, if warranted. Thus, such Big data can assist government entities to produce an objective decision and action to establish or contract business with foreign partners. The examples are e-DB for international economics and trade.

3) **Information Common Utilization for Civil Service.** The ultimate goal of e-Government is to provide a convenient public service for citizen. In Korea, the development of e-Government hastens the information sharing for effective and reliable public service. The creation of internet or web portals integrated various government agencies' websites and the presence of the main government's internet portal, especially the name of 'Alim Ma-dang (Notice Plantform)' could supply necessary information requested by the people. Thus, it allows citizens to access and use information in accordance with law and statutes.

Strategies and Tasks

Information common utilization must go away with the traditional and voluminous protocols that hamper smooth sharing and joint utilization of information. The strategies and policy tasks to improve information common utilization includes:

1) Clear Policy Goal Setting: The national policy on information common utilization is required as this policy need a comprehensive planning and coordination among the entire government ministries and agencies.

2) Information Common Utilization Policy Mechanism as Government Reform System: Strategic Policy Mechanism associated with information common utilization should be implemented as a means of government reform. Therefore the authoritative agency should have a powerful authority to command and coordinate the related agencies.

3) Reengineering of Government Personnel Function: Information common utilization policy does not only mean the technical aspect of e-Government functions such as technological infrastructure. Rather it includes the culture and attitudes of the public officials willing to cooperate with other agencies. Hence, the authority of

implementing information common utilization should have the power of reforming personnel functions. For example, it is required to have a government reinvention by recreating the capabilities to solve the problem of intolerance to collaborate with other ministries (called sectionalism or parochialism) or to enhance the professional expertise of government personnel.

4) Reengineering of Government Work Process: For the effective and efficient information common utilization, it is also required to have a government reinvention by effectively proceeding business process reengineering. Without a proper work process of government affairs, we could not expect an appropriate information common utilization.

5) Updating Legal Framework: Government should investigate the legal elements hampering information common utilization among agencies and should continue to update the legal framework.

In summary, the promotion of e-Government according to the rapid development of the Smart information technology is not avoidable and the activation of information common utilization is the essential foundation of realizing the most updated e-Government model.

Recent Trends: Government Information Common Utilizatlon Center in Korea

1) Concept

Korean government installed the government information common utilization center to promote information sharing and information common utilization among government agencies, thereby facilitating e-Government services without the requirement of a hard document. Accordingly, government information common utilization center eliminates the traditional bricks and mortar system search for public offices that are responsible for specific governmental works. The burden and annoying standard operating procedures that are required for a government document are likewise removed. Thus, citizens, business and government officials are freed from waste of time and unnecessary burdens that was brought by government bureaucratic processes.

2) Main Service

(1) Customized Information Inquiry System

The customized information inquiry system is a service that provides business processes on one screen. In order to strengthen the protection of personal information, only the minimum amount of information should be enough. To take a simple example, veteran status or tax information will be ascertained with Y/N confirmation only.

(2) Electronic Document Management system

Electronic document management system is a system for registering, keeping, and viewing applications utilizing digital document system. To support no visit administrative services, it is required to convert documents into electronic document; thereby it is easier to process and to verify the results by the whole process of online. It will significantly lead to less time and administrative burden required to visiting the government agencies for civil applications or petitions.

3) Strategies and Challenges

Since April 2011, the Ministry of Public Administration and Security in Korea builds a distribution hub of central government agencies to provide services using Smart information sharing and common utilization. Smart personalized information distribution services and the scope of the information sharing policy have been expanded. Also, customized information look ups (One Screen) has been expanded. This kind of user-oriented services, as a result, has enhanced the convenience of the information sharing and common utilization system.

But one thing should be recognized to further promoting information sharing and information common utilization services, is a culture. If we could not cultivate the proper culture of information sharing or information common utilization to promote sharing or collaboration among agencies, we could never realize the vision and dreams brought by the most updated model of Smart e-Government.

Collaboration and E-Government 3.0

Concept

Collaboration is indicating the situation that the number of government workers is performing tasks collaboratively by using the means of Smart information technologies. Collaboration is an important concept in realizing the advanced version of e-Government. In this modern society, there is an increasing demand of a complex public service that requires a joint or collaborative work of many related government agencies. Therefore, to achieve the people's happiness, an ultimate goal of e-Government 3.0, collaboration is a prerequisite concept.

E-Government 3.0

We are living in a more democratic society that the people's participation and demands are increasing. The people have been requesting for the correction of government failures and wanting more choices from the public service that suit their needs. They expect that the quality of public service should coequal with that of private sector. As shown in the 〈Figure 9-2〉, the citizen, after reaching the basic expectations of material service, through the value-added service of customization and personalization, moves toward the best the top-level leading service of "Involve me, Inspire me, and Remember me!"

Therefore they are more sensitive about the cost and benefit of taxes they are paying, more critical about the bureaucratic and inefficient administration. As a result, they are demanding more competitive government with greater citizen satisfaction, which could be expected to be fully realized in the e-Government 3.0.

Figure 9-2 The Changing Patterns of Citizen Expectation

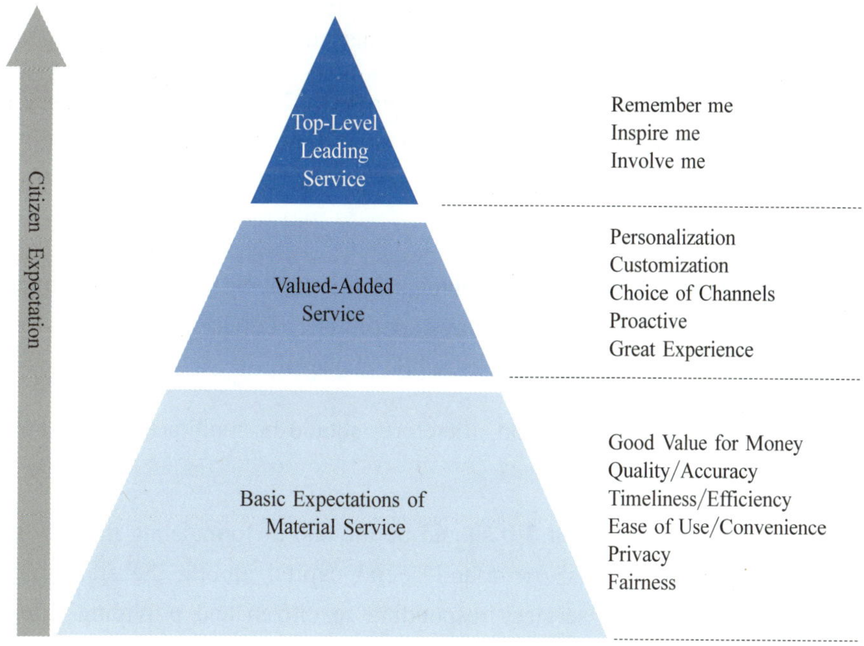

* Source: Revised from the Citizen Concept of UAE Government Service

Public Value Management Model and Government 3.0

Mark Moore (1995) presented the public value management model as the third generation governance model. If we call the bureaucratic government as the first generation model, and the NPM (New Public Management) model as the second generation model, the PVM (Public Value Model) could be called as the third generation model of governance or Government model 3.0. This PVM model emphasizes the public value compared to the market value emphasized by the NPM model (see Figure 9-1〉

The paradigm of this model is as follows:

First, the public value of government 3.0 is the preferences of all individuals of the nation, which might be derived by the process of deliberative democracy.

Second, the performance objective of government 3.0 is to consider the diverse aspects of satisfaction, outcome, trust, transparency, and accountability from the public services, rather than the mere consideration of input and output of the previous models.

Third, the accountability mechanism of government 3.0 highlights the active role of citizen. Citizen should play the role of monitoring or inspecting government, beyond the roles of just tax-payers or clients/customers as users.

Fourth, the service delivering system of government 3.0 highlights the public-private partnership or collaborative governance among the diverse stakeholders including government agencies, public enterprises, private companies, interest groups, or local communities.

Fifth, the public service ethos of government 3.0 is to avoid government monopoly or to think that no one ethos is always appropriate. Public good and services, as a community resource, should be carefully managed.

Six, the role of public participation, therefore, should be multifaceted as a tax-payer, client, customer, or citizen.

Seven, the goal of government 3.0 should be the one of formulating the new network governance to establish trust and social capital among the stakeholders by guaranteeing quality services responding to citizen and providing a legal and regulatory framework (Kelly and Muers, 2002).

Table 9-1 The Paradigm of Government 3.0

	Traditional Bureaucratic Model	New Public Management	Public Value Management
Public Interest	Defined by Politicians/ Government	Aggregation of Individual Preferences Demonstrated by Customer Choice	Individual and Public Preferences Derived from the Political Process of Deliberative Democracy
Performance Objective	Managing Inputs	Managing Inputs and Outputs	Multiple Objectives: • Outputs • Outcome • Satisfaction • Trust • Transparency • Accountability
Accountability Mechanism	Upwards through Department to Politicians and through them to Parliament	Upwards through Performance Contracts; Sometimes Outward to the Customers through Market Mechanisms	Multiple: • Citizens as Inspector of Government • Customers as users • Taxpayers as funders
Public Service Delivering System	Bureaucracy Hierarchical System (Command & Control)	Private Sector or Special Agency (Market Mechanism)	Menu of Alternatives Selected Contextually (Government Agencies, Public Enterprises, Private Companies, Interest Groups, Local Community)
Public Service Ethos	Public Sector has Monopoly on Service Ethos	Skeptical of Public Sector Ethos(Leads to Inefficiency and Empire Building) – Favors Customer Service by Market Mechanism	No One Ethos Always Appropriate. Public Good and Services, as a Community Resource, Should be Carefully Managed.
Role of Public Participation	Limited to Voting in Elections and Pressure on Elected Representatives	Limited Expressed only in the form of Customer Satisfaction	Crucial-multifaceted Stakeholders(Citizen, Customer/client, Taxpayer)
Goal of Government	Respond to Political Direction	Focusing on Performance Targets	Trust Building by Forming Network Governance Providing a Legal and Regulatory Framework Responding to Citizen by Guaranteeing Quality Services.

* Source: Revised from Mark Moore(1995); Kelly and Muers(2002).

Government 3.0 and E-Government 3.0

E-Government 3.0, based on the paradigm of Government 3.0, highlights the strategic setting and transformation by utilizing the Smart knowledge management of big data, sensor-based technologies, and semantic-based algorism. If e-Government 1.0 emphasized the government internal efficiency by using the concept of BPR, G2B, G2G, and G4C, e-Government 2.0 emphasizes the Open Platform of participation, sharing, open, and collective intelligence, highlighted by Web 2.0(see Table 9-1).

Korean E-Government Model of 3.0

Korean e-Government 3.0 has been evolutionarily developed by the precedent models of e-government 1.0 and 2.0.

The first generation of e-Government, that is, e-Government 1.0 was from the late 1990s to 2002 in Korea when the President Kim Dae-Jung government initially constructs the infrastructure of e-Government. Of course, these were possible by the efforts of the previous regimes such as the economic development of President Park Jung-Hee among others.

In this period of e-Government 1.0, Korean government established the basic infrastructure of administrative information networks and information superhighway. Notably, Kim Dae-Jung government established the special committee of e-Government which was very helpful to set up a comprehensive and systematic blue print of Korean e-Government at the time. Basically in this period e-Government 1.0 tried to enhance effectiveness and efficiency by implementing government integrated e-Procurement system and the project of 'government for citizen.' The major policy instruments used in this period is BPR, IRM, and ERP to enhance the public services of G2B, G2C, and G4C.

The second generation of e-Government, that is, e-Government 2.0 was from 2003 to 2012 in Korea when the Korean government had developed e-Government at the advanced stage of Web 2.0 of open, participation, and sharing level. People started to use and participated the new online services such as online banking system and 'Cheo-Man-Sang-Sang Oasis' (http://oasis.seoul.go.kr) utilizing the advanced technology of web 2.0. In this period of e-Government 2.0, Korean government tried to enhance innovation and participation by enhancing the online services in which people could freely participate and suggest the new policy ideas. In addition, Government expanded the project of public information sharing and government information common utilization. The major policy instruments used in this period is Web 2.0 of open, participation, and collective intelligence.

Figure 9-3 The Evolution Stage of e-Government 3.0

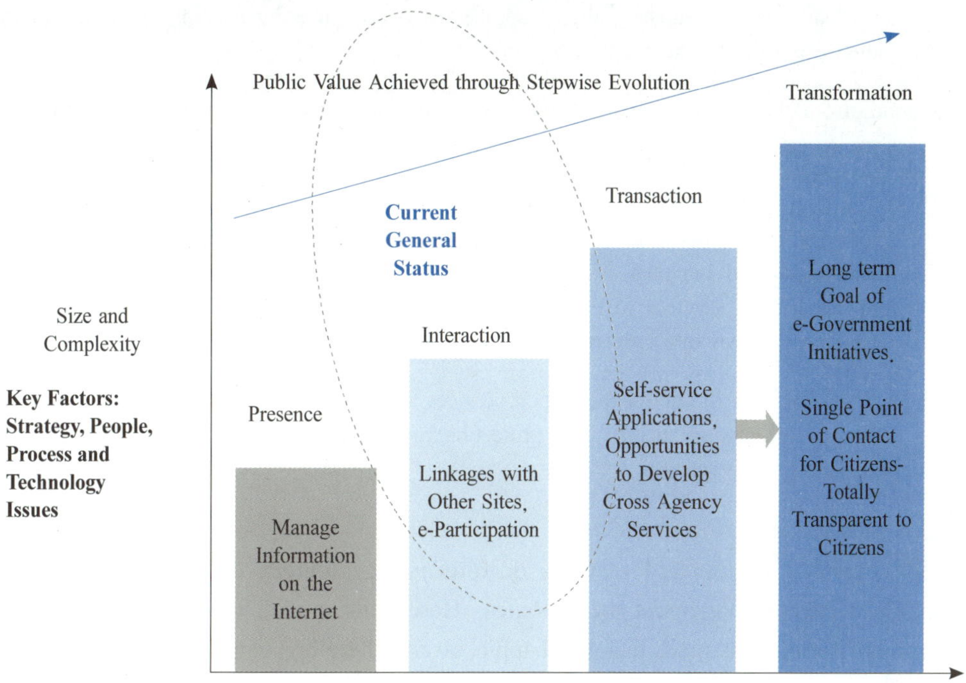

*Source: Revised from Gartner Research (2010).

The third generation of e-Government, that is, e-Government 3.0 is from 2013 and it is in the currently progress based on the development of the previous achievement of 1.0 and 2.0. It is the model attempted in the Korean President Park Geun-Hae government. E-Government 3.0 highlights strategic directional-setting and transformation by utilizing the new smart technologies such as big data, Sementic Web based algorism, RFID/Sensor based u-technologies and KMS system. It really emphasizes "Do the Right Things" rather than "Do Things Right" and therefore it is not searching for a mere efficiency but the right direction of national transformation or government reinvention. In this regard, the ideology aimed by this model 3.0 is trust, accountability, and reflexivity.

The vision of e-Government 3.0 is to achieve the humanity-based society in which people's human dignity and quality of life are enhanced based on the democratic governance of transparency, accountability and reflexivity.

To achieve this vision and goals, e-Government 3.0 should have the following policy strategies:

First, from the perspective of government management, e-Government 3.0 should be a really smart one of transforming government by removing the walls of agencies and sectionalism. It emphasizes to upgrade total intelligence of the nation by rearranging the information, knowledge, and resources scattered around the nation, thereby meeting the vision of the nation expressed by the people's happiness.

Second, from the perspective of public service, e-Government 3.0 emphasizes information sharing, openness, and collective intelligence.

Third, from the perspective of big data, e-Government 3.0 emphasizes the right decision-making and collaboration based on the systematic knowledge management of smart technologies and big data. It is an upgraded model to serve pre-emptive, forecasting, and customized services to each people, which is one-step developed beyond the just interactive services of e-Government 2.0.

Finally, to guarantee the above-mentioned services, trust and security should be prerequisite. That is, information security and protection of personal information are very important foundation of the services.

In a nutshell, e-Government 3.0 is the advanced model of e-Government that could provide personal customized services or forecasting services utilizing big data and smart knowledge management technologies. Here, this model highlights the value of government services to meet people's happiness and therefore emphasizes the citizen as the main actor of democratic governance, not just a taxpayer or client as a user. Base on the spirit of open, participation, and network, people as a citizen is encouraged to participate and suggest new policy ideas to the democratic political processes by using new smart ICT technologies and Social Network Services.

Table 9-2 The Paradigm of e-Government 3.0

	e-Government 1.0	e-Government 2.0	e-Government 3.0
Focal Points	• Government Internal Efficiency	• Interface • Web 2.0: Open Platform, Participation, Sharing, Collective Intelligence	• Strategic Setting • Transformation • Policy Decision-Making with Big Data
Policy Instruments	• BRP, IRM, ERP • G2B, G2G, G4C	• Web 2.0 • Open Platform	• Big Data • Collaboration • Information Sharing • Smart Technologies (KMS, Sementic Web, Algorism, Sensor/RFID)
Policy Ideas	• Effectiveness • Efficiency	• Innovation • Participation • Democracy	• Trust • Transparency • Accountability • Reflexivity

Recent Trends: Smart Work

1) Concept

The concept of smart work is a future-oriented work system to do the work regardless of places and time. Due to the rapid development of information and communication technologies and the emergence of a variety of media, including smart phones, the concept of smart work is required. Remote collaboration and problem solving process should be possible based on the real-time communication (Jeong, Myung-Soo et. al, 2011).

Table 9-3 Typology of Smart Work

Category	Type of Work	Advantages	Disadvantages
Working at Home	• Work performed at home using information network connected to the Headquarters	• Separate office space is not needed • Commuting time and transportation burden reduction	• Increased isolation of the workers and reduce the synergies of collaboration • Reduced job satisfaction due to isolation • Limited due to insufficient security
Mobile Office	• Work performed in the field using mobile devices	• Useful for face-to-face business or mobile environments	• Insecure work environment • Location tracking from Smartphone
Work at Smart Work Center	• Work performed at Smart Work Center	• Similar level of working environment with Headquarters • Keep filing of performance management • Ensure Security	• Separate office space is needed • Need to build a system

* Source: Modified from Jae sung Lee, et al (2010: 79).

2) Challenges and Tasks

Smart work doesn't mean only piecemeal changes in the business and should not be understood as a situation that a smart phone is using in the business. Rather, it means the overall change of business style by using smart technologies. Therefore, for an effective smart work, government should provide the basic facilities and smart information system, such as Wi-Fi, BcN, or wide-area wireless networks.

BPR: Business Process Reengineering

Concept

BPR, first introduced by Michael Hammer and immediately followed by P. Drucker, M. Porter, and E. Deming, means a fundamental redesign of business process. The philosophy of BPR is based on the innovative thoughts that if we want to survive in the competition, it requires a fundamental rethinking from the basic way of doing business.

BPR is defined to rebuild the system by changing the people, process, and technology utilizing the smart information technology that fundamentally reconsiders the traditional way in all parts of business process.

Features

BPR has the following features:

First, BPR is an innovation. It redesigns internal business process to enhance innovation, thus increasing customer satisfaction. Time-saving, cost reduction and downsizing is an associated effect.

Second, BPR pursues a Zero-based approach. It requires a fundamental reconsideration in all the ways of existing approach.

Third, BPR focuses on the process. It makes business processes innovated and fast to enhance customer satisfaction.

Fourth, BPR pursues innovative goal setting, say, at least 30%, or from 50% to 100% increase of goal achievement.

Finally, BPR actively utilizes the new information technology. It utilizes smart ICT as a tool of innovation, standardizes the results of innovation and proliferated them to the other parts of the organization.

Strategies

The critical success factors for BPR include three key elements: People, Process, and Information technology.

1) People

If a person does not change, we can never expect the successful result of BPR. Consider the following strategies:

- Change process involving key stakeholders and internal work flow.
- Eliminate duplicate or redundant business processes.
- Redesign the business process from the viewpoint of customer satisfaction.
- Perform organizational restructuring from the process efficiency.
- Review laws and regulatory framework to support the above activities.

2) Process

Reengineering the business process is the key to the successful BPR. Consider the following strategies:

- Target to focus on time-consuming process.
- Attention to the process of paperwork involving several departments.
- Distinguish high-value, low-value-added process.
- Distinguish high-risk, low-risk process.
- Distinguish high-accountability, low-accountability process.
- Remove unnecessary, duplicate, and redundant non value-added work.
- Readjust business range according to the level of risk.
- Reengineer business process for performing work with high accountability.

3) Information Technology

Information technology is the key instrument for the successful BPR. Consider the following strategies:

- Establish the smart ICT infrastructure for innovating and shortening business process.
- Redesign and Integrate business process by utilizing ICT to speed up and to prevent from disconnected knowledge flow.
- Establish IRM system for knowledge creation and utilization.
- Establish integrated DB or DW system for knowledge accumulation and sharing.
- Establish overall-company, ERP system for knowledge learning and proliferation by including customers and suppliers, or citizen, stakeholders and other related agencies.

4) Operating Strategies

To operating BPR properly, we should take note of the following BPR establishing stages:

(1) Strategic Planning Stage

In this stage, the strategies, plans, and a specific schedule of future activities of BPR are developed. Here, establish project strategy, define project success factors, construct the project infrastructure, plan detailed schedule, BPR initiated meetings, training and education, and basic benchmarking activity, are performed.

(2) Diagnostic Stage

In this stage, the authoritative agency is trying to diagnose the status of organization itself by analyzing for its strength and weakness, opportunities and threats. Based on the analysis, the organization performs the workshop brainstorming how to remedy the problematic points of the process. In the workshop, select the target process, job analysis, discuss how to remove and readjust unnecessary, duplicate, and redundant processes, are performed.

(3) Re-design Stage

In this stage, the agency is redesigning the future process analyzed by the previous steps. Here, re-design the future process; establish the action plan and action-resolution meeting are performed.

(4) Implementation Stage

In this stage, the agency is implementing the concrete actions by performing the action of the suggested personnel and function readjustment. Here, action of reengineering, reform activities, monitoring and feedback, standardization, selects the best practice, and wrapping up session, are performed.

(5) Maintenance & Update Stage

In this stage, the agency is finishing the first step of BPR and establishes the plan the next step of the second stage of BPR for the continuous innovation of the organizational process.

5) Failure Points

The BPR strategies and implementation usually involve the downsizing activities and therefore it is a difficult task facing the strong resistance of organization members which may end in failure. The followings are the some of the points to pay attention to prevent the failures in BPR process.

(1) Give the Full Power: BPR activities, as noted, are not the easy tasks. The authoritative agency in charge of this task should have a powerful authority in accordance with the Reengineering activities. The CEO of the organization should give the full power associated with it.

(2) Special Agency is better: It might be more appropriate to perform the BPR activities by the special outsourcing or independent team rather than the internal team. The target process in the BPR usually involves many departments and they may be more resistant to the suggestion raised by the internal BPR team.

(3) Need a Full Communication: The BPR team should have a full communication with the people in the process and should avoid the problems raised by miscommunication or lack of understanding.

(4) Consider Morale of the workers: It is more natural for human to prefer the status quo and therefore BPR should be sensitive matters dealing with the re-engineering. These kinds of psychological factors should be carefully taken into account in the BPR process and select the reasonable and feasible set of reengineering reform. Otherwise, after the BPR is done, the overall morale of the organization might be severely downward, which may end in failure of the BPR reform anyway.

6) E-Government and BPR

When we apply BPR to the government organizations, much more careful considerations should be paid. As BPR is to highlight the rapid changes of business process across the organizations, it makes the risk of failure greater. Especially the characteristics of the public administrative organizations are status-quo oriented and risk-aversive.

In addition, the government organization is not like the business organization as it should take into account of the diverse values of democratic regime such as democracy, equality, fairness, legitimacy, and accountability. It is unlike that private organization mainly considers the mere efficiency and profitability. This had been the reason that BPR could not be easily adopted in the government organizations.

However, things have been changed. National governance model has been changed searching for a more competitive, productive, and customer-oriented one. Especially with the adoption of e-Government and knowledge government, the main issues of government innovation become more similar to the ones of entrepreneurial business organizations. For example, e-Government now concerns such issues like, how to kindly treat citizen as a customer or client, how to transparently involve them to the policy processes, how to utilize smart ICT technologies to cut down the red tapes and unnecessary processes to conveniently provide them with one-stop, any-stop, or non-stop services, which would lead to enhance the people's quality of life and people's happiness.

Nevertheless, we should pay a careful attention when we apply BPR to the government organizations. Special attentions should include the following points:

(1) Do not consider only the narrow economic values like efficiency.

(2) Consider public interest by accommodating a variety of values like democracy and equity.

(3) Consider public interest by accommodating a variety of stakeholders.

(4) Consider the modest strategies. It is possible that BPR damages the public interest.
It may be more difficult to take a zero-based approach in the government agencies. Therefore, it is more advisable to take a modest strategy of BPR and consider a more flexible approach of BPR taking into account the laws, regulations, and institutional tradition to a certain level. It is important to form a special team of agency and do the brainstorming workshop to select the wise set of strategic actions.

TQM: Total Quality Management

Concept

The concept of TQM is a comprehensive quality management of the organization. It takes a quite similar process with BPR when it analyzes the fundamental process of work flows. However, TQM is more a broader concept than BPR as it includes analyzing public personnel system, budget system, policy management, MBO and other management system.

Logic

The theoretical foundation of TQM is based on NPM (New Public Management), which is to reform government activities by using the concepts of economics and business administration like downsizing, privatization, contracting out, and outsourcing. TQM tries to analyze continuously the government employee's work process to improve their job performance, and to remove anomalies and inefficiencies on the work process. It also tries to maintain close communication with customers to identify what they want, and to understand how they define the quality of public services.

Therefore, like BPR, TQM is a good instrument to enhance the organization performance and efficiency in this knowledge-based economy as long as it approaches to the government reform by understanding the fundamental nature of public values and services, as mentioned in the BPR discussion.

Limitation and Strategy

P. Drucker (1980) pointed out the obstacles of TQM when it applied to the government sector: 1) The absence of clear performance standards, 2) Attempting too many things at once, 3) Use too many workforce to solve the problem, 4) The lack of the spirit of experimentation, 5) Low-effect of training due to the lack of proper evaluation, and 6) Path-dependency problem: Once a public program started, it is hard to abolish. E. Deming (1986) also pointed out the obstacles as: 1) The absence of clear goal and consistency, 2) Myopic vision, 3) Lack of proper incentive system, 4) Frequent turnover of high-ranking officials, 5) Too much dependency on the tangible numbers, and 6) Displacement of goal and instruments. In other words, these are the issues and points to be considered when we apply TQM to the government sectors.

ERP: Enterprise Resource Planning

Concept

ERP refers to an integrated management system that maximizes the utilization of all resources, including the human resources and financial resources by utilizing the smart information technologies. In the private organizations, it means to integrate the business processes of the organization's financial, human resources, accounting, production, and marketing.

Evolution of ERP

The ERP system appeared from MRP-I in the 1970s, MRP-II in the 1980s, and CIM and since the mid-1990s; various functions have been integrated to manage within the

Figure 9-4 The Evolution of ERP System

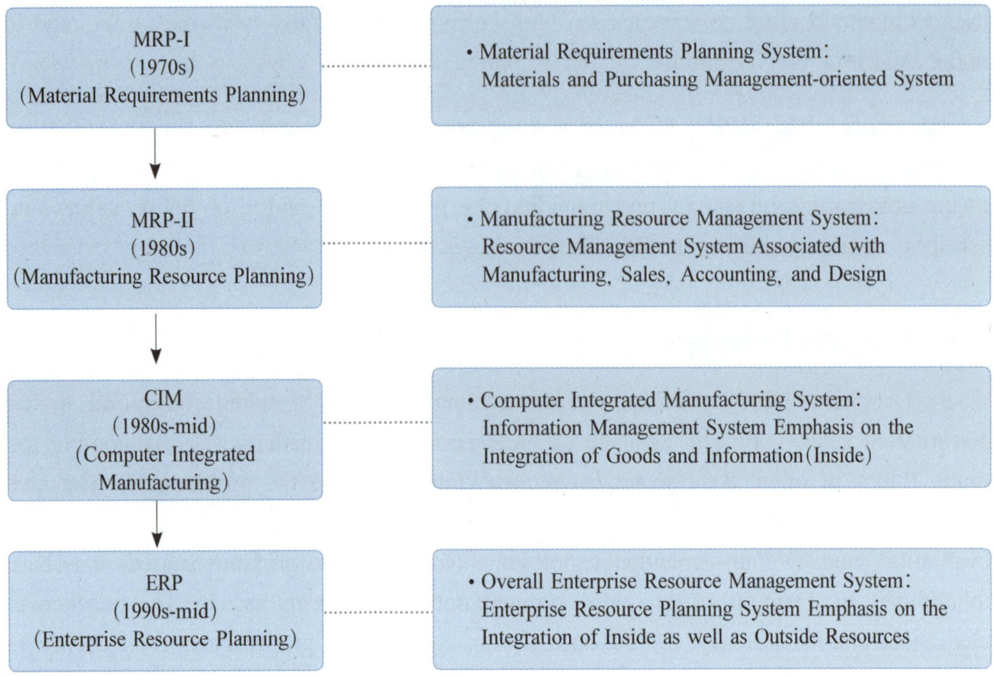

organization as an ERP system.

ERP and BPR

BPR and ERP has a close mutual relationship. If the organization wants to promote BPR as well as the ERP system, it is desirable that the organization integrates to proceed with building activities of ERP and BPR activities. In other words, it is desirable to perform the procedure of BPR by considering the possibility of the introduction of the ERP system soon to support. The integrative effects of the ERP system from the perspective of the BPR are as follows:

1) Efficient Work Flow from the System Integration:

   From the system integration, it is possible to have a real-time exchange of information between departments, abolition of redundant work, and integration of splitted work, overcoming geographic matters, and shortening business processes.

2) Efficient Knowledge Management from the Database Integration:

   From the database integration, it is possible to have a real-time exchange of information between departments, abolition of redundant work, integration of splitted work, and maintaining the accuracy of the information.

3) Cost Savings from the Business Process Integration:

From the process integration, it is possible to have cost and time savings, and reduction of personnel. Eventually these kinds of ERP efforts will be very useful to pursue the streamlining of business process re-engineering of the government organization.

IRM: Information Resource Management

Concept

Information resource management can be defined a set of management strategy relating with e-Government from information creation, sharing, utilization, learning, proliferation, and storage. Therefore, IRM is a concept that includes not only the management of the information itself, but also the management of resource related to personnel, budget, policy, and data processing. While TQM and ERP is the concept rather more applicable to the private business enterprises, BPR and IRM is more like the comprehensive concept which can be applied to enhance the productivity of the public sectors.

Necessity

Information resource management will be used to consistently manage a series of processes of e-Governance at the national level from the introduction of information technology, operation, maintenance, and disposal. In this way, we can provide the national ICT management system to ensure investment efficiency, to guarantee interoperability between systems, and to reduce the waste elements. To gain these effects and to accelerate administrative innovation, IRM emphasizes the legal framework to ensure the coherent management system envisioned above.

Strategy

The followings are the strategies for successful management of information resources (Caudle, 1996).

1) Leadership: The top management should guide the change in information resource

management as this change management is so pivotal for the organizational performance. The CEO should select and empower CIO to direct all the IRM process. After examining the application and information resources management strategies, it is required to justify the necessity and changes of IRM. Establish standards of implementing IRM.

2) Strategic Management: It is required to set up the strategic management plan which includes the changes of personnel, budgeting, and performance evaluation in association with IRM.

3) Performance Management: It is required to set up the performance management plan which evaluates the performance of IRM that contributed to the extent to organizational goals and mission.

4) Recognizing as an investment rather than a cost: Successful organization considered IRM as an investment, not as a cost, that will provide a long-term effect to the organization.

5) Innovation Process: In order to operate an efficient information resource management, the organization should analyze the business processes first by using BPR methodology. Successful organization should first analyze the current process and recognized the inefficient and weak points of the process, thereby improving the process in conjunction with information resource management.

6) Coordination and Communication: The CIO who is in charge of IRM should closely communicate with the line officers.

Recent Trends: IRM and EA

Some Strategic Issues

To achieve a more goal-oriented and effective e-Government, IRM should be considered as a prerequisite. If IRM is a overall governance scheme or strategic map, EA (Enterprise Architecture), based on this overall picture, is a technical design or blueprint for the e-Government. To have an effective IRM and EA, we need to consider the following strategies:

First, Clarification of Roles and Responsibilities. In the IRM process, many stakeholders are involved including the chief agency officer, ICT Administrator including CIO, middle management, line workers, public service users, and ICT service providers. IRM emphasizes the relevant role of each parties and the performance and accountability associated with the results should be accredited to each actors.

Second, Contribution to Organizational Goals. Even if information effort is development of new technologies and systems, it must be driven in the direction that contributes to the goals of organization. Consequentially, a systematic management control plan from planning to implementation and evaluation such as other capital investment should be applied.

Third, Co-management of Information Resources. Information and knowledge resources are valuable resources of the organization and therefore should be shared by the members of organization. Information resources, in this regard, should be commonly managed by the related agencies.

Fourth, Use of the Effective Means. IRM should be supported by the effective EA. The successful IRM cases, from the previous literature and research, were the ones that tried to continuously review the scheme that is able to reform and innovate agencies or MDAs(Ministries, Departments, and Agencies). In addition, by actively utilizing the BPs(best practices) and by setting up certain criteria and standards for managing information resources, the IRM was able to respond systematically to the changes of technology and operational environment. In this perspective, EA should reflect this kind of the basic principles in its technical design and architecture. When the IRM could be integrated with EA, the productivity of e-Government will be maximized(see Figure 9-4).

Figure 9-5 The Strategic Components of IRM

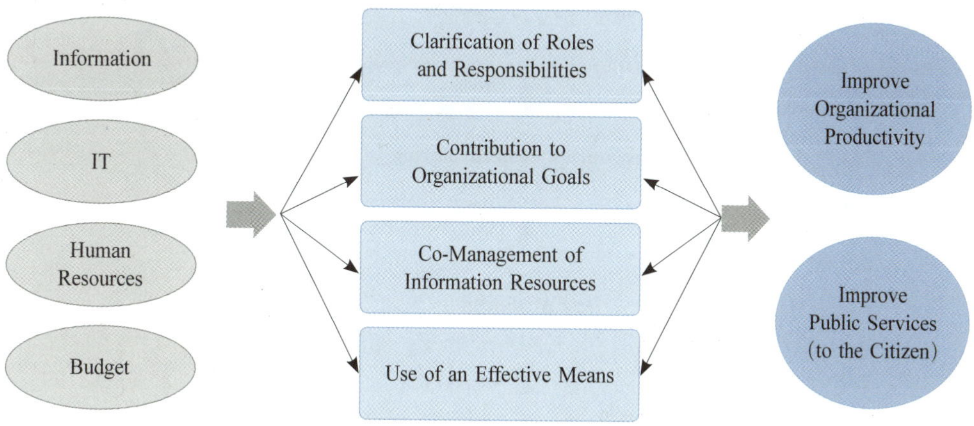

* Source: Revised from Kim, Seung-Keun(2007: 3-6).

Integration of IRM and EA

In the IRM process of the agency, EA is to carry out the role to support the technical scheme of the e-Government, especially by setting up the technical principles and criteria. If there is no criterion provided by EA, we cannot expect the effective IRM as individual business, organization, information systems, and data of agency will be separately operated. Therefore, IRM and EA should be integrated to ensure the reuse, joint use, integration, partnership and interoperability of e-Government. The followings are some strategies to integrate IRM and EA.

First, the authoritative agency should establish the overall IRM strategy and plan in conjunction with the vision and strategy of the organization. The agency also identifies the relationship between information systems and business operations using the technical architecture of EA. In this way, it should elastically respond to the radical changes of external environment such as the large-scale government restructuring or the large-scale business transfer due to the change of legal system or government reform.

Figure 9-6 The Technical Structure of EA

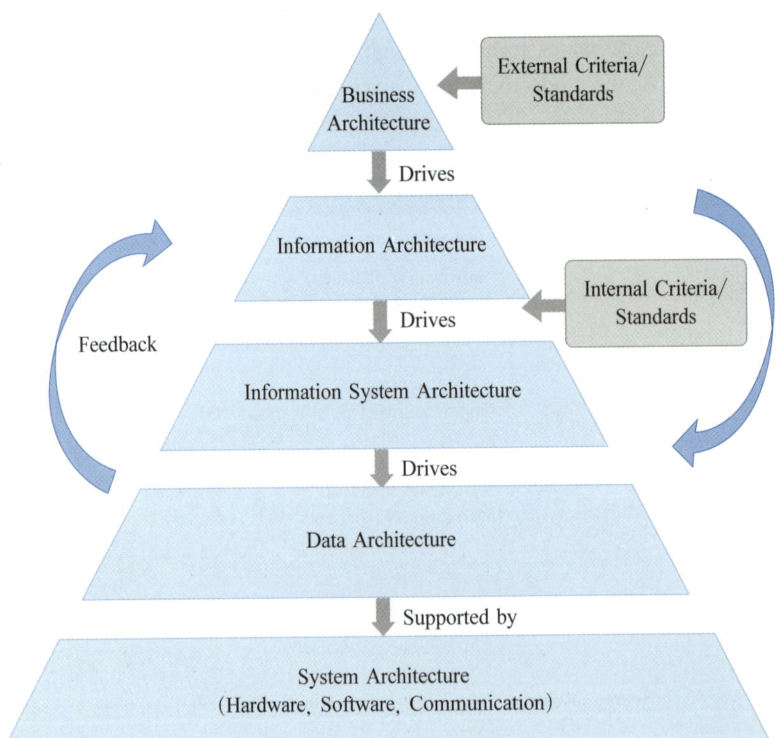

*Source: Revised from Kim, Jin-Hee(2002).

Second, the authoritative agency should establish a new e-Government business plan. In this process, the agency should check that the validity of the new ICT investment plan by investigating whether it conforms to the agency's policy goals. The agency should also investigate the new plan whether it is consistent with the specific goal of the current architecture of EA. In this way, the agency should avoid inefficiency or duplication of the ICT investment in the e-Government project (Choe, Jin-myeong, 2007: 31-32).

The Overall Scheme of IRM e-Governace in Korea

Along with the Vision and Leadership of the top management of national governance, which is the President, the strategic management level of each MDAs should be carried out. At this juncture, the overall scheme of IRM governance is the concept that makes it possible to achieve the strategic utilization of national information and knowledge resources. It is an integrated concept of overall scheme to support the business activities of knowledge management at the national level, from its creation, accumulation, and utilization, sharing and learning. It is an overall scheme of national laws, policies, technologies, and management relating with national allocation of information and knowledge resources.

The IRM laws and policies set up at the overall governance level should control and guide the information resource management plan at each agency level. And each agency should implement the ICT or e-Government initiatives in accordance with the overall

Figure 9-7 The Overall Scheme of IRM Governance

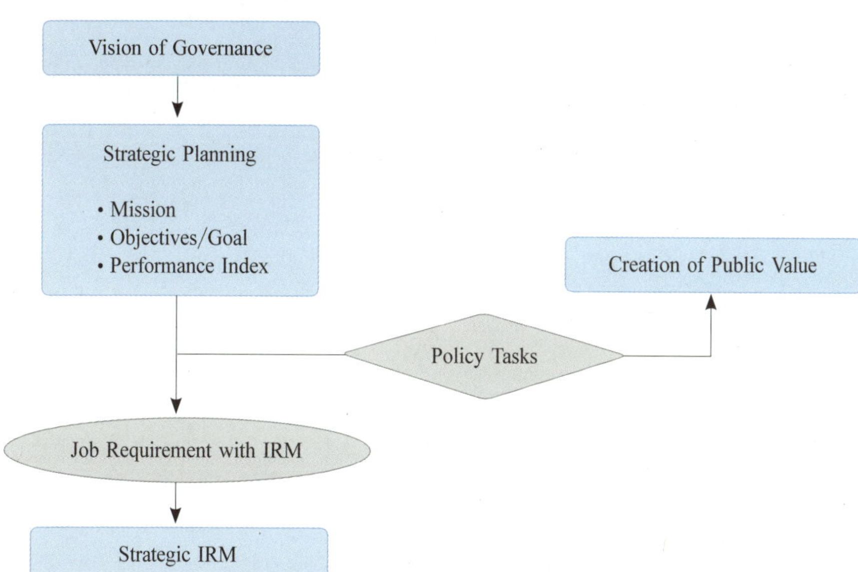

scheme of IRM governance to achieve the specific mission and goals of the organization. In a nutshell, IRM, in this regard, can be understood as an overall scheme to support the creation and innovation of public value in the national governance. The following figure presents the overall scheme of IRM governance in Korea.

Summary and Conclusion

This chapter highlighted e-Government Operational Strategy from the back-office building perspective. The chapter looks at how back-office building strategy can be employed to improve effectiveness and efficiency of the e-Government.

To improve productivity using e-Government's Back Office building strategy, this chapter examined the following concepts: e-documents, public official's digital literacy, government information common utilization, collaboration and e-Government 3.0, TQM, BPR, ERP, and IRM. The chapter further discusses about Electronic Document Distribution System, CIO, Government Common Utilization Center, Smart Work, and IRM and EA as recent trends of Korean e-Government initiatives.

Key Point!

◎ BACK-OFFICE STRATEGY

◎ Electronic Document

◘ Necessity and Importance

- The general concept of electronic document is the sharing of characters, symbols, or electronic records via computer network in order to convey ideas or opinions. This includes all official documents, email records and contents of conversations that are shared over computer networks or through internet.
- In order to improve business process, reduction of time spent on document processing must be in place.

◘ Policy Issues

- It is required to have a government-wide infrastructure management system.
- It is required to have an Inter-Agency consultation for such document processing, and distribution system.
- It is required to improve the documentation system.

◘ Recent Trends: Recent Trends: Government e-Document Distribution System

◎ Digital Literacy of Government Officials

◘ Concept

- In the information and knowledge society, literacy is determined by the ability to solve their immediate problems by utilizing information technology.

◘ Necessity

- Public official's digital literacy is an important factor in determining the speed and breadth of e-government implementation.

◘ Strategy

- This is a user-centric strategy that emphasizes on the users, comparing to the initial focus on infrastructure.

- One important strategy is to appoint an effective CIO to enhance digital literacy and competence of government staff.

Recent Trends: Chief Information Officer (CIO)

◎ Public Information Common Utilization

Concept and Significance

- Public information common utilization is to share and utilize information in a collaborative way between departments within the government agency, agency and citizen, or agency and enterprise to achieve the common value of government, that is to say human dignity or the happiness of the people.

Typology

- Common internal administrative functions of government agencies
- Common use of information for decision support
- Information common utilization for Civil Service

Strategies and Tasks

- Clear Policy Goal Setting
- Information Common Utilization Policy Mechanism as Government Reform System
- Reengineering of Government Personnel Function
- Reengineering of Government Work Process
- Updating Legal Framework

Recent Trends: Government Information Common Utilization Center in Korea

◎ Collaboration and E-Government 3.0

Concept

- Collaboration is indicating the situation that the number of government workers is performing tasks collaboratively by using the means of Smart information technologies.

◘ Public Value Management Model and Government 3.0

- Mark Moore(1995) presented the public value management model as the third generation governance model
- This PVM model emphasizes the public value compared to the market value emphasized by the NPM model

◘ Government 3.0 and e-Government 3.0

- E-Government 3.0, based on the paradigm of Government 3.0, highlights the strategic setting and transformation by utilizing the Smart knowledge management of Big data, sensor-based technologies, and semantic-based algorism. If e-Government 1.0 emphasized the government internal efficiency by using the concept of BPR, G2B, G2G, and G4C, e-Government 2.0 emphasizes the Open Platform of participation, sharing, open, and collective intelligence, highlighted by Web 2.0.

◘ Korean e-Government Model of 3.0

- The vision of e-Government 3.0 is to achieve the humanity-based society in which people's human dignity and quality of life are enhanced based on the democratic governance of transparency, accountability and reflexivity.

◘ Recent Trends: Smart Work

◎ BPR (Business Process Reengineering)

◘ Concept

- BPR is defined to rebuild the system by changing the people, process, and technology utilizing the Smart information technology that fundamentally reconsider the traditional way in all parts of business process.

◘ Features

- BPR is an innovation.
- BPR pursues a Zero-based approach.
- BPR focuses on the process.
- BPR pursues innovative goal setting, say, at least 30%, or from 50% to 100% increase of goal achievement.

- BPR actively utilizes the new information technology.

Strategies

- People:
  - Change process involving key stakeholders and internal work flow
  - Eliminate duplicate or redundant business processes
  - Redesign the business process from the viewpoint of citizen satisfaction
  - Perform organizational restructuring from the process efficiency
  - Review laws and regulatory framework to support the above activities

- Process:
  - Target to focus on time-consuming process
  - Attention to the process of paperwork involving several departments
  - Distinguish high-value, low-value-added process
  - Distinguish high-risk, low-risk process
  - Distinguish high-accountability, low-accountability process
  - Remove unnecessary, duplicate, and redundant non value-added work
  - Readjust business range according to the level of risk
  - Reengineer business process for performing work with high accountability

Technology:

- Establish the Smart ICT infrastructure for innovating and shortening business process
- Redesign and Integrate business process by utilizing ICT to speed up and to prevent from disconnected knowledge flow
- Establish IRM system for knowledge creation and utilization
- Establish integrated DB or DW system for knowledge accumulation and sharing
- Establish overall-company, ERP system for knowledge learning and proliferation by including customers and suppliers, or citizen, stakeholders and other related agencies

BPR failure factors

- Problems of communication: the department of work-site lacks the understanding on information processing departments
- Carried out within the existing organization: reengineering business team are more effective if to employ professional team

- Officers Rights: Failure may be attributed to the weakened director's authority
- Morale Issues: members of organization prefer the status quo more than change

◎ TQM (Total Quality Management)

◪ Concept

- TQM improves the employee's ability to do the job on the course of action and to eliminate the skill variation between employees. Continue to work to analyze the process of communication with customers and improve the quality of policy.

◪ Limitation(P. Drucker, 1980)

- The absence of clear performance standards
- Attempting to do many things at once
- Use too many workforce to solve the problem
- The lack of the spirit of experimentation
- Low-effect of training due to the lack of proper evaluation
- Path-dependency problem

◎ ERP (Enterprise Resource Planning)

◪ Concept

- Integrated management system that integrates into a single system standardization and implementation of information technology business functions and processes of the organization that is operated independently, try to maximize the utilization of various resources of the organization.

◪ ERP and BPR

- Efficient Work Flow from the System Integration
- Efficient Knowledge Management from the Database Integration
- Cost Savings from the Business Process Integration

◎ Information Resource Management(IRM)

◪ Concept

- Information resource management can be defined a set of management functions related to the disposal and the information creation, collection, processing, transmission, distribution, use, and storage.

Strategy

- Leadership
- Strategic management
- Performance management
- Recognizing as an investment rather than a cost
- Innovation process (BPR)
- Coordination between the person in charge of IRM and line

◎ Recent Trends: IRM and EA

- To achieve a more goal-oriented and effective e-Government, IRM should be considered as a prerequisite. If IRM is a overall governance scheme or strategic map, EA(Enterprise Architecture), based on this overall picture, is a technical design or blueprint for the e-Government.

- To have an effective IRM and EA, we need to consider the following strategies:
  - Contribution to Organizational Goals
  - Co-management of Information Resources
  - Use of the Effective Means

- **Integration of IRM and EA:**
  - The authoritative agency should establish the overall IRM strategy and plan in conjuction with the vision and strategy of the organization.
  - The authoritative agency should establish a new e-Government business plan.

- **The Overall Scheme of IRM e-Governance in Korea:**
  - Along with the Vision and Leadership of the top management of national governance, which is the President, the strategic management level of each MDAs should be carried out.
  - At this juncture, the overall scheme of IRM governance is the concept that makes it possible to achieve the strategic utilization of national information and knowledge resources.

- It is an overall scheme of national laws, policies, technologies, and management relating with national allocation of information and knowledge resources.
- The IRM laws and policies set up at the overall governance level should control and guide the information resource management plan at each agency level. And each agency should implement the ICT or e-Government initiatives in accordance with the overall scheme of IRM governance to achieve the specific mission and goals of the organization.

Key Question!

◎ Consider what methods can increase productivity is. Disucss Back Office building strategies of e-government.

◎ What is Information Literacy of officials? Let's discuss the necessities and roles for information literacy of civil servants in the knowledge-based society.

◎ Look at the concept and role of Chief Information Officer (CIO), problems and ways to improve operational guidelines of the current CIO system.

◎ Think about the concept of the critical elements of Total Quality Management (TQM). What are the possible ways to solve the problem and successfully realize effective management?

◎ Examines the concepts and key factors for a successful BPR.

◎ Let's discuss the concepts and components of Information Resource Management (IRM). What are the successful factors of IRM?

Chapter 10

OPERATIONAL STRATEGY OF E-GOVERNMENT(II): FRONT-OFFICE STRATEGY

Without a proper set up of the back-office foundation, e-Government could not achieve effectiveness and accountability of the government work processes.

››› Objectives

The purpose of this chapter is to explain the operational strategy of e-Government from the standpoint of the front office.

First, it will examine how to build front-office innovation strategy to enhance democracy and transparency by using the concept of Information Opening Policy, G4C, G2B, Green technology as the recent trend of G4C, electronic corruption (e-Corruption), and electronic participation (e-Participation). As a recent trend, it will discuss e-Green and e-OASIS of Seoul City Government.

Second, it will examine the law and institutional-based foundation to implement the successful Front-Office Innovation Strategy. It will discuss the strategic legal framework of e-Government in Korea and will derive the successful conditions and implications from the Korean e-Government development.

The strategy to set up a good e-Government can be divided by the criteria whether the work activities take place inside or outside of government. The Back Office is the main activities mainly take place at the inside of government and the Front Office is the main activities mainly take place at the interface of government and people.

While the Back Office activities will enhance productivity through G2G (Government to Government) or inside of government activities like CIO, BPR, TQM, ERP, IRM, the Front Office activities will enhance democracy and transparency of e-Government through the contact point activities of government like G4C (Government for Citizen) and G2B (Government to Business).

Information Opening Policy

Significance

Information opening policy is very important as it will facilitate the information utilization and accessibility of the people by ensuring free flow and open access of information. It will also make possible to criticize and control of the governmental activities, thereby enhancing policy participation in the democratic governance.

Strategy

1) The Information Opening Promotion through the Smart phone

The internet is used every day especially through the mobile devices like the smart phone. Therefore the internet is good tool for information opening. The internet makes people search all kind of information easily and the information opening policy should also provide the legal system to support this kind of mobile activities.

2) The Limit of the traditional Public Information Opening Act

It needs to minimize the limit of application of the Public Information Opening Act. The principle should be open and unavoidable non-disclosure must be minimized as far as possible. The specification of the list of the closed information is required.

3) Establishing the electronic information opening management system

In this era of information society, there is a need to revitalize the release of electronic documents. However, the legal framework to support this system is required.

4) Single Window for Information Access

The one window to information access is required. In case of opening information through internet, one URL is needed. For example, in Australia, the people can access information what they want at http://www.fed.gov.au and In USA, GILS(Government Information Location System) is operating.

G4C (Government for Citizen)

Concept

G4C is the project which tries to enhance the services of the public petition areas (e.g. residents, real estate, automobiles, tax and business enterprises etc) by building the internet portal site and by utilizing Government Information Common Center. The project called "the Single Window of e-Government" and "the innovation of the public petition" are the successful cases of "G4C(Government for Citizen)" project in Korea. The purpose of G4C is to electronize and informatize the public complaint or civil petition process and improve the quality of the public grievance service essentially corresponding to the rapid change of the policy environment.

Strategy

G4C is the project that intends to fundamentally innovate public complaints or civil petitions and to improve quality of life from the national life and business activities.

The effective strategies of G4C project are as follows:

1) The Innovation of the Civil Service Process

G4C should provide one-stop service to the area such as residents, real estate, automobiles, tax and business enterprises etc, by combining or deleting unnecessary documents or by using the Government Information Common Utilization Center.

2) Building A Single Window for Civil Petitions

G4C should provide the unified single window for civil petitions can deal with the application and issue of civil complaints through the internet. By doing so, people can apply various civil complaints and receive its result through the internet-based unified single window platform.

3) Building the Government Information Common Utilization Center

G4C should build the Government information common utilization center that can utilize the core national information. To this end, G4C should designate the core national information as the basic national information to be included in the Government Information Common Utilization Center. The core national information is a national strategic resource. The joint utilization of those resources will enhance the effectiveness and transparency of national e-Governance.

4) Improvement of Legal System

The legal framework must be prepared to clearly define the legal liabilities and accountabilities associated with electronic transactions of e-Document. The e-Security system and e-Certification system should also be provided to block illegal access or forgery of e-Document.

The Recent Trends: e-Green Service

The e-Green service is the paperless green civil service policy that contribute the low-carbon green growth through online civil service advancement plan. This project started in April, 2009 in Korea aiming to minimize public grievance and to improve e-Governance

Figure 10-1 Green Customer Services

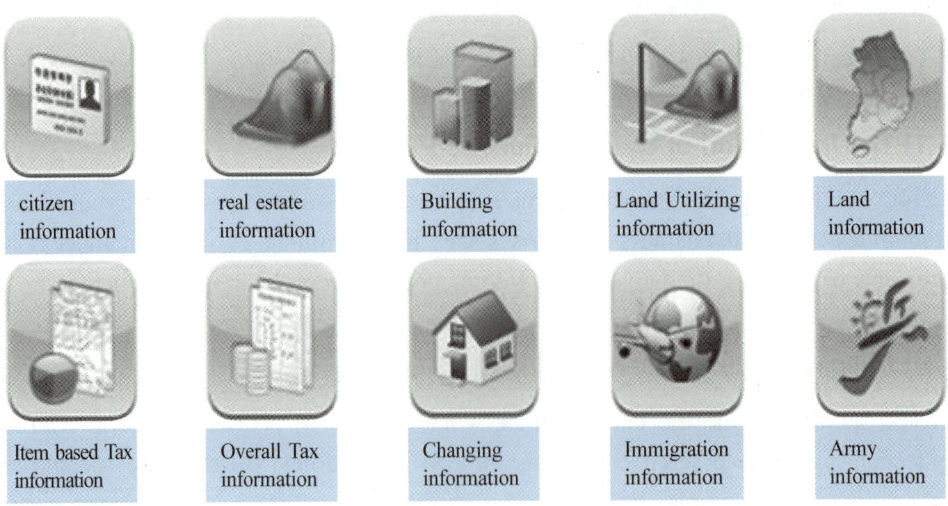

* Sources: http://www.minwon.go.kr.

system corresponding to the global standard of the low-carbon green growth.

The e-Green service is realized by the "civil service 24((http://www.minwon.go.kr)," the Korean government information service. The civil service 24 is the online service that guides the necessary information to people without visiting the office whenever and wherever they want for 24 hours and 365 days. This online civil service is including the guide the civil complaints, online reviewing of the civil complaints, online issue of the civil complaints, the package service of the civil complaints related to living, and online visiting whenever and wherever they want.

G2B(Government to Business)

Concept

G2B is the project that try to innovate the e-service delivering to the business enterprises. The purpose of G2B is to electronize and informatize the public procurement and improve the quality of the public service essentially corresponding to the rapid change of the policy environment. E-Procurement is the successful case of "G2B(Government to Business)" project in Korea.

Strategy

G2B system has 9 operational strategies as follows:

① To eliminate duplication and implement standardization (BPR)
② To implement own Database for effective G2B and e-procurement
③ To develop strategic plan for future integration of e-procurement
④ To integrate related MDAs Procurement System
⑤ To re-design of hardware and software for e-procurement system
⑥ To develop proper legal framework
⑦ To review comments from users/clients and evaluate the system
⑧ To increase interoperability
⑨ To assure for security, privacy and backup of the system

Expected Effects of G2B

The expected effects of G2B are as follows.

1) Improving the Business Efficiency

By constructing the G2B system, various information is provided online to users in a lump through the integrated bidding function, as a result, there are no necessity for checking one by one to get needed information through various media.

2) Enhancing the Process Transparency

By constructing G2B system, the public offices can accumulate and manage the business-related information systematically. Then it can send the electronic standard document to the business enterprises at high speed. Business enterprises can prepare the electronic document remotely and monitor the results by the one-stop process. Therefore the fairness and transparency of the decision is assured in the government related bidding or procurement processes.

3) Increasing the Business Competitiveness

By constructing G2B system, public relation(PR) is possible by registering goods at shopping mall, the private B2B is revitalized based on e-commerce and the market of procurements is expanded. As reducing unnecessary works through electronic process and it make the business enterprises concentrate their own business, as a result, the business competitiveness and the quality of goods will be improved.

E-Corruption

Concept

The electronic corruption (e-Corruption) is defined as "the misdeed, corruption or crime of the public official, the private contractor or authorized person through the computer system of the public organizations"(ICAC, 2001; Lee, Tae-Young, 2008: 50-51). "e-Corruption" is the concept appeared after e-Government was introduced.

'Corruption' means illegal actions when the public official offends the legal statute through abusing or exerting their governmental authority directly and indirectly for their selfish interests or desires. Therefore, e-Corruption can be understood as that the public official, who has authorities accessing to national information system, damages to the people through rigging the information and communication system for their selfish interests or desires.

Vulnerability and Causing Factors of e-Corruption

The followings are the vulnerability and causing factors of e-Corruption and the authoritative agency should respond to these crimes by understanding these typologies first:

Table 10-1 Vulnerability and Causing Factors of e-Corruption

Vulnerability	Explanation
Automation & immediacy	The automated work process and speed in the e-Gov makes more difficult to audit and inspection with the existing methods
Loss of collateral information	The absence of face-to-face in the governmental trading limits the standard of judgment to other party of transaction in cyber-space, as a result, the government office is cheated the online trick by conspire with inner government official
Accessibility and Ubiquity	By realizing e-Gov, the service can provide at any time and anywhere, but it also offers the same potential opportunities to the corrupt government officials
New business models	By making service be difficult and hard to understand at the first process of business, the intermediate groups can cheat or make a profit
Encryption	By cryptographic technique being complicated and renewed day by day, the investigation of corruptive behavior is also getting difficult

* Source: Revised from Choi, Young-Hoon et. al(2003: 152).

E-Participation

E-participation is the concept of citizens to participate in various government decision-making processes by utilizing the smart ICT devices. The purpose of e-participation is to enhance transparency and democracy in the democratic governance.

E-participation is related to the evolving stages of e-Government. E-Government oriented ideology has a step-by-step maturity. As shown in 〈Figure 10-2〉, the first stage is to improve the effectiveness and efficiency of government operations. The second stage is to provide customer-oriented government service. The third stage is to achieve democracy, transparency, and reflexivity through the smart e-devices. E-Participation is a very important requirement to achieve a trusted and matured society, which is the highest vision and purpose of e-Government that is shown as democracy and reflexivity in the Figure(Kwon, Gi-Heon, 2008a: 60).

Figure 10-2 E-Participation and E-Government

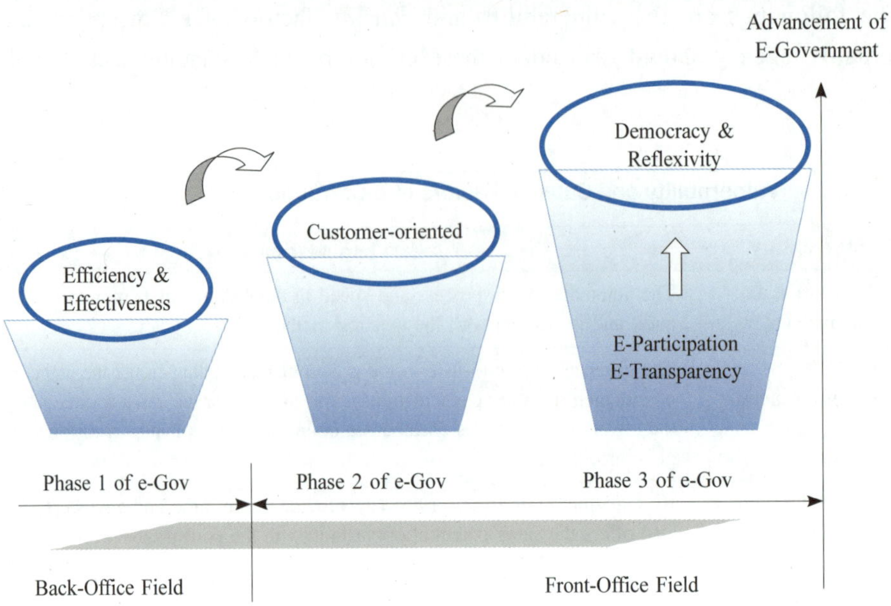

* Source: Revised from Kim, Sun-Kyung(2007:36).

Significance

The importance of e-participation is raised by the following ideological aspects of democracy and efficiency.

First, it is necessary for e-participation to cope with the crisis of representative democracy, where the power and functions of the administration greatly expanded up, representative politics is fading out, and the traditional administrative control by the legislature or the judiciary is not able to function as it should be. In this regard, e-participation, as a direct democracy instrument, is expected to supplement the limitation of representative democracy.

Second, it is necessary for e-participation in order to ensure the efficiency of the administration. As e-participation can be utilized as the channels of new policy ideas or suggestions raised by the citizen, it can help to improve the quality of the policy management or to break the government's inertia or path dependency by infusing new airs to the stagnant bureaucracy.

Recent Trends: The Policy Case of OASIS: Seoul City Government

1) Concept

OASIS is one of the successful e-Government program operating by Seoul City Government.

Using this web-site, over ten million citizens of Seoul city are able to offer the policy ideas. The name of program means citizen can imagine city's policies whatever they want which indicates that the public policy space of Seoul City Government is opened for all the citizen.

2) Features

OASIS has the following four features:

First, in terms of offering creative ideas for city's policies through the Internet, it is a kind of on-line civic suggestion system on policy ideas.

Second, it is also citizen participation in terms of being able to receive pros-cons debate by diverse stakeholders of policy.

Third, it is a two-way communication system that Seoul government and citizens could react to interactively.

Finally, it is a collaborative governance system that Seoul citizen could directly participate in city policy making and administration.

3) Operational Process

The operational process of OASIS is divided into the following five stages:

(1) Suggestion (Step for Idea Suggestion): Once an idea is suggested, citizen and a group of citizen in the online system evaluate it and put it on the discussion menu in the online system.

(2) Discussion (Step for Supplemented by Discussion): Citizens, experts, and government officials will discuss and comment about the suggested ideas. At working-level meeting, they analyze the results of the discussion and decide whether to put to the formal meeting agenda.

(3) Review Feasibility (Step for Realization Meeting): The preliminary report on the suggested agenda will be made and discussed whether it will be implemented based on feasibility analysis. All the process of this realization meeting is to broadcast live over the Internet.

(4) Project Implementation (Step for Implementing Project): The planning for the new project will be made and revise the related laws and rules, if necessary.

(5) Project Completion (Step for Project Evaluation and Rewards): Seoul City government will reward to citizen who propose the project or dedicate them in the Hall of Fame Award. In 2010, approximately 157 cases were brought to the realization meetings, 90 cases of them have been completed, the 42 cases of them are on the progress of realization, and 20 cases of them are in the planning stage.

Figure 10-3 The Operational Process of OASIS

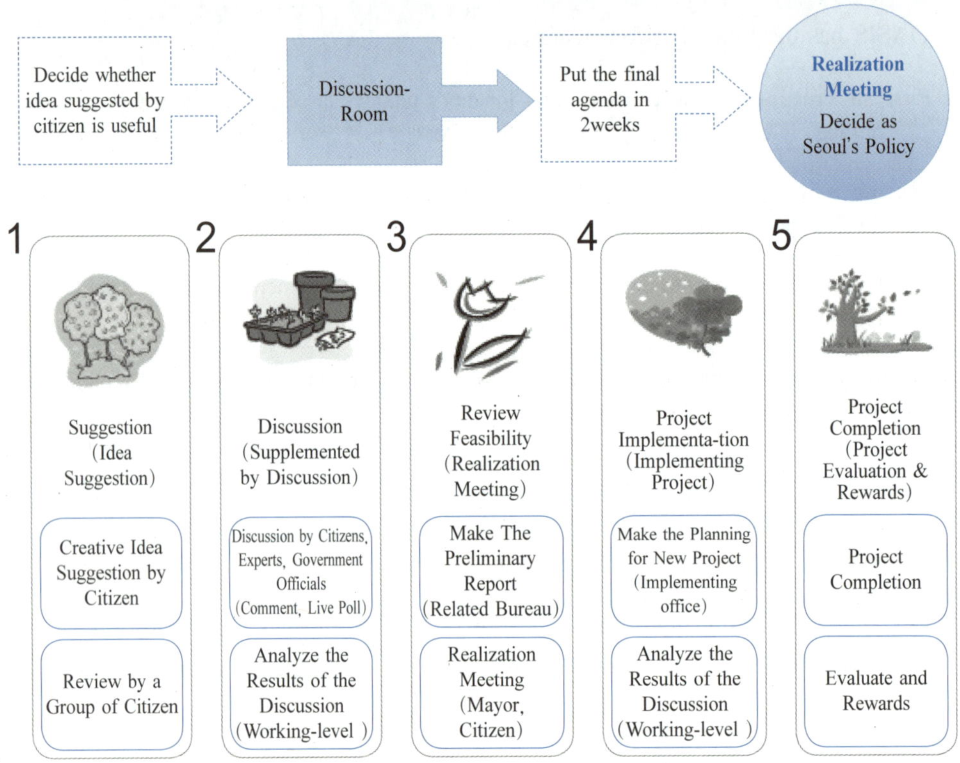

* Source: Revised from http://oasis.seoul.go.kr

Basic Legal System of E-Government

Korea's E-Government Strategies: Overview

In the 1970's, Korea's informatization initiative was driven by the government with the start of the Administration Computerization Project. Since 1978, the 1st (78-82) and 2nd (83-87) Administration Computerization Projects, and the 1st (87-91) and 2nd (92-96) National Basic Information System Projects have been progressed, and until the mid-1990s, the foundation of Korea's national informatization was established.

Following the administration computerization and national basic information system project, Korean government could be able to focus more on information superhighway projects starting 1995(1st: 95-97; 2nd: 98-2000; 3rd: 2001-2005).

And then Korean government enacted the "Framework Act on Informatization Promotion" in August 1995, and proceeded the "Basic Planning on Informatization Promotion" (1st: 96-98; 2nd: 99-2001; 3rd: 2002-2006). This was the foundation of information and knowledge society in Korea.

In addition Korean government enacted the "e-Government Act" in 2001, and embarked on "e-Government Project" (1st: 2001-2001; 2nd: 2003-2007). This was the foundation of e-Government advancement in Korea.

Especially, under the Kim Dae-Jung Government, Korean government established the "Special Committee on e-Government" under the Presidential Office in 2001, and preceded 11 e-Government projects such as e-Civil Petition, e-Procurement, and e-Home Tax System. At this time, Korean government improved the government process toward the people and business enterprises, and suggested the blue print of the world best model of e-Government providing efficient and transparent public services.

The notable project at this time was to promote the "Creative Knowledge-based Nation," and to accomplish the "10 Million Information Education for People" in response to the digital divide and to enlarge the demand basis of national informatization. This was an important turning point to consider the demand sides of e-Policy and e-Strategy compared to the previous efforts focusing on the supply sides of e-Policy and e-Strategy, such as providing information bask-bone system and information infrastructure in Korea.

Subsequently, under the Ryo Mu-Hyun Government, Korean government embarked on 31 e-Government projects. This government focused on building up a participatory e-Governance by innovating the way of work process in the government, such as e-Document, e-Finance, e-Local Government, e-Audit, e-Congress, e-Court, e-Personnel, e-Diplomacy, and e-Governance Management.

Under the Lee Myung-Bak Government of 2008-2013, Korean government enacted the "Basic Act on National Informatization" in 2009, and at the same time, accomplished the "Basic Planning on National Informatization" (2008-2012). This government initiated Smart e-Government project based on openness, sharing, and collaboration and highlighted the new initiatives like e-Green promoting the low-carbon, green growth strategy and e-Strategies responding to the low-birth, aging trends of the Korean society. In addition, this government changed the paradigm of Korean e-Policy and e-Strategy from promotion to utilization by providing the safe and trustful legal framework of e-Government, especially in the areas of personal information protection and privacy, e-Security, e-Authorization, and e-Property Right. At the same time, government rearranged the regulatory framework in the areas of software, online digital contents, broadcasting, and internet multimedia broadcasting.

The notable system change of e-Government in Lee Myung-Bak regime was to create National Informatization Promotion Committee under the governance of Presidential Office. This was a significant movement because its status was upgraded to the Presidential level, although the regular meeting is managed by the Co-chairmanship of Prime Minister and civilian expert (see Figure 10-4).

Under the Park Geun-Hye Government of 2013-2018, Korean government is now pursuing the new initiatives of e-Government 3.0 which emphasizes transformation and new direction that serves for creative economy and happiness of all people in Korea. This government is emphasizing the government working process by removing walls between MDAs or sectionalism to create a better public value for the people. At the same time, based on Big Data and smart technologies founded on knowledge management system, Korean government is trying to upgrade policy decision-making system and the activities of collaboration.

Framework Act on National Informatization

"Framework Act on National Informatization" is divided into the following three areas of Informatization Promotion of National Society: Sustainable Development of ICT, Technology and Industry, and Upgrading ICT Infrastructure.

First, the Informatization Promotion of National Society includes: 1) The area of e-Government such as Electronic Government Act, Regulations Governing Efficient Management of Administrative Affairs, and Civil Petitions Treatment

Figure 10-4 Legal Framework for Korean National Informatization Strategy

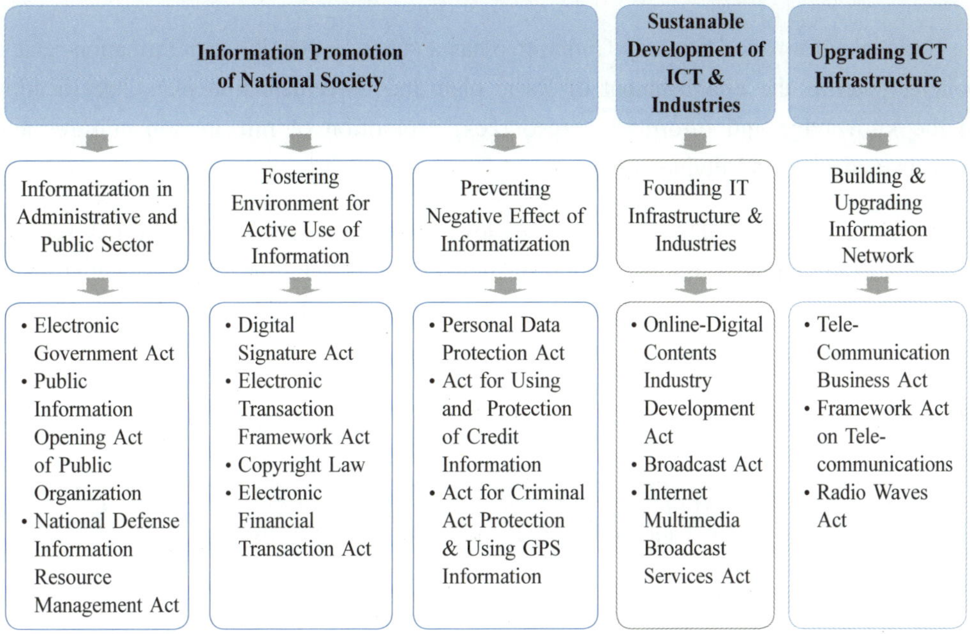

Act; 2) The area of Information Utilization Environment such as Digital Signature Act, Framework Act on Electronic Commerce, and Copyright Act; 3) The area of Information Dysfunction Prevention such as Protection of Personal Information, The Use and Protection of Credit Information Act, and Protection of Communications Secrets Act.

Second, the Sustainable Development of ICT Technology and Industry includes Software Industry Promotion Act, Online Digital Contents Industry Development Act, Broadcasting Act, and Internet Multimedia Broadcast Services Act.

Third, upgrading ICT Infrastructure includes the promotion of ICT Network Use and Protection, Framework Act on Telecommunications, and Radio Waves Act.

The Framework Act on National Informatization is drawn as the following 〈Figure 10-3〉.

Korean E-Government Strategic Governance System

Under the Framework Act on National Informatization, Lee Myung-bak government established a National Information Strategy Committee as the national informatization strategic governance system in November 2009. National Information Strategy Committee established under the President to deliberate on matters related to the promotion of national information.

National Information Strategy Committee has a supreme position in information-related policies such as the establishment of Basic plan and implementation plan, specification of the knowledge and information resources, promotion of information culture, and prioritization of digital divide policy.

It can be evaluated that the Korean e-Government Strategic Committee has secured its status as the national informatization of the Control Tower from the Presidential level. It identifies and promotes the future-oriented information policy agenda according to the paradigm of the new information and knowledge society.

Co-chair of the National Information Strategy Committee consists of the Prime

Figure 10-5 Korean e-Government Strategic Governance System: The Korean National Informatization Strategic Committee

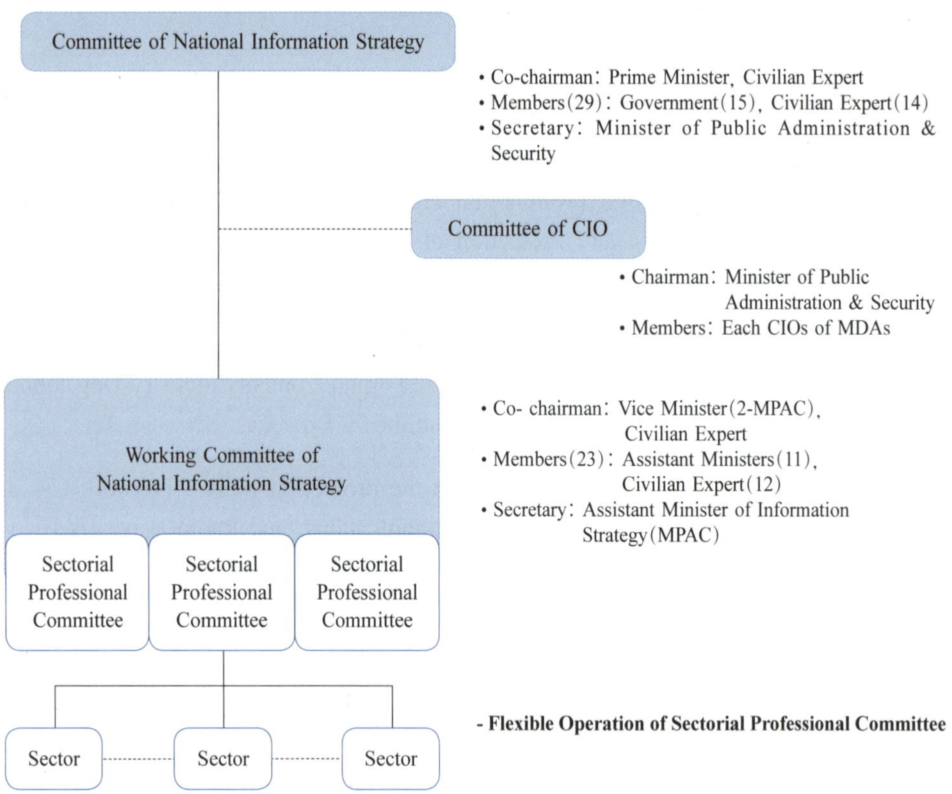

* Source: Revised from Ministry of Public Administration & Security(2010: 47).

Minister and civilian expert. Total of 31 people, including the 15 ex-officio government members and 14 civilian experts in the ICT area have been involved. National Information Strategy Working Committee is composed by a panel of experts (total 10) to review the agenda submitted to the National Information Strategy Committee.

The Korean National Informatization Strategic Committee as the Korean e-Government Strategic Governance System is drawn as the following 〈Figure 10-4〉.

Vision & Strategy

The vision of Korean National Informatization is to realize advanced knowledge and information society that ensures the convenience and safety of the people by information based on creativity and trust. Here, 'creativity' means to create a new value-added and to improve the efficiency of each sector of national society by the creative use of Smart ICT devices. 'Trust' means to create an environment of sustainable information promotion based on the sound information culture. Ultimately, it aims to contribute to the realization of a leading & advanced nation.

To achieve this vision and goal, Korean government has established the following four implementation strategies based on the creativity and confidence unlike in the past: 1) The utilization-centered informatization, 2) The convergence and communication of informatization, 3) The active response for information dysfunction, and 4) The promotion of public-private collaborative e-governance system. The vision and strategy of Korean National Informatization are drawn as the following 〈Figure 10-5〉.

These overall scheme can be interpreted as giving credits for informatization promotion achievement in the past Korean governments, recognizing the limitations and problems from the top-down drive of Korean government initiatives, the Korean e-Government strategy should establish a new direction as a strategic setting for the future Korean informatization to realize the genuine human-centered society.

The successful factors of Korean e-Government could be summarized:

1) Strong Information Infrastructure based on economic development especially in the electronics, semi-conductor and heavy-equipped industries, which was early pursued by the strong and committed leadership of President Park Jung-Hee.
2) Consistent ICT Infrastructure Projects and e-Government Initiatives uninhibited by the changes of the political regimes.
3) Combination of Supply(Government-drive) and Demand(Social needs based on People's education and awareness) Strategies.

Figure 10-6 Vision and Strategy of Korean National Informatization

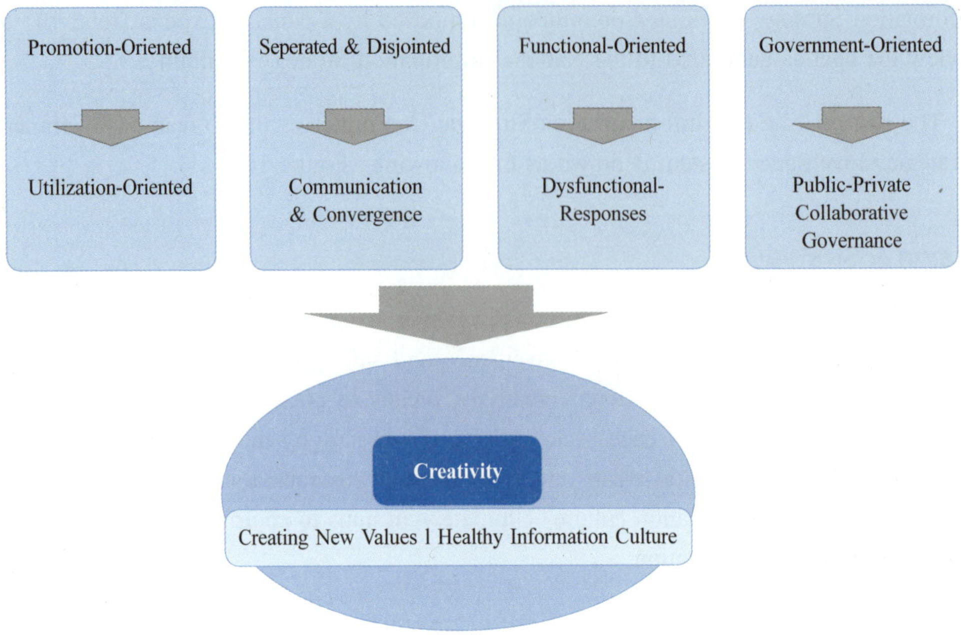

* Source: Revised from Ministry of Public Administration & Security(2010: 36).

4) Combination of Top-down Government Drive and Incentive-based Public-Private Partnership.
5) Strong Promotion Committee supported by the national highest level of Governance, such as President and Prime Minister.

Summary and Conclusions

In this chapter, we reviewed the second part of operating strategies of e-Government, that is, e-Government strategy for upgrading the front-office strategy to enhance democracy and transparency. The key elements of each part can be summarized as follows:

First, this chapter examined the front office strategy for enhancing democracy and transparency by reviewing information openness policy, G4C and G2B. Green Civil services is highlighted as a recent trend for G2C. E-Participation was also discussed at the democracy and transparency dimension.

Secondly, this chapter also examined the legal foundation of e-Government. These foundations include the basic law of informatization promotion and the future vision and strategy of Korean national informatization and e-Government. In addition, the successful factors of Korean e-Government were also analyzed and presented.

Key Point!

◎ FRONT-OFFICE STRATEGY

◎ Information Opening Policy

Significance

- Information opening policy is very important as it will facilitate the information utilization and accessibility of the people by ensuring free flow and open access of information.
- It will also make possible to criticize and control of the governmental activities, thereby enhancing policy participation in the democratic governance.

Strategy

- The Information Opening Promotion through the Smart phone
- The Limit of the traditional Public Information Opening Act
- Establishing the electronic information opening management system
- Single Window for Information Access

◎ G4C (Government for Citizen)

Concept

- G4C is the project that try to innovate the service of the public petition areas(e.g. residents, real estate, automobiles, tax and business enterprises etc) by building the internet portal site and by utilizing Government Information Common Utilization Center.

Strategy

- The Innovation of the Civil Service Process
- Building A Single Window for Civil Petitions
- Building the Government Information Common Utilization Center
- Improvement of Legal System

The Recent Trends: e-Green Service

◎ G2B (Government to Business)

◘ Concepts

- G2B is the project that try to innovate the e-service delivering to the business enterprises.
- The purpose of G2B is to computerize and informatize the public procurement and improve the quality of the public service essentially corresponding to the rapid change of the policy environment.

◘ Strategy

- To eliminate duplication and implement standardization (BPR)
- To implement own Database for effective G2B and e-procurement
- To develop strategic plan for future integration of e-procurement
- To integrate related MDAs Procurement System
- To re-design of hardware and software for e-procurement system
- To develop proper legal framework
- To review comments from users/clients and evaluate the system
- To increase interoperability
- To assure for security, privacy and backup of the system

◘ Expected Effects of G2B

- Improving the Business Efficiency
- Enhancing the Process Transparency
- Increasing the Business Competitiveness

◎ E-Corruption

◘ Concept

- The electronic corruption(e-Corruption) is defined as "the misdeed, corruption or crime of the public official, the private contractor or authorized person through the computer system of the public organizations."

◘ Vulnerability and Causing Factors of e-Corruption

- Automation & immediacy
- Loss of collateral information

- Accessibility and Ubiquity
- New business models
- Encryption

◎ E-Participation

Concept

- E-participation is the concept of citizens to participate in various government decision-making process by utilizing the Smart ICT devices. The purpose of e-participation is to enhance transparency and democracy in the democratic governance.
- The purpose of e-participation is to enhance transparency and democracy in the democratic governance.

Significance

- It is necessary for e-participation to cope with the crisis of representative democracy.
- It is necessary for e-participation in order to ensure the efficiency of the administration.

Recent Trends: The Policy Case of OASIS: Seoul City Government

◎ Basic Legal System of e-Government

Korea e-Government Legal System Overview

- In the 1970's, Korea's informatization initiative was driven by the government with the start of the Administration Computerization Project.
- And then Koean government enacted the "Framework Act on Informatization Promotion" in August 1995, and proceeded the "Basic Planning on Informatization Promotion"(1st: 96-98; 2nd: 99-2001; 3rd: 2002-2006). This was the foundation of information and knowledge society in Korea.
- Under the Kim Dae-Jung Government, Korean government established the "Special Committee on e-Government" under the Presidential Office in 2001, and proceeded 11 e-Government projects such as e-Civil Petition, e-Procurement, and

e-Home Tax System.

▸ Subsequently, under the Ryo Mu-Hyun Government, Korean government embarked on 31 e-Government projects.

▸ Under the Lee Myung-Bak Government of 2008-2013, Korean government initiated Smart e-Government project based on openness, sharing, and collaboration; and highlighted the new initiatives like e-Green promoting the low-carbon, green growth strategy and e-Strategies responding to the low-birth, aging trends of the Korean society.

▸ The notable system change of e-Government in Lee Myung-Bak regime was to create National Informatization Promotion Committee under the leadership of Presidential Office.

▸ Under the Park Geun-Hae Government of 2013-2018, Korean government is pursuing the new initiatives of e-Government 3.0 which emphasizes transformation and new direction that serves for creative economy and happiness of all people in Korea. This government is emphasizing the way of government working flow by removing walls between MDAs and sectionalism to create better public value for the people. At the same time, based on Big Data and smart technologies based knowledge management system, Korean government is trying to upgrade policy decision-making capacity based on the activities of collaboration.

Framework Act on National Informatization

▸ The Informatization Promotion of National Society includes:

- The area of e-Government such as Electronic Government Act, Regulations Governing Efficient Management of Administrative Affairs, and Civil Petitions Treatment Act.
- The area of Information Utilization Environment such as Digital Signature Act, Framework Act on Electronic Commerce, and Copyright Act.
- The area of Information Dysfunction Prevention such as Protection of Personal Information, The Use and Protection of Credit Information Act, and Protection of Communications Secrets Act.

▸ The Sustainable Development of ICT Technology and Industry includes Software Industry Promotion Act, Online Digital Contents Industry Development Act, Broadcasting Act, and Internet Multimedia Broadcast Services Act.

- The Upgrading ICT Infrastructure includes the Promotion of ICT Network Use and Protection, Framework Act on Telecommunications, and Radio Waves Act.

Vision & Strategy

- Vision
  - The vision of Korean National Informatization is to realize advanced knowledge and information society that ensures the convenience and safety of the people by information based on creativity and trust. Here, 'creativity' means to create a new value-added and to improve the efficiency of each sector of national society by the creative use of Smart ICT devices. 'Trust' means to create an environment of sustainable information promotion based on the sound information culture. Ultimately, it aims to contribute to the realization of a leading & advanced nation.
- Strategy
  - To achieve this vision and goal, Korean government has established the following four implementation strategies based on the creativity, trust and confidence unlike in the past: 1) the utilization-centered informatization, 2) the convergence and communication of informatization, 3) the active response for information dysfunction, and 4) the promotion of public-private collaborative e-governance system.

Successful Factors of Korean E-Government

- Strong Information Infrastructure based on economic development especially in the electronics, semi-conductor and heavy-equipped industries, which was early pursued by the strong and committed leadership of President Park Jung-Hee.
- Consistent ICT Infrastructure Projects and e-Government Initiatives uninhibited by the changes of the political regimes
- Combination of Supply and Demand e-Policy and e-Strategies
- Combination of Top-down Government Drive and Incentive-based Public-Private Partnership
- Strong Promotion Committee supported by the highest level of Governance, such as President and Prime Minister

Key Question!

◎ Let's discuss the way to enhance the ability to decision-making as Front Office Building Strategies for e-government.

◎ What are the concept of G2B and G4C?

◎ Let's think about Korea e-Government Legal System?

◎ What are the Successful Factors of Korean E-Government? Discuss it and think about what could be lessons & implications relevant for your own country.

Chapter 11

THE NEXT GENERATION OF E-GOVERNMENT MODEL

The Next Generation of e-Government should integrate world by connecting the current technology to the future dream.

Objectives

The purpose of this chapter is to discuss the next generation of e-Government model. It will discuss the changes in the Information Technology environment, e-Government and Information Technology, Mobile Government, and Ubiquitous Government.

First, it will examine the government technology trends, ICT development, and the lessons and prospects casting to the development of the next generation of e-Government.

Second, it will examine the emerging concept of Mobile government, the characteristics and relationship between e-Government and mobile government. It will further discuss the development and policy direction of mobile government in Korea.

Third, it will examine the emerging concept of Ubiquitous Government. In this section, it will review the drivers on the development of ubiquitous government from the perspective of technical supply and service demand. Also, it will touch on the issues such as ubiquitous government technological trends. Finally, it will further discuss the vision and strategies of Korean Ubiquitous Government to derive the clear lessons and implications about the success factors of Korean e-Government.

Information Technology and E-Government

ICT development has brought major changes in the Internet world. There is an increasing demand for technological development for real time support in the field of software technology, mobility, multi-media, intelligence, integration, knowledge, and personalized applications. The demand is to increase real-time services of large-capacity multimedia data on high-speed communication; it is expected to become a significant real-time high-capacity data processing technology, real-time video processing technology, and synchronization technology.

In addition, because of the development of mobile technology, it can be connected regardless of time, place, devices, and network. The new GIS technology, which connects the virtual space and real space, are expected to change significantly in the aspect of openness, network and internet, four-dimensional factors, mobile and video integration.

Real-time services of large multimedia big data, wired and wireless made the services faster and more convenient and can be accessed anytime, anywhere. It is possible to build a four-dimensional and realistic in administrative services in the e-government mechanism. The development of real-time high-capacity processing technology, synchronization technology, and the mobile environment support technology made possible the process of the large amounts of big data and applications in the e-government mechanism.

Due to these rapid development of smart information technologies, the smart e-Government environments were changed as follows: 1) An environment where there is no spatial, geographical restrictions, 2) An environment where there is no constraint of communication capacity, 3) An environment where there is no restriction on the network, terminals, and contents selection, and 4) An environment where there is no constraint of communication target.

It is expected that the striking development of the smart e-technologies will enhance the overall mobility, convenience, efficiency, and safety by transforming the business process of the internal government operations. The smart technologies will also be transformed in a interconnected way and will be appeared as a new phenomenon of new era. We may called the e-government embodied those new technologies "M-Government," "U-Government," or "Smart Government."

Mobile Government (M-Government)

Concept

Mobile government is the process wherein various government services through a mobile terminal based on the wireless internet. M-Government ensures the mobility and/or portability, and provides ease of access, timeliness, security, and personalization for business and citizen. M-Government provides mobile public services (G2C), mobile business services (G2B), and mobile administrative services (G2G) to take advantage of wireless interne (Im, Soo-Jung, 2010).

Figure 11-1 Mobile Government Services

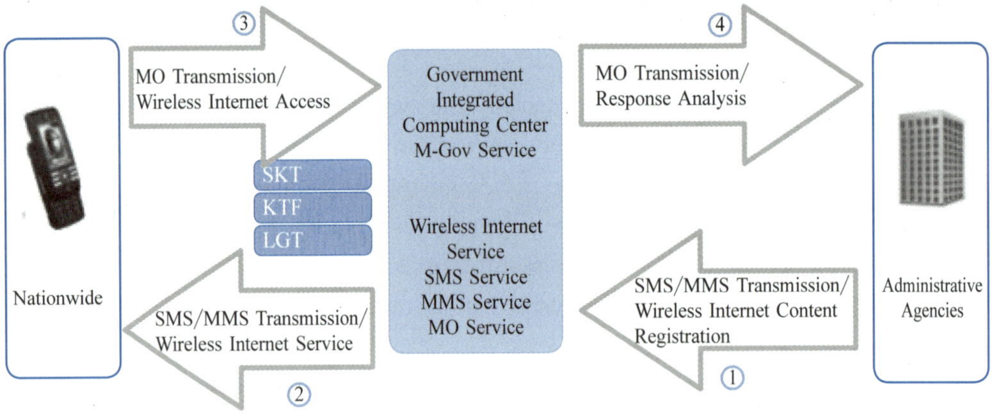

* MO Service: Message-Oriented Service

Features

The features of mobile government services are as follows:

First, M-government can provide public services of high quality at low cost.

Second, M-government can provide various public services through realization of a mobile two-way transfer of SMS-MMS services. A wide range of services are available, such as the sending and receiving lengthy, short, and video messages.

Third, M-government can provide the ongoing quality of service management. It maintains and repairs the system in a systematic and sustained way through quality management of the mobile service.

Fourth, M-government can provide public services thorough security management system. Using mobile communication integration center and a leased government line, a tight security management of government agencies is operating.

Korean Mobile Government Service

The m-Government services based on the smart phone recently has been advocating smart work and effective government, which may be called as smart government. Smart government provides various forms of communication channels to people through the smart phone based online applications. Smart m-government, based on a two-way communications, evolves to provide proactive communication with people through a variety of smart media. Smart m-Government services are focusing on the customized, individual-based services, while e-Government services in the past were largely the public-based services.

The following 〈Figure 11-2〉 indicates the direction of the next generation e-Government services. Since 1996, government services based on the PC began to be spread and expansion. Since the beginning of the 2000s, government services based on the mobile began to be increasing. In the future, government services based on the fusion of broadcasting and communications using smart phones, tablet PC, and smart TV will be spread out.

〈Figure 11-3〉 shows the growing trends in the use of mobile government. Looking at the trend of mobile government agencies, from 2007 until the end of 2009, mobile government agencies and the number of services had been remarkably increasing. It also appeared larger during the years 2008-2009 than the increase in 2007 to 2008. Due to

Figure 11-2 The Next Generation of E-Government Services

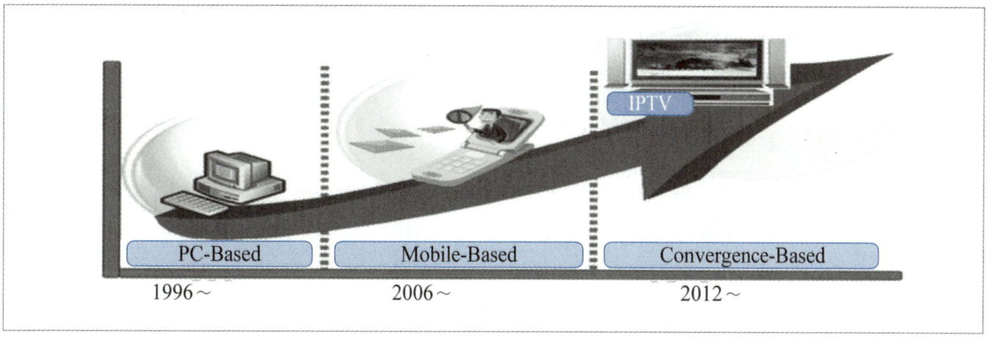

* Source: Korean Government Integrated Information Center (2010).

Figure 11-3 Mobile Government Agencies and Services

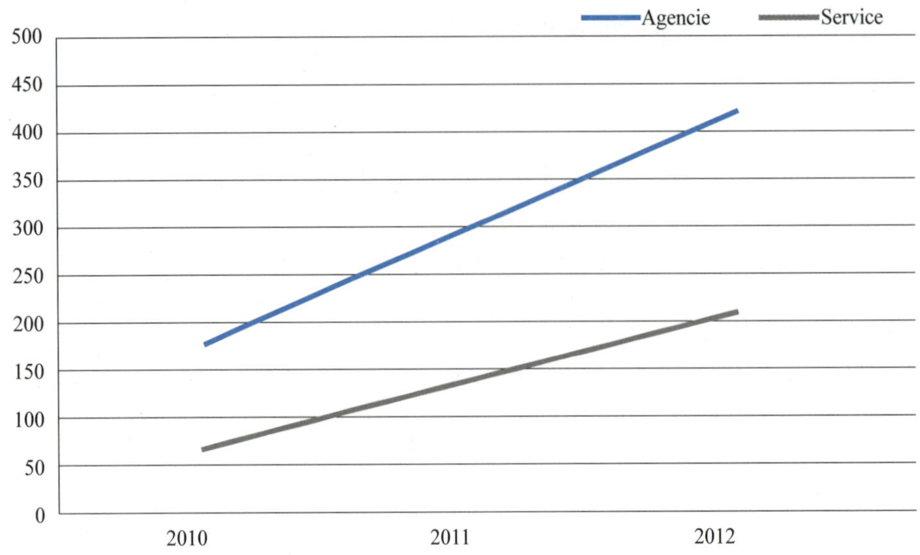

* Source: National Information Agency (2013)

the increase of smart phone users, the increasing trends of m-Government users will be phenomenal.

M-government services can provide flexible services to people anytime and anywhere. Service providers overcome the limitations of place due to the features of mobile enhancing interactivity with clients. As the information society evolves, Mobile communication services will be more popularized. As wireless communication technology evolves, the public services will be more developed to a personalized and customized.

Ubiquitous Government (U-Government)

Concept

Ubiquitous government is the government to process various government services with so-called 5 Any, Anywhere, Anytime, Anyplace, Any device, and Any network. In this u-Government people can get their desired service freely regardless of time, place and devices.

U-Government is more advanced form than m-Government because u-Government can

Figure 11-4 Concept of U-Government

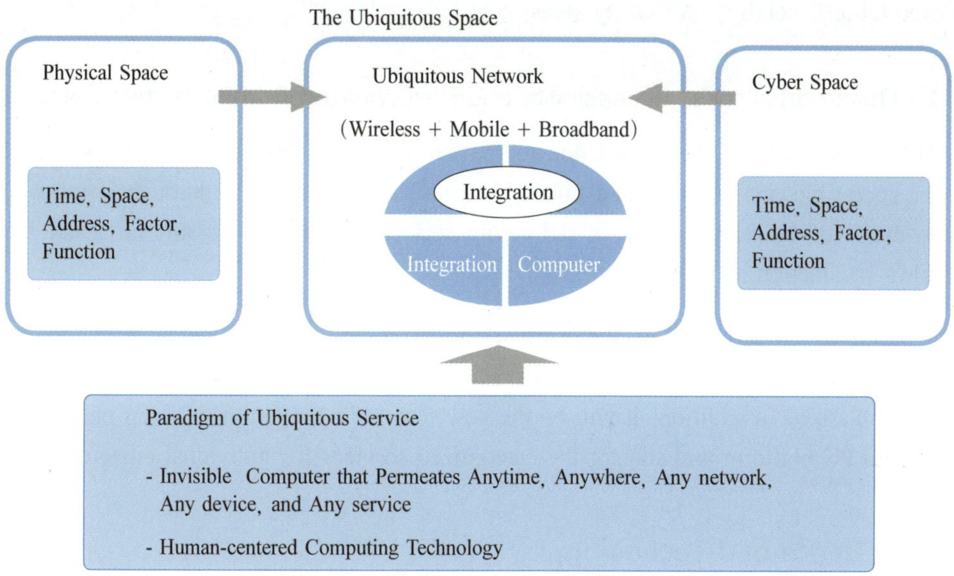

* Source: Revised from Bae, Kang-Won(2009).

utilize the more diversified devices than m-Government. U-Government can utilize not only Mobile terminals but many kinds of RFID/Sensors based services so that the various devices like mobile terminals, DTV, KIOSK, and smart phones will be used to improve the accessibility of u-Government. Therefore u-Government is a kind of the most updated form of e-Government opening a new era of e-Government to provide people with the necessary services anywhere and anytime.

The Drivers of U-Government

The drivers of the Ubiquitous Government are divided by supply factors and demand factors as follows:

1) Supply Factors: Sensor Technology RFID

U-Government is possible due to the development of sensor technology, especially called RFID. Due to the development of sensor technology, RFID (Radio Frequency Identification) is a system that processes information attached to things in the non-contact ways through radio signals to identify the tag in the form of thin and flat. RFID composes of 1) The reader to read and decrypt functions (RF reader), 2) RF tags (RFID tag) containing a unique ID information, and 3) The operating software and network. These RFID technologies are utilized in a variety of applications such as logistics, transportation, security, and safety areas.

2) Demand Factors: Accessibility and Personalized Administrative Services

U-Government was developed due to the demand of the better services such as the better accessible and personalized public services. E-Government, although it innovated many ways of traditional ways of delivering services to people, is still far away from people's satisfaction and utilization level.

Ubiquitous Government is the form of government 'always exist everywhere' and it will stimulates the demand for public services by reducing the reluctance of digital illiteracy classes. In addition, it will be the new form of e-Government using personalized tools than PC platform and suit for the customized services for individual citizen.

Recent Trends of U-Technology

The recent trends of technologies for enabling the ubiquitous government are as follows:

1) IPv6

IPv6 is short of the "Internet Protocol Version 6". By increased use of the internet, IPv6 is an advanced form of Internet protocol, called the next generation Internet.

2) Giga Internet

Giga Internet is to provide internet service a class of up to 1Gbps to their subscribers by using ultra-broadband subscriber networks technologies (FTTx, HFC, LAN). It is an advanced form of internet services compared to BcN(see Table 11-1).

Table 11-1 Comparison of BcN and Giga Internet Services

Division	BcN service	Giga internet service
Subscriber Network Speed	50M~100M	100M~up to 1G
Representative Service	Video Phone, IPTV	Multi-Angle TV, 3DTV, Giga P2P/Web Hard

* Source: The Korea Communications Commission, Korea Information Society Agency (2009)

3) IP-USN

IP-USN is the abbreviation for Internet Protocol Ubiquitous Sensor Network. The USN service provides the various services based on the Internet infrastructure like BcN (the next generation of intelligent networks), IPv6 (next generation Internet address system), WiBro, and Wireless LAN (Oh, Se-Geun, 2007).

4) Cloud Computing

(1) Concept

Cloud Computing is a computer technology that borrows the computing resources (hardware, software), as much as a user wants, existing in the form of intangible like Cloud. Using virtual technologies, it provides by integrating computing resources that exist in different physical locations. Therefore, it means the computer environment that information resources are permanently stored in the Main Servers on the Internet while they are temporarily stored in the Client Servers like Desktop, Tablet PC, Laptop, Net books, and Smart phones, etc. In other words, Clouding Computer is a computer based on cloud computing technology, which makes possible storing and retrieving data on the Internet Server Computer.

(2) Advantages

The advantages of cloud computing is as follows:

Figure 11-5 Implementation Concept Map of Cloud Computing

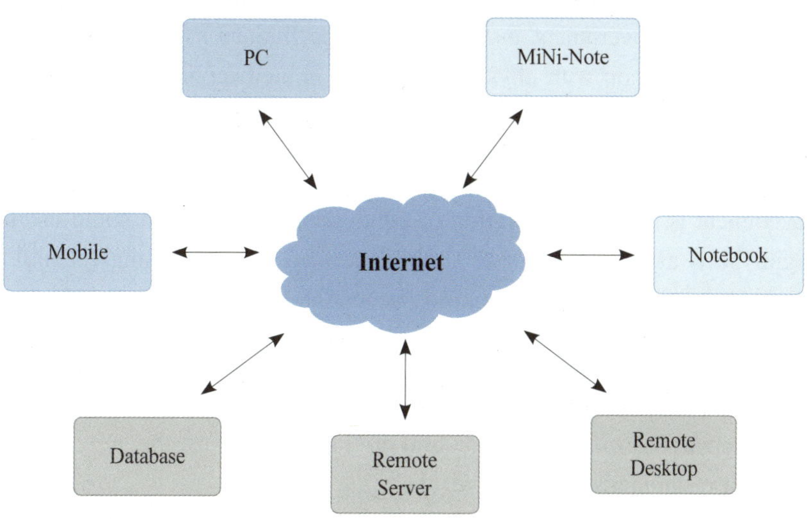

First, Cloud Computing ensures to store data securely by storing the data on an external server, while storing the data on the PC can be damaged by the hard disk failures.

Second, Cloud Computing can overcome the constraints of storage space.

Third, Cloud Computing has a strong security foundation as the records are not being saved in the personal storage media.

Fourth, Cloud Computing allows reviewing and revising document anytime, anywhere.

(3) Disadvantages

The disadvantages of cloud computing is as follows:

First, if the server is hacked, there is a high risk of leakage of personal information.

Second, if the server fails or breaks down, the materials may not be available.

E-Government vs. U-Government

Until now, the concept of e-Government was to overcome the existing physical space through Internet-based information technology by providing operations and services on the electronic space. However, if the e-space is not linked with the physical space, the development and growth of e-space must face limitations. Electronic space is the virtual and incomplete space as the e-space cannot exist in independently disconnected from the physical space.

The key challenges of new information strategy were to link and converge between the physical space and the electronic space. Ubiquitous information technology suggested a new direction for how the physical space and the electronic space will be linked. If the next generation of e-government is to overcome the limitations of today's e-government caused by poor connection with physical space and limited services to e-space, ubiquitous e-government can provide a new solution and this is the reason why we call u-Government as the next generation of e-Government.

U-Government is the next generation of e-Government because it could use ubiquitous technologies such as the wireless & mobile networks, and sensing technologies and RFID. In addition, ubiquitous technologies enable to overcome the functional and essential limitations of physical and electronic space by integrating electronic space and physical space.

The differences of e-Government and u-Government as the next generation of e-government are summarized in 〈Table 11-2〉.

Table 11-2 Comparison between E-Government and U-Government

Classification	E-Government	U-Government
Technical Aspect	Information Super-highway Network or Internet Technology	Broadband, Wireless & Mobile Networks, Sensing Technology(RFID)
Government Service Delivery	Immediate and Transparent Service Delivery	Intelligent Work Process, Providing Customized/Personalized Public Services
Operational Method	Immediacy, Transparency, Efficiency, Democracy	Intelligence, Equity, Real-time, Customer Orientation

Differences of the next generation e-government can be understood in terms of the possibility of a new service from the development of ubiquitous information technology. The conceptual meaning is basically identified as an extension of the past.

Strategies for Realizing the Vision of Ubiquitous Government

Strategies for realizing the vision of the next generation of u-Government will be able to be promoted from three perspectives: public service, government efficiency, and infrastructure (Oh, Kwang-Suk, 2003).

1) Public Service

In terms of the public service, u-Government should consider for digital divide for information alienation, information accessibility, and direct democracy. In particular, the basic strategy should expand of the information accessibility on the e-Government by enlarging media aside from the PC Internet.

2) Government Efficiency

In terms of the government efficiency, u-Government should seriously consider for the collaboration as the collaboration will assure government transparency and efficiency. On the technical side, ubiquitous technologies like P2P technology, wireless, or mobile communication technologies will be useful for enhancing collaboration.

3) Technology Infrastructure

In terms of infrastructure, u-Government should consider for the government-wide integrated computing environment based on the standardization. It is necessary to enhance the capacity of broadband in wire environments, while spreading out the wireless based technologies. In particular, the spread of wireless and mobile technology and the

Figure 11-6 The Base Technology for Ubiquitous Government

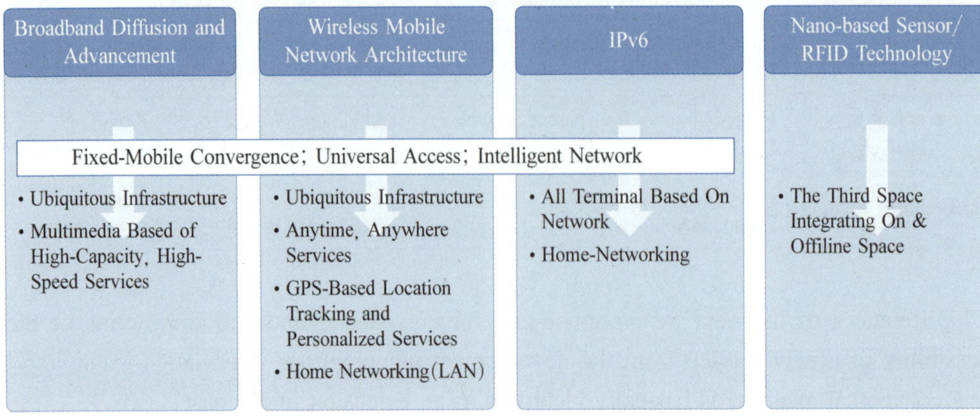

transition to IPv6, the internet address system, is the prerequisite for the realization of u-Government. The base technologies for u-Government are suggested as 〈Figure 11-6〉.

Vision and Strategies of the Korean U-Government

Ubiquitous Government proceed to the following four stages: advancement stage of one-stop services of electronic government, entry stage of intelligent U-Government, development stage of customized service of U-Government, and advancement stage of U-Government. 〈Table 11-3〉 shows the detailed contents of the development stages of U-Government. Also, 〈Figure 11-7〉 shows the vision and strategies of the Korean U-Government.

Table 11-3 The Development Stage of U-Government

Period	Information Means	Range of Information Utilization in Public Sector
2005-2007 (Advancement Stage of One-stop Services of E-Government)	(Wired and Wireless Integrated Internet, Broadband and Ubiquitous Element)	• Provide integrated services, linked online and offline • Provide personalized service to fit the demands of the citizens and businesses • Change the policy of e-Government services to u-Government services: Prepare the basic policies and information protection scheme for the u-Government

2007~ (Entry Stage of Intelligent U-Government)	(Ubiquitous Information Technology)	• Intellectual approach of e-government services through a variety of media accesses, such as online, mobile, sensor, voice, and chip etc. • Innovate e-Government infrastructure toward customer-oriented and invisible e-Government services through the basic concept, Anytime, Anywhere, Any networks, Any devices, and Any service (5Any). • Provide the required security elements
2010- (Development Stage of Customized Service of U-Government)	Highly Developed U-Technology	• Real-time and comprehensive means of service innovation • Provide two-way personalized service by implementing ubiquitous sensors into important national infrastructure • Changes in the concept of participation of e-Governance
2013- (Advancement Stage of U-Government)	Full Range of Ubiquitous Information Technology	• The highly developed sensor and chip is embedded in all things, the concept of access media is meaninglessness, e-Gov services can be provided by voice or other means • Through second ubiquitous information technology, the service area is expanded to all areas of invisible government functions

* Source: Revised from Do, Kyeong-Hwa(2005).

Figure 11-7 Vision & Strategy of the Korean U-Government

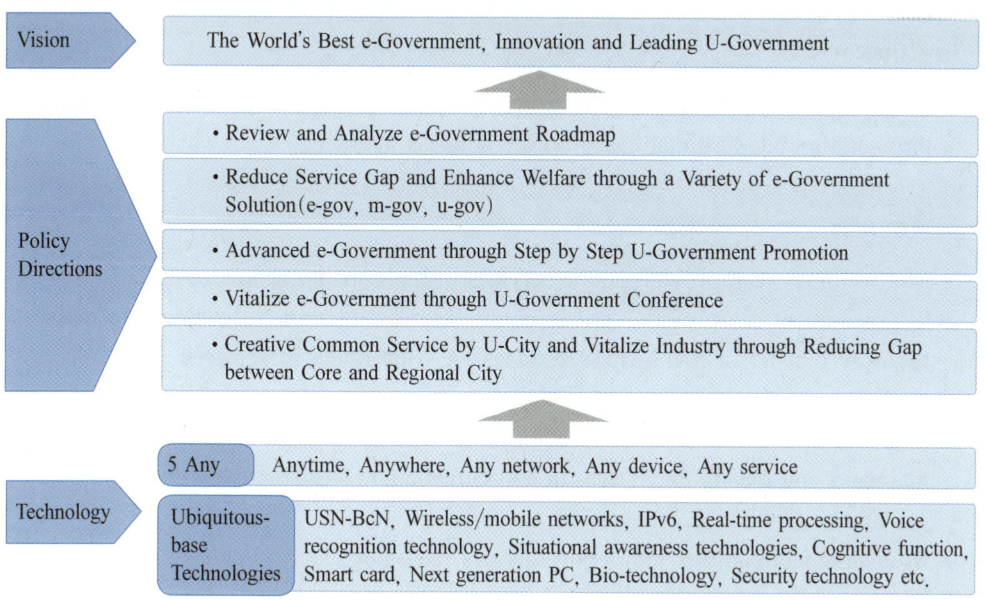

* Source: Revised from Do Kyeong Hwa (2005).

Key Point!

◎ Information Technology and E-Government

▸ ICT development has brought major changes in the Internet world. There is an increasing demand for technological development for real time support in the field of software technology, mobility, multi-media, intelligence, integration, knowledge, and personalized applications.

▸ General environment change of e-Government result from development of information technology

- An environment where there is no spatial, geographical restrictions
- An environment where there is no constraint of communication capacity
- An environment where there is no restriction on the network, terminals, and contents selection
- An environment where there is no constraint of communication target.

◎ Mobile Government(M-Government)

Concept

▸ Mobile government is the government to process various government services through a mobile terminal based on the wireless internet.

Features

▸ M-government can provide public services of high quality at low cost.

▸ M-government can provide various public services through realization of a mobile two-way transfer of SMS-MMS services. A wide range of services are available, such as the sending and receiving lengthy, short, and video messages.

▸ M-government can provide the ongoing quality of service management. It maintains and repairs the system in a systematic and sustained way through quality management of the mobile service.

▸ M-government can provide public services thorough security management system. Using mobile communication integration center and a leased government line, a tight security management of government agencies is operating.

◎ Ubiquitous Government (U-Government)

Concept

- Ubiquitous government is the government to process various government services with so-called 5 Any, Anywhere, Anytime, Anyplace, Any device, and Any network. In this u-Government people can get their desired service freely regardless of time, place and devices.

The Drivers of U-Government

- Supply Factors: Sensor Technology RFID
- Demand Factors: Accessibility and Personalized Administrative Services

Recent Trends of U-Technology

- IPv6
- Giga Internet
- IP-USN
- Cloud Computing

E-Government vs. U-Government

- U-Government is the next generation of e-Government because it could use ubiquitous technologies such as the wireless & mobile networks, and sensing technologies and RFID.
- Ubiquitous technologies enable to overcome the functional and essential limitations of physical and electronic space by integrating electronic space and physical space.

Strategies for Realizing the Ubiquitous Government

- Public service: U-Government should be considered for digital divide for information alienation, information accessibility, and direct democracy. In particular, the basic strategy should expand of the information accessibility on the e-Government by enlarging media aside from the PC Internet.
- Government efficiency: U-Government should be seriously considered for the collaboration as the collaboration will assure government transparency and efficiency.
- Technology Infrastructure: U-Government should be considered for the government-wide integrated computing environment based on the standardization.

Key Question!

◎ What influenced does ICT has in the development of e-Government?

◎ What is Mobile Government? What is the difference between e-Government and Mobile government?

◎ Summarize strategic and successful development of Mobile government and Ubiquitous government.

◎ What is U-Government? Which is the different between E-Government and U-Government?

PART 4

THEORY & STRATEGY OF KNOWLEDGE GOVERNMENT

In Part IV, Theory and Strategy of Knowledge Government, the various aspects of Knowledge Government theory will be explored.

First, we will discuss the concept and vision of Knowledge Government.

Second, we will discuss the operational strategies of Knowledge Government, including the management components such as compensation or incentives, HRD system, business processes, and organizational culture.

Knowledge government highlights the management factors other than the technological factors of e-Government. To create and utilize knowledge, we need to move beyond the technical paradigm of e-Government.

Informational system or technological infrastructure itself, however smart they are, could not solve the problem. Therefore, we need some of the compensation or incentive system, human resources, and other management factors to make e-Government fully knowledge-creating and problem-solving intelligent model. Entrepreneur government and learning government, in addition to the paradigm of e-Government, are required to be supplemented for a better problem-solving knowledge government. To explore these issues of focal points, the paradigm of knowledge government will be explored in this Part.

Chapter 12

THE THEORY OF KNOWLEDGE GOVERNMENT

The management environment of the 21st century is charactrized by time, speed and uncertainty;
For organizations to survive in these environment,
learning must be realized consistently through digital neutral networks.

- Bill Gates

››› Objectives

The purpose of this chapter is to elucidate the theory of knowledge government. This chapter will cover the theoretical background, definition and visions of knowledge government. Subsequently, it will evaluate the framework of knowledge government of Korea, and drawing some important policy implications.

First, it will explore the rise of knowledge government starting from the need of national innovation system, change of international order, development of ICT, and change of the people's demand perspective.

Secondly, it will explore the concept and vision of knowledge government based on the concept of knowledge.

Thirdly, it will evaluate the process of knowledge government in Korea and thereby learning important lessons and implications from the analysis. For this purpose, in this section, it will first present the analytical framework and then assess the process of knowledge government.

Problem Definition

Knowledge has been appeared as a core paradigm of the 21st century. As P. Drucker (1993: 29) properly predicted, the post-Capital society is coming in which knowledge, not capital or natural resources which was the dominant resources in the Capitalist society last 250 years, becomes the most important key resource of the nation. Knowledge has become the key element of national competitiveness; Knowledge society, knowledge-based economy, and knowledge-based government are the most important buzz words in these days.

In this background, this chapter consists of two research objectives. First, we will theoretically explore the definition of 'knowledge government' which is the core concept of the knowledge and information society. Secondly, we will evaluate the progress of knowledge government in Korea and derive some important lessons and implications from the analysis. For this purpose, we will first draw the assessment framework of the knowledge government from the knowledge and knowledge-based perspective.

Theoretical Background

First, let's examine some of the important theoretical background that caused the emergence of Knowledge Government. There are four factors as shown below.

The Necessity of the National Innovation System

The bureaucratic paradigm of government was appropriate to lead the huge industrial society during the last 200 years. The policy decision-making was mainly at the top of the bureaucratic organization and could move the huge bureaucratic organization effectively as if the large machine of huge factory was operating. This hierarchical pyramid was effective in leading the industrial state.

But the time is over. The throad-cutting competition of world markets was heightening, the speed of technological development was ever accelerating, and the diversity of social organization was ever increasing. The rigid, hierachinal machine system is not effective to cope with these kinds of multidimensional change of the knowledge society.

Figure 12-1 Change of Government Paradigm

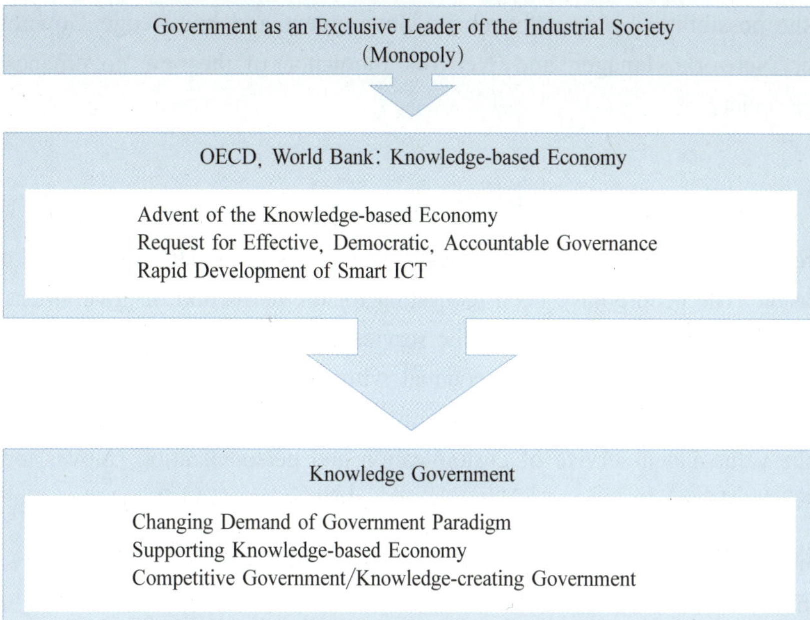

Adapting to the rapid environmental change means that preparing organization to respond to all these changes at all times. The national innovation system is the phrase of the words indicating the national knowledge system reacting those rapid changes of the environment; the system of knowledge governance that diffusing innovation by creating and sharing information and knowledge scattering all the sub-units of national society. The paradigm of knowledge government was highlighted with this backdrop of environmental change.

Change of an International Order

At the spatial axis as well as the temporal axis, the world market has been changing radically. After the Cold War between East and West, the new trade regime of WTO appreared. These open trading systems meant that all economic/industrial sectors were to operate transparently, with no sectoral boundaries, including every regulation of domestic industry, law, procedure and business practices.

The Development of ICT

The development of information and communication technology, as a tool of promoting changes, plays an important role of stimulating the bigger change of knowledge society. The introduction of ICT suggested extensively new ways of doing the job process. It promoted changes in governmental roles and organizational structures, opening the possibilities of transforming e-Government and knowledge Government as the proper 'Network Manager' and 'Network Innovator' of the new governance in this knowledge society.

The Increase of the People's Demand

We are living in a more democratic society that the people's participation and demands are increasing. The people have been requesting for the correction of government failures and wanting more choices from the public service that suit their needs. They expect that the quality of public service should coequal with that of private sector. As shown in the 〈Figure 12-2〉, the citizen, after reaching the basic expectations of material service, through the value-added service of customization and personalization, moves toward the best the top-level leading service of "Involve me, Inspire me, and Remember me!"

Therefore they are more sensitive about the cost and benefit of taxes they are paying, more critical about the bureaucratic and inefficient administration. As a result, they are

Figure 12-2 The Changing Patterns of Citizen Expectation

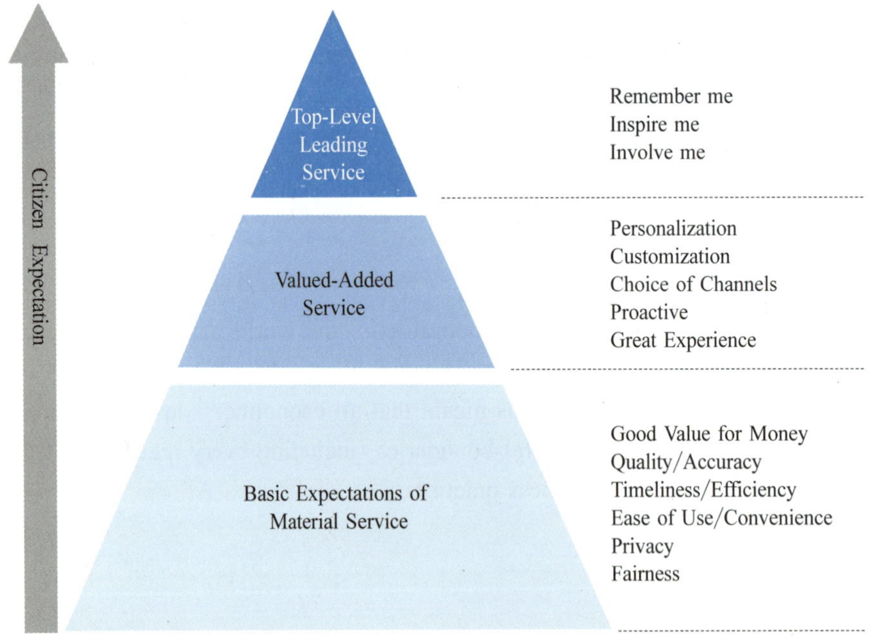

*Source: Revised from the Citizen Concept of UAE Government Service

demanding more competitive government with greater customer satisfaction, which might be realized in a form of knowledge government.

Definition and Vision of Knowledgy Government

Knowledge

OECD defined knowledge by four types. First, 'know-what' as a kind of fact often called the 'Information.' It distinguishes the expert from somebody who has much information or not. Second, 'know-why' is the natural law or scientific knowledge often called 'systematic knowledge.' It is produced from research institutes and applied to the production process. Third, 'know-how' is the ability to do something. Lastly, 'know-who' is the knowledge about who can do something.

The former two types of knowledge, called codified knowledge, can be gained by reading books or accessing related DBs, but the latter two types of knowledge, called tacit knowledge, can be gained by real experiences. Kwon, Gi-Heon (2000) explained this process of knowledge activities to the process of 'creation-accumulation-sharing-utilization-learning.' (See Figure 12-3).

Figure 12-3 Life Cycle of Knowledge Activities

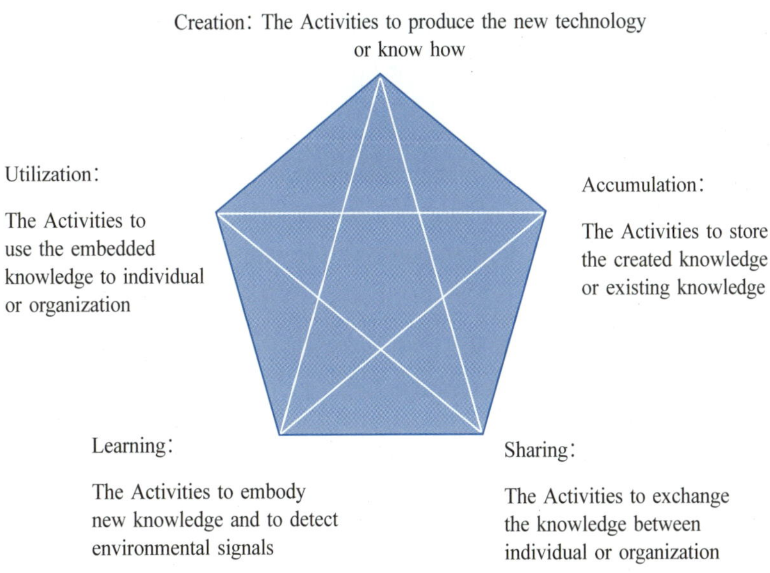

Table 12-1 The Knowledge Activities in the Government

KNOWLEDGE PROCESS	KNOWLEDGE PROCESS OF GOVERNMENT	
	KNOWLEDGE PROCESS OF ORGANIZATION	KNOWLEDGE PROCESS OF INDIVIDUAL
Creation	The knowledge that is produced through R&D activities, monitoring, policy evlaution, and analyzing people's needs	The individual know-how to enhance administrative efficiency
Diffusion	The public use of knowledge through e-Government	Open access to the individual knowledge store
Utilization	The application to the policy decision-making	Increase productivity through the use of diffused knowledge
Accumulation	Classification and management of e-documents that are produced in e-Government	Accumulation in the knowledge store

The knowledge activities in the government can be divided to the organizational knowledge activities and individual knowledge activities of the officials. The organizational knowledge activities are for achieving policy goals effectively, while the individual knowledge activities are for improving official's own productivity.

Knowledge and Knowledge Government

The meaning of knowledge in the company's intellectual capital as a key resource means an intangible asset. Knowledge and intellectural capital in organizations helps quick and accurate decision-making and management activities as these kinds of knowledge are embodied in an individual or organization, technology, know-how, type, and systems.

Knowledge management in government operations creates a huge value. These values are related with a proper decision-making and setting strategies for a nation's future blue print because knowledge is the key resource in the entire policy-making processes of national governance.

Definition of Knowledge Government

Knowledge government is defined "a new form of government that maximizing productivity of public services by increasing and accelerating knowledge cycle activities, that is, knowledge creating-accumulating-sharing-utilizing-learning (Kwon, Gi-Heon, 2000). To have these effects, three critical prerequisites should be met.

Table 12-2 Definition of Knowledge

Researchers	Content
Nonaka & Takuechi (1995)	The skill acquired by one's own true experience and belief.
Wiig (1995)	The accumulated knowledge of truth, faith, outlook, concepts, judgments, expectations, methods, and know-how to be applied to particular situations and problem-solving.
Leibeskind (1996)	The information to gain validity throught the verified process.
Heibeler (1996)	The meaningful information of an organization to use and implement to the action.
Davenport, Long, Beers (1998)	The information associated with experience, situation(context), judgments, and ideas.
Leonard & Sensiper (1998)	The information based on the experience to be utilized immediately to soleve the problem at hand.

Table 12-3 Definition of Government Knowledge

Core Knowledge	Key Contents
Problem Definition	Investigate Peoples Needs Define the Proper Government Role Cost-Benefit & Cost-Effectiveness Analysis
Institution Building	Setting up Incentives Institutionalizing Key Actors Rearraging Law and Institution
Strategy Setting	Leadership Skills Setting Strategic Direction & Vision Sharing Government Knowledge Understanding Peoples Needs

* Source: Revised from Samsung Economic Research Institute (1999).

First, Incentive system with Entreprenuer Government. The organization should set up a fair and effective incentive system to create knowledge. To create knowledge in the typical bureaucratic settings is not an easy task because information and knowledge involves risks and uncertainty. To overcome the risk and uncertainty especially under the environment of bureaucracy, special incentive system is required. If individuals are forced to obey strict bureaucratic hierarchical system, such as a rigid audit and inspection system, not many public officials would attempt to create knowledge under the risk of personal sacrifces.

Second, Learning with Learning Government. Once created, created knowledge should be utilized in the organization. To be utilized and learned, there should be an organizational culture to learn something. Knowledge is useless if it is not learned and utilized. Therefore, it is very critical to create an open organizational culture encouraging individuals to learn. Also it is important to create a flexible organizational structure to adapt the constantly changing external environment.

Third, Information Infrastructure with e-government. Obviously, E-government is the core foundation for knowledge government. E-government should set up information network to accumulate and diffuse the learned knowledge. The smart policy decision-making based on knowledg sharing and collaboration, which is one of the main fuction of e-Government, is the key foundation of knowledge government.

This insight indicates that knowledge government should have three basic elements of entrepreneur government, learning government, and e-government. In other words, knowledge government should have 1) Entrepreneur government to set up the internal incentive system to create knowledge under the personnel and budget constraints; 2) Learning government to set up the learning system to constantly reacting with the external signals; and 3) E-government to set up the information system to coordinate and integrate information and knowledge to be properly utilized and shared in the entire policy processes (see Figure 12-4).

Figure 12-4 Knowledge Government: Conceptual Framework

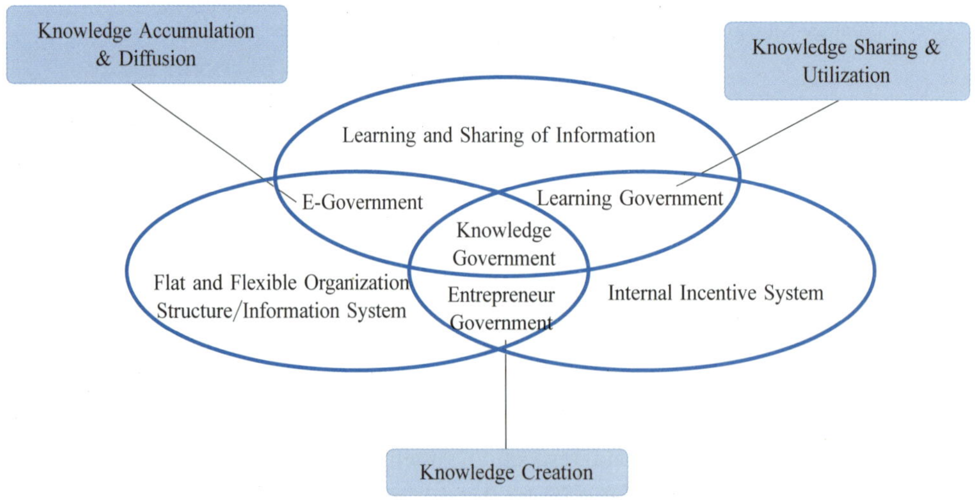

Evaluation of Knowledge Government: Case of Korea

This section will present the evaluation framework of knowledge government from the two perspectives, one with government foundation and the other with government reform.

Knowledge Government Framework: Government Foundation

The transition to the knowledge government should be based on four core factors of government foundation: 1) Organizational culture, 2) Leadership, 3) Organizational members as the key knowledge agents, and 4) Information technology (Samsung Economic Research Institute, 1999).

The first is organizational culture. For knowledge government to be successful, it should be accepted and embedded in organizational culture. Therefore organizational culture is important. Government should encourage an open organizational culture, information and knowledge sharing, and collaboration.

The second is leadership. For the successful transition to the knowledge government, leadership is the second key element. Top policy makers should be equipped with knowledge and leadership skills, with vision and goals to meet the desired direction of the nation. In fact, transformational leadership, utilizing energy, mobilization, and spontaneity, is needed within the organization in order to effectively advance the new paradigm of knowledge government.

The third is organizational members because they must be the key change agent. The collective patterns of government officials' behavior will be consist of the organizational culture in the end.

The final is information technology. This book is about e-government. Information technology is the key foundation of open system and network organization which should be the critical basis of knowledge government.

Knowledge Government Framework: Government Reform

As described earlier, knowledge government is a sharing point of e-government, entrepreneur government, and learning government. To have a proper process of knowledge creation, diffusion, utilization, and accumulation, government reform should be prerequisite. The overall knowledge government framework, base on the discussion up until now, is as follows(see Figure 12-5).

Figure 12-5 Knowedge Government: Evaluation Framework

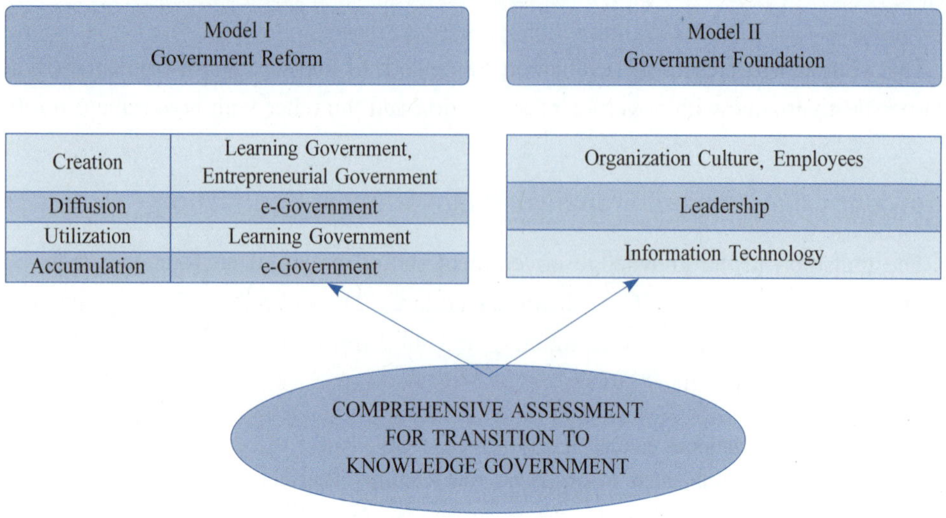

Evaluation I: Knowledge-based Government Foundation

1) Organization Culture and Organization Members

Organizational culture that is shared by members of an organization consists of values, beliefs, learning, and norms. It is difficult to effectively enforce a new system if the new system is not suitable for the organizational culture. And In order to circulate knowledge within an organization, there is need for an incentive system and a flat and flexible organizational structure. The maintenance of seniority system in Korea, for example, is a huddle to the successful transition to the knowledge government.

2) Leadership

Leadership is important. In Korea, since 1996, the Informatization Promotion Committee which was chaired by the Prime Minister has been the key leadership institution to promote knowledge government. But sometimes, President himself chairs the commit in the Presidential Office.

Informatization Promotion Committee set the basic direction in the promotion of e-Government in Korea and the individual ministries promote informatization projects. Also, the Minister of Security and Administrative Affairs takes a role of coordinating and its agencies, NCA has been responsible for implementing e-Government. Therefore, the features of promoting e-Government in Korea take the form of a vertical system with highly top-down approach.

Ministry of Security and Administrative Affairs, nevertheless, is only one of the ministries and lack of budgetary power, has no ability to powerfully adjust policies among agencies. Also the weak leadership capacity of the Office of the Prime Minister is to be criticized for the effective policy implementation of knowledge government in Korea.

3) Information Technology and Information Resource

Organization needs information to reduce the uncertainty and ambiguity. Therefore, it is important that information technology and information resource could effectively support the organization. In Korea, hardware and infrastructure of e-government has been relatively successful while software and knowledge sharing is to be criticized as a poor condition.

Evaluation II: Knowledge-based Government Reform

1) Learning Government: Knowledge Creation and Utilization

(1) Learning Government as the Knowledge Creator

Learning government is important as learning is the key for knowledge creation. For knowledge creation, it is important to have invisible insights and thoughts of the organization which comes from learning. The creative activities of Korean government have been evaluated as a weak point. It has been suggested to have a stronger role of policy evaluation committee in Prime Minister Office as policy evaluation plays very important role to promote learning among government agencies. In the current administration of President Park Geun-Hae, in the same context, Government 3.0, emphasizing learning and collaboration to promote creative economy, is mostly highlighted.

(2) Learning Government as the Knowledge Utilizer

Learning government is also important as learning is the key for knowledge utilization. For knowledge utilization, it is important to invisible experiences and knowledge of the organization which comes from learning. The utilizing activities of Korean government have also been evaluated as another weak point. The exemplar policy failure was IMF financial crisis and Korea-Japan Fishery Negotiation. Also, the knowledge storage such as Data Base in Korean knowledge system is noted as a relatively poor. Sectionalism among ministries is also pointed to be the problem of knowledge sharing.

Figure 12-6 The Contents of National Level of Knowledge Government

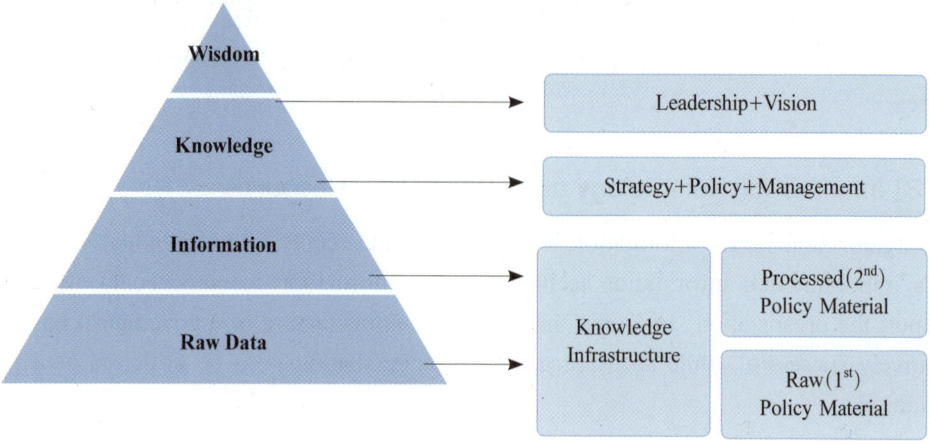

Source: Revised from the Samsung Economic Research Institute(1999).

2) Entrepreneur Government as the Knowledge Creator

Entrepreneurial government is the government who encourage innovation utilizing incentives. To have a proper knowledge creation, an effective incentive system is essential. Therefore, entrepreneur government is very closely related with the function of knowledge creation. This function is also poor in Korean government. Although the incentive system was first introduced in Korea in 1996, it has not been effectively implemented because of the Korean seniority culture.

3) E-government as the Knowledge Accumulation and Diffusion

E-government, by definition, has the function of data base and knowledge proliferation. As has been evaluated the world top in the UN assessment in 2010 and 2012 consequtively, the implementation of e-Government from the point of knowledge accumulation and diffusion can be assessed as the most successful function in Korea. In other words, knowledge accumulation and diffusion, compared to creation and utilization, are the relatively successful parts of the knowledge government process in Korea.

Conclusions and Implications

There are three prerequisites for building Knowledge Government, which are: 1) Information system (E-Government), 2) Incentive system (Entrepreneur government), and 3) Learning mechanism (Learning government).

Knowledge Government is defined as a government to have an effective knowledge creation based on the incentives of entrepreneur government and to have an effective knowledge utilization based on the sharing and learning activities of learning government. Of course, all these activities should be based on the smart information system of e-government.

Korean government should accelerate this kind of grand vision of knowledge government. To this end, we need to redefine the whole meaning of governance based on the study of the entire policy processes. And knowledge learning should be activating on a continous basis based on smart information technologies.

Knowledge is the key currency of 21st knowledge society. To prepare the full knowledge activities in the e-government, we need a national strategy to support the knowledge foundation of e-government, which is the critical sources of national strength.

Key Point!

◎ Theoretical Background of Knowledge Government

- The Necessity of the National Innovation System
- Change of an International Order
- The Development of ICT
- The Increase of the People's Demand

◎ Definition and Vision of Knowledge Government

Four concepts of knowledge (OECD)

- Know-what: a kind of fact, we often referred to as information.
- Know-why: produced knowledge in research institute as law of nature or science knowledge.
- Know-how: the ability to do something.
- Know-who; knowledge concerning who, what, how much can do.

Knowledge Activity

- Creation
- Diffusion
- Utilization
- Accumulation

Definition of Knowledge Government

- Knowledge government is defined as "a new form of government that maximizing productivity of public services by increasing knowledge cycle activities, that is, knowledge creating-accumulating-sharing-utilizing-learning.

◎ Evaluation of Knowledge Government: Case of Korea

- Knowledge Government Framework: Government Foundation
- Knowledge Government Framework: Government Reform

Evaluation I: Knowledge-based Government Foundation

- Organization Culture and Organization Members
- Leadership
- Information Technology and Information Resource

Evaluation II: Knowledge-based Government Reform

- Learning Government: Knowledge Creation and Utilization
- Entrepreneur Government as the Knowledge Creator
- E-government as the Knowledge Accumulation and Diffusion

Key Question!

◎ What is concept of knowledge?

◎ What is the concept of knowledge government, and what is its difference with e-government?

◎ What are the three essential conditions of knowledge government?

◎ Let evaluate knowledge government as learning government from knowledge creation viewpoint, entrepreneurial government from incentive viewpoint, and e-government from spread of knowledge and accumulation viewpoint.

Chapter 13

OPERATING STRATEGY OF KNOWLEDGE GOVERNMENT

The heart of knowledge management is not just information technology, but related with how to foster the knowledge-created culture in the organization.

Objectives

The purpose of this chapter is to discuss the operating strategy of knowledge government. It will cover the concept of Knowledge Management System (KMS) and the role of Chief Knowledge Officer (CKO). It will also examine the institutional components such as reward systems, personnel management and organizational culture as one of the strategy to effectively operate the KMS, the core element of knowledge government.

First, it will examine the concept and role of Knowledge Management System (KMS) and search for the developing stages of KMS. It will then analyze the success factors of Knowledge Management System.

Second, it will discuss the concept and role of Chief Knowledge Manager (CKO) for promoting knowledge-oriented culture in the government organization.

Third, it will discuss the institutional components that can contribute to build an effective knowledge management system. They include reward and incentive system, personnel and e-HRD system, and setting up an efficient business process. In addition, it will further discuss the knowledge-oriented organizational culture, one of the most critical factors for successful knowledge government.

Knowledge Management

There are two types of knowledge management, human-oriented knowledge management and technology-oriented knowledge management. Human-oriented knowledge management emphasizes on the human factors. The key of the successful knowledge management depends on the good human relationship in the process of knowledge creation and utilization; therefore the Chief Knowledge Officer should focus on creating the favorable working environment of collaboration and cooperation to have an effective knowledge management.

Technology-oriented knowledge management system, on the other hand, emphasizes on the technology factors. The key of the successful knowledge management depends on the good technological foundation; therefore the Chief Knowledge Officer should focus on providing good knowledge classification and system to have an uninhibited knowledge sharing and utilization.

Literature Review

Gartner Group presented the success factors of knowledge management as: 1) Planning and control at an early stage of knowledge management, 2) Continuous support, 3) Strong commitment and leadership of the Top Management, 4) Appointment of CKO, 5) Proper monitoring, 6) Best project team members for the knowledge project, and 7) Quality assurance.

Jang, Young-Chul (2001) defined the success factors of knowledge management as: 1) Creating knowledge-oriented culture, 2) Building up knowledge infrastructure, 3) Developing effective motivation and reward system, 4) Top management support, 5) Knowledge diffusion through a variety of channels, 6) Clarifying purpose, 7) Classifying knowledge system, and 8) Integrating with the value of the organization.

Korea Computer Center (1999) argued that Knowledge Management System failed in Korean government at the time, because of the lack of connection between knowledge management and its supporting elements. Among these supporting elements, it reported, especially human resource management policies are the most important factor. Therefore, it suggested that it is necessary to develop the incentive framework for changing the attitude and behavior of organization members toward the more active knowledge creation and utilization.

Summary and Implications

Anderson Consulting (1997) suggested the success factors of knowledge management as Strategy, People, Process, and Information Technology. Productivity Association of America (APQC, 1998) argued as leadership and strategy, culture, measurement and evaluation, information technology. Samsung Economic Research Institute (1999) described as goals, strategy, leadership, knowledge activities, and knowledge infrastructure. Kang, Hwang-Sun (2002) suggested the success factors of knowledge management as: 1) Acquiring Professional HR, 2) Institutional support and culture building, and 3) Utilizing KMS based on the integrated information technology.

The critical successful factors of knowledge management, as we wrap up and summarize the above discussions, are boiled down to three factors, 1) People, 2) Management and Culture, and 3) Technology. Or, if we describe more specifically, a) Leadership, b) Strategy, c) Process, d) Culture, and e) Technology.

In a nutshell, it may not be the most critical issue that how many factors we will select. The more important issue is to notice that the heart of knowledge management is not just information technology, but human factor; how to develop the knowledge-oriented culture and system in which knowledge workers are more inclined to create and share knowledge among them.

Knowledge Management System

Concept and Significance

Data is described as a fragmentary combination of letters, numbers, and symbols. Analysis of data is needed to understand events, circumstances or state. Information is described as a significant combination of data that describe, explain, and predict events, circumstances or state. Knowledge is developed into a more valuable form of information systematically processed by judgment, experience, and the theories. It is used to create new information and knowledge which is critical to make the better policy decision-making.

Knowledge Management System is the system to manage knowledge sharing at organizational level with the use of information technology. Knowledge sharing and management is much easier and effective with the help of ICT, especially the development of Internet and Smart technologies. With the advance of Smart information technologies, it was able to manage to share the knowledge of the all member of organization, which is one of the critical conditions for the knowledge creation and utilization.

Development Stages of Knowledge Management System

1) Preparation Stage: Preparation Committee

It is very critical to have a full review and consultation from the preparation stage for the success of Knowledge Management System. It is desirable to set up an organization-wide preparation committee composed of capable personnel with dedication and knowledgeable about the business process very well. In addition, personnel should know the working process of information technology and design the KMS model feasibly; otherwise, it would be too much idealistic.

2) Consulting & Analyzing Stage: Analysis of Internal Capacity & External Environment

It is necessary to analyze the internal capacities such as its own strength and weakness relating especially with its internal knowledge assets. It is also necessary to analyze the external environment such as its opportunity and threat. For the internal analysis, it is critical to have a strategy setting for selecting core competencies after analyzing the entire enterprise resource planning (ERP) and business process reengineering (BPR). It is also critical to have a change management perspective. For the external analysis, it is critical to perform a sensitivity analysis on the external conditions and search for a proper role model of the organization (benchmarking) by investigating the best practices of the other organizations.

3) Development and Diffusion Stage: KMS Development and Feedback

In Development and diffusion stage, it is important to design the basic architecture of KMS model, regarding how to structure the overall work process, what kinds of information technologies will be introduced, and what kinds of packaged system will be utilized. In this process, the systematic training about KMS development should be implemented. In addition, the continuous monitoring and feedback to correct and revise the KMS system should be performed.

4) Advancement Stage: The Most Updated Version of KMS Model

The best KMS model is to flexibly change in accordance with the ever-changing

Figure 13-1 The Development Stages of Knowledge Management System

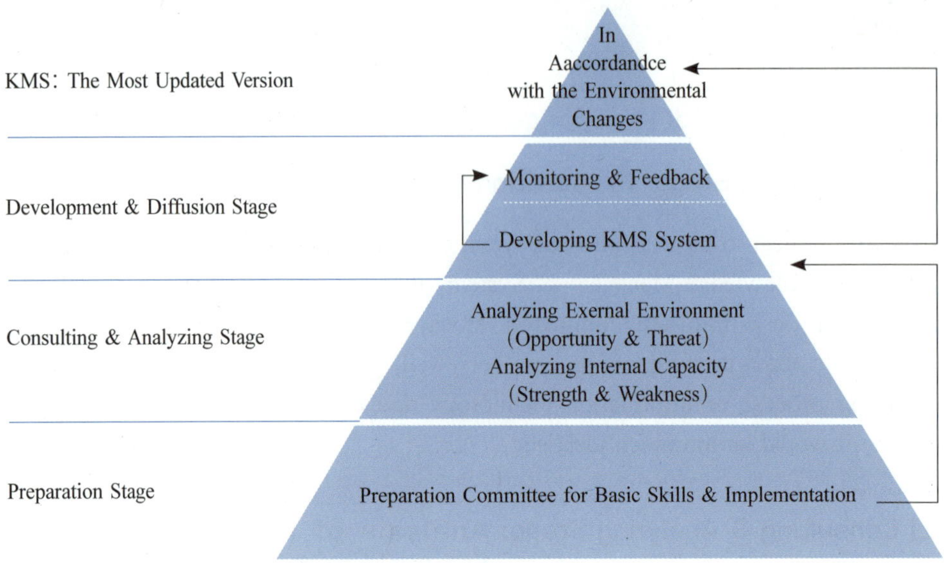

nature of organization environment. In other words, it is necessary to revise and update the model to correspond with the increase of organization knowledge, the change of users and stakeholders, and the change of organization vision and goal. It is important therefore to monitor and upgrade the KMS model to reflect the ongoing changes of Smart technologies and to have the proper model fitting the organizational realities.

Critical Success Factors of Knowledge Management System (KMS)

The most fundamental function of KMS is to create knowledge; otherwise, it is useless. Creating knowledge should take place not only at the individual level but more importantly at the organization level. Therefore, the most critical success factor (CSF) of KMS depends on how to transform the tacit knowledge, embedded at each individual's brain and finger-tips, into the codified knowledge to be shared at the organizational level. For this purpose, a holistic strategy is required.

The first one is Culture. It is to create organizational culture to share knowledge. To have successful knowledge governance, the entire team members of organization should be willing to share the new knowledge acquired in the process of business. Therefore, the top leader or CKO of the organization should encourage those kinds of knowledge-oriented culture.

The second one is Institutionalizing Incentive System. In fact, people do not share their knowledge with other person if there are no proper incentives to back up those activities.

Therefore, it is important to develop and institutionalize the incentive system to support those knowledge-creating or sharing activities by utilizing personnel evaluation system including promotion, salary, or other non-material reward plan. The most important thing is to induce an active participation, sharing, and utilization of knowledge among the entire members of organization.

The third one is Setting-up the Best KMS System. The final one is to set up the best KMS system using Smart information technology. This should be the system to clearly reflect the vision and goal of the organization. It is also the flexible one to be realistically feasible to the existing structure, procedures, and norms of the organization.

Evaluation of the Government KMS Policy

In Korea, the Ministry of Security & Government Administration is in charge of KMS policy. They established the initial version of "government knowledge management system: basic plan" to operate knowledge management system. Through the knowledge management system of government and the implementation of knowledge management center, Korean government could maximize the efficiency of the administration. It created a synergy effect by promoting knowledge sharing among agencies, thus spreading the best practices of policy success and offering the learning opportunities for the good governance.

Figure 13-2 Government Knowledge Management Center

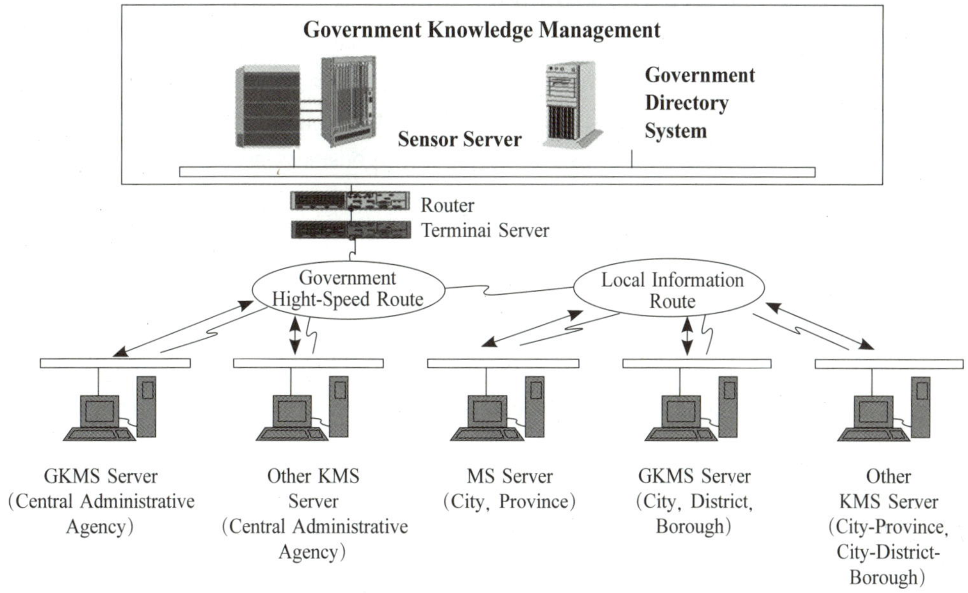

Policy Strategy and Priorities

The knowledge management of the government sector still lags behind that of the private sector. To name a few, the problems are: 1) Technology-oriented approach, 2) Sectionalism between ministries/agencies, and 3) Lack of rewarding system to the creative performance. Therefore, we have to develop the KMS strategy reflecting the characteristics of the public institutions. Those strategies and tasks are as follows:

1) Establishing Master Plan of Knowledge Management. Master plan is required. In this plan, the concrete directions at each step should be included. Core business, core user, and core knowledge and their sources should also be included.

2) Strong and Commitment of Top Leadership. The most important factor is Top leadership. The success of knowledge management depends on the attitudes and leadership of Top management. His perception, attitude, and consistent support for the knowledge management process is the key. In this regard, CEO should appoint CKO as a competent, real able man of the organization, not in name only.

3) Quality Management. The current state of knowledge management in public agencies is only at the level of e-document, file management, or e-authorization[i]. Strategic policy-setting or Creative transformation based on Big Data management, or Real collaboration based on knowledge sharing, which are the key direction of e-Government or knowledge government 3.0 versions does not take place.

4) Knowledge-oriented Organization Culture. All cases and every expert on knowledge management emphasize this point of organizational culture. But there is no one simple, easy solution. Knowledge-oriented culture is the one to be making with time. Do not try to make a big, risky successful project at one time; Try to build small but meaningful cases at daily practices of work flow in the business processes.

5) Benchmarking the Best Practice Model. It is necessary to search for the best practice model of KMS all over the world and to monitor the performance assessment on a daily basis in the business.

6) Establishing Knowledge Work Process. The CKO and his team should analyze the business process reengineering, especially relating with knowledge-oriented work

---

i) These kinds of knowledge activities of data base, file keeping, or file management, are called as the stage of Content at the development process of knowledge management. The next stage of Content is Communication, which is the prerequisite of Collaboration. This is corresponding to the evolutionary stage of e-Government: Bureaucracy (Paper-oriented file management), MIS(e-document), Participatory e-Government(e-Participation), Transaction(e-Banking or e-Tax), and Integration & Transformation(e-Transformation or e-Government 3.0 version).

process: select target knowledge, evaluate the target knowledge, how and where to utilize, reward and incentives, and feedback. Select the best practices and reward the best knowledge activities. By doing so, knowledge activities will be activated and promoted at the organizational level. In the process, the team should also analyze all the knowledge and information resources scattered in the entire enterprise, which is called Enterprise Resource Planning. These kinds of BPR, ERP, and stimulating knowledge circulation are the core prerequisite for the Communication and Collaboration, the next stage of mere Content in the knowledge management process.

Chief Knowledge Officer: CKO

Background

In the increasing discussion about Knowledge Management since the late 1990s, CKO (Chief Knowledge Officer) has emerged instead of the existing CIO (Chief Information Officer). As CIO has evolved and developed to CKO, Information from a personal computer or a data warehouse should be able to convert knowledge to action. Information is just information; when information is combined and refined to a meaning set of theories that is useful for problem-solving and decision-making, we call it knowledge.

Concept of CKO

The concept of CKO is created in an attempt to excavate and manage the valuable intellectual capitals scattered around the organization by utilizing the systematic organization operating system. ⟨Figure 13-3⟩ explains the conceptual difference among CKO (Chief Knowledge Officer), CLO (Chief Labor Officer) and CIO (Chief

Figure 13-3 CKO, CLO, and CIO

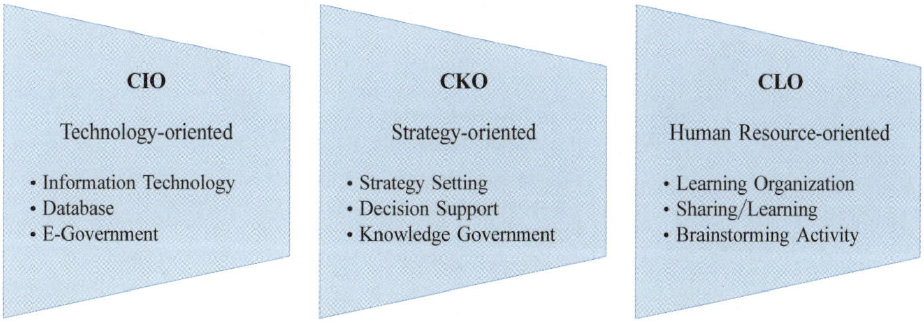

Information Officer).

The Role of the CKO

CKO has the following roles at the four development stages:

1) Excavating and Sharing of Knowledge

Government agencies need organizational innovation in order to adapt to a rapidly changing external environment. Success of organizational innovation is determined by setting clear goals and excavating the knowledge relevant for achieving those goals. CKO should play this kind of roles; excavating the valuable knowledge to achieve the organizational goals by applying the Smart ICT; and diffusing the excavated knowledge to the whole organization for sharing and solving the problems faced by the organization.

The following 〈Figure 13-4〉 & 〈Figure 13-5〉 show the various sources of the

Figure 13-4 The Contents of National Level of Knowledge Government

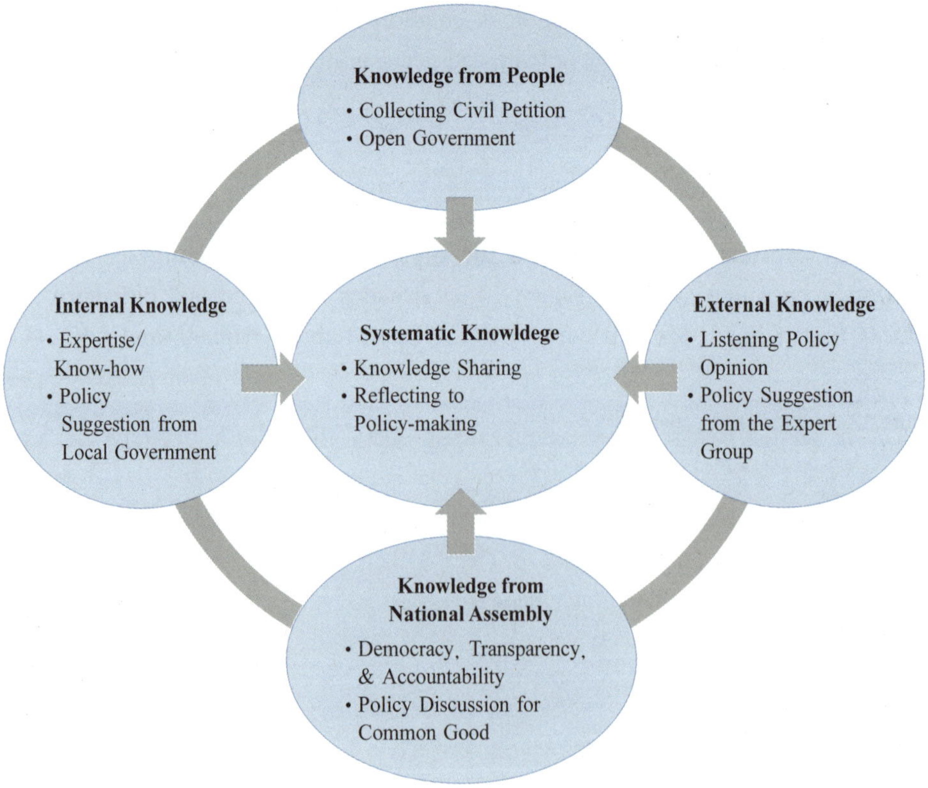

systematic knowledge for good governance and the process of knowledge and knowledge government.

2) Designing and Managing KMS Infrastructure.

CKO is an officer who is to design and manages KMS infrastructure (i.e., knowledge-based archive, human resources, computer networks & data centers, research centers, etc.). In addition, CKO plays the role of the acquisition and dissemination of knowledge-base that exists within and outside the organization. Here, the knowledge-base, one of the core elements of the KMS, is a kind of data-base about problem-solving methodologies and problem-solving best-practice cases. By systematically applying these best-practice cases to the newly emerging problem, knowledge-base of the KMS helps to find the optimum solution of the organization. This kind of knowledge-based problem-solving capacity is the core of the organization capacity. The following ⟨Figure 13-5⟩ show the process of knowledge and knowledge – base.

Figure 13-5 Process of Knowledge and Knowledge-Base

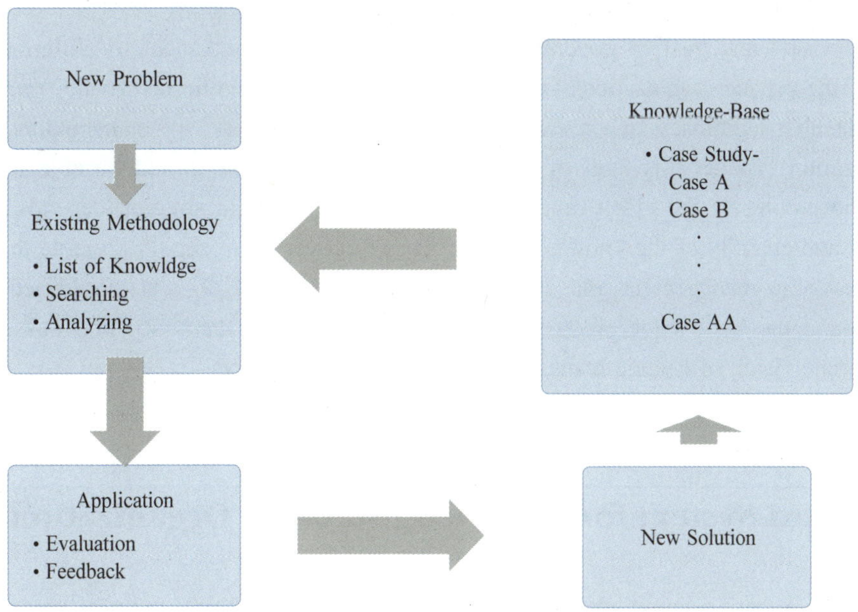

3) Bridging Key Members of Organization Network.

The CKO should play an important role to contact decision-makers and discuss the on-going problems & solutions of the organization. Therefore, he should be a bridge-connector and network-builder among the key members of the organization.

4) Measuring Strategic Performance and Getting Feedback.

With respect to the organizational performance, CKO is playing two roles. First, in order to measure the organization's performance, CKO is building a systematic knowledge management system. Second, CKO is playing a role to get feedback and to enhance problem-solving and decision-making capacity by bridging the inter-organizational knowledge gap.

"Why our organization has a poor problem-solving capacity even though having a lot of competent human resources with full dedication?" If an organization faces this kind of question and problem that means the proper function of the CKO is not working. Conversely, this means that if the CKO plays an appropriate role in the organization, he could effectively connect the capable human resources abilities and passion to the elevation of productivity thereby enhancing organization capacity.

CKO Strategy in Governmental Organizations

The vision and goal of government organization is not fundamentally different from that of the private organization. Organization, whether it is public or private, must earn its existential legitimacy by providing the values for its clients, the stakeholders of the organization. To get this kind of legitimacy, the organization should be able to solve its basic problems; the effectiveness and efficiency of problem solution depends on the quality and quantity of the knowledge-base. Hence, government should promote this kind of knowledge management and search for the competent CKO, who could accurately understand the knowledge, required for the government of the time, and possess the appropriate vision of change management and future governance.

Reward System for Knowledge-created Organization

For an effective knowledge government, the institutional and cultural components (i.e., reward system, personnel system, and work process) should be appropriate for knowledge creation. As we have discussed the KMS infrastructure and CKO, here we will discuss the issue of how to promote the knowledge-created culture of government.

Performance-Oriented Pay System

The policy strategies and tasks for capacity development and the performance-oriented pay system are as follows:

① Reform the pay system in connection with job performance;

② The personnel reward must be provided according to the standards that how knowledge contributes to the productivity development. But the productivity of administrative service isn't easy to measure with traditional input-output analysis. Therefore pay system of government must consider these governmental characters carefully.

③ One way to overcome this basic limitation is to measure the performance of changing tacit knowledge to explicit knowledge.

Performance-Oriented Budget System

Korean government had revolutionarily reformed input-oriented budget system through the introduction of performance-oriented budget system. This performance system basically evaluates how each department achieves their goals in accordance with fundamental goal, community condition indexes, objectives, and performance indicators.

It measures each department's quality of service and productivity and provide bonus to the managers who excess their objectives with the incentives of within 10% of their pay. In this way, the government can provide a high-quality service with lower human resources than in the past.

Personnel System for Knowledge-created Organization

To construct personnel system fitted with knowledge-created organization, we will discuss the ways to remove the inner-oriented consciousness, emphasis of professionalism, reinforcement of career path development of public officials.

Getting Rid of the Inner-oriented Bureaucratic Mind

The strategies to get rid of the inner-oriented bureaucratic mindset are as follows:

① Government cannot respond effectively to the 21st Mega-trends of globalization and knowledge revolution unless government officials remove its inner-oriented mindset

② Remove the barriers of the existing bureaucratic system, institutions, and culture: Restructure the government system to an open personnel system and recruit the external experts so as to infuse fresh airs and professionalism to the government system.

③ Remove sectionalism and bureaucratic inerti: Break down an old system and norms to set up a real no-boundary spanning organization.

Professionalism

The strategies to reinforce the professionalism of knowledge government officials are as follows:

① Recruit fresh talented experts with professional knowledge and action power in the government agencies.

② Set-up the open personnel system. To achieve this, recruit the external experts to the positions of professional service, and increase the quota enough to interchange cross-working system between public officials and private enterprises (or research institutes and universities).

③ Reform the Senior Government Service Examination System. In addition to the current written test, utilize the various evaluation systems of allowing the work experiences of private sectors or overseas assignments. In addition, introduce the special recruitments on a regular basis.

Career Management

The strategies to reinforce the career management of knowledge government officials are as follows:

① Set-up the promotion path in a rational way. Institutionalize the long service system to work for a long time in the same or similar positions. To be a knowledge servant, or to be a real expert on his tasks, the public official should not turn over his position too frequently.

② Reform the current Generalist system and cultivate T-shaped higher policy experts who have both general administrative abilities with professional special abilities.

Work Process for Knowledge-created Organization

Definition

The work process of Knowledge Management is to reform the business process to effectively manage the resources and knowledge scattered in the organization. Also it is to have a free and fluent knowledge cycle in which the knowledge circulation of creation, accumulation, sharing, utilizing, and learning could be accelerated. Therefore, it is a strategic concept to strengthen organization competency by means of sharing knowledge in their organization.

The work process of Knowledge Management is defined differently by scholars. Ruggles (1997) explained the knowledge work process as three parts: "creation, formalization, and spread." Myers (1996) defined knowledge work process as "creation, encoding, and transfer of knowledge" and Vacernport, et al. (1998) defined it as "acquisition, storage, sharing, and utilization of knowledge." Kwon, Gi-Heon (2000) defined it as "creation, accumulation, sharing, utilization and learning of knowledge." Kwon (2000) emphasized the importance of the "learning" of knowledge process.

Contents

The knowledge management work process is a cyclic chain of process connected organically than a sequential or linear process. Individual knowledge management work process is not mutuality independent or exclusive, but is mutuality overlapping and complementary. And by this repetitive cycle, the value of knowledge in the organization increases tremendously.

Knowledge created by each person, in the knowledge management perspective, must accumulate in the organization and share and utilize by the whole members of the organization. Unless knowledge created by each person is shared extensively in the organization level, the value that an organization is seeking as an intellectual capital is limited. Therefore the knowledge management in the organization level must be communicated and crystallized through communication, discussion, and experience. And the creation, accumulation, sharing, utilization, and learning of knowledge must be repeated consistently.

1) Creation of Knowledge

The creation of knowledge is the stage that creates knowledge. And it means the intellectualization of data or information. Concretely, the creation of knowledge is the creative activities that make new skills, ideas, know-how, procedures and solutions help problem solving based on individual learning and experiences (Oldham & Cummings, 1996: 607).

2) Accumulation of Knowledge

The accumulation of knowledge is the activities that verify and classify created knowledge, and register and store it. In other words, the accumulation of knowledge is the process that store created knowledge at the knowledge storage and help it share by all organization members. The implementation of information technology infrastructure such as a knowledge management system is core component of knowledge storage.

3) Sharing of Knowledge

The sharing of knowledge is the process that created and accumulated knowledge is shared and embedded through interaction among organization members. It is an important interactive process being foundation for securing competitive edge.

The knowledge sharing is core component to establish the knowledge management. It must focus on not only sharing explicit knowledge based on business guideline or manual, but also sharing tacit knowledge depending individual know-how. Unless knowledge isn't shared in spite of accumulation, this knowledge is limited as an organizational value.

4) Utilization of Knowledge

The utilization of knowledge is the activities that include all process of adaptation, use, application and evaluation of knowledge obtained by knowledge sharing work process. It contributes directly to the performance of members and problem solving skills. In other words, the utilization of knowledge in the organization is crystallized into the utilization of knowledge for efficient work process, for providing a better government service, and for effective problem solving and rational policy decision making.

5) Learning of Knowledge

The learning of knowledge is the activities to add new knowledge into organization. Obviously, learning is one of the most important concept in the knowledge society. These activities would easily take place for an open system of the organization as the open system is easier to detect the external signals of environment in a vigilant way. Therefore, we need to make an open, flexible system of the organization that encourages learning by all organization members.

Organizational Culture for Knowledge-created Organization

Definition

The organizational culture is defined as the "whole body of consciousness structure comprising of values, perception, and attitude that particular organization's members are sharing"(Min Jin, 2004: 420-421). Robbin (2001) defined the organizational culture as the set of values, beliefs and norms shared by personnel in an organization. The culture is the pattern and appearance of human life in a large sense, but in a narrow sense, it means the consciousness structure, values, and attitude that members of society have in common.

Functions

The organizational culture has four functions are as follows:

First, the organizational culture provides identities to members of organization. In other words, it provides unique homogeneity that members of organization are commonly sharing.

Second, the organizational culture makes collective immersion. Because it justifies members' behavior, the immersion of members is elevated in the organization with strong culture.

Third, the organizational culture provides stability of organizational system. In the organization with strong culture, the regulations and controls are increasing to reinforce cultural homogeneity.

Lastly, the organizational culture forms members' behavior. In other words, it forms members' behavior the way the organization wanted as providing solutions about what organization want to them. Thus, the organizational culture plays a role as a kind of learning instrument (Kim, In-Su, 1991: 597-602; Park, Jae-Hee, 1996: 461).

Knowledge Management and Organizational Culture

If the organization highly appreciates working hard but is cynical about new ideas or suggestion at the same time, members don't pay attention to creation of new knowledge. Therefore, to make the best model of knowledge management, the mindset about knowledge must be changed first. The mindset of the organization should encourage knowledge activities of the organization. The strategies to make knowledge creation-type organizational culture are as follows:

First, Create knowledge-oriented organizational culture that highly appreciates the values of creative knowledge. The attitudes which are accustomed to work process by rules or the routine SOPs must be transformed. In these cultures, although smart information network is constructed, it is limited to create and utilize knowledge of organization. Therefore, the learning attitude in the process of work is very important.

Second, Build trust and cooperative organizational culture. If the creation and utilization of knowledge are more revitalized by members' interaction rather than individual's independent role, the culture that puts emphasis on cooperation among members is essential. Only in this culture, each person is willing to provide and share his or her knowledge on a voluntary basis.

Third, the perception about mistake must be changed. Anyone doesn't like to make mistakes, but everyone makes mistakes. If someone doesn't accept or hide other's mistakes, those mistakes become corruption and crime. But if someone investigates the fundamental reason of mistakes and attempts to prevent recurrence all together, the shining creative energy fields of knowledge creation will be unfolded. In the organization that does not allow any mistake, the bold, future-oriented, experimental attempts could not be tried. Mistake could be the source of new idea and inspiration; as long as an organization is learning from its failures or mistakes, there is no failed attempt (Marquardt & Reynolds, 1995: 101).

Summary and Conclusion

In this chapter, we discussed and identified the operating strategies of knowledge management system that is the critical foundation of knowledge Government. In particular, we defined the roles and operating strategies of CKO. Also we examined the personnel system, reward system, work process and organizational culture supporting the knowledge management.

The critical successful factors of knowledge management, as we wrap up and summarize the discussions of this chapter, are boiled down to three factors, 1) People, 2) Management and Culture, and 3) Technology. Or, if we describe more specifically, a) Leadership, b) Strategy, c) Process, d) Culture, and e) Technology.

The strong commitment and consistent leadership is the most crucial factor to set up and implement the successful Knowledge Management System. The second important thing is the organizational culture. In other words, the existing bureaucratic culture must be transformed to knowledge-created organizational culture to encourage knowledge activities of the knowledge government. To make knowledge-created organization culture, a lot of management factors such as the personnel system, reward system, and work process must be transformed. Therefore, when all these human, management and culture, and technological factors are transformed, we could surely achieve the successful knowledge government.

Key Point!

◎ Knowledge Management

- Human-Oriented Knowledge Management
  - Focus of human aspect for the absorption of knowledge and application as an emphasis on cooperation and collaboration.
- Technology-Oriented Knowledge Management
  - Focus of information technology for knowledge sharing and utilization emphasizes on the support and management.

◎ Knowledge Management System

Concept and significance

- Knowledge Management System is the system to manage knowledge sharing at organizational level with the use of information technological supports.

Development Stages of Knowledge Management System

- Preparation Stage: Preparation Committee
- Consulting & Analyzing Stage: Analysis of Internal Capacity & External Environment
- Development and Diffusion Stage: KMS Development and Feedback
- Advancement Stage: The Most Updated Version of KMS Model

Critical Success Factors of Knowledge Management System (KMS)

- Culture: Organizational culture to share knowledge
- Incentive System: Incentives allow to effectively create knowledge
- Setting Up the Best KMS System: Information technology infrastructure building

Policy Strategy and Tasks

- Establishing Master Plan of Knowledge Management
- Strong and Commitment of Top Leadership
- Quality Management
- Knowledge-oriented Organization Culture

- Benchmarking the Best Practice Model
- Establishing Knowledge Work Process

◎ Chief Knowledge Officer: CKO

Concept of CKO

- Manager is responsible for information technology and computer system of organization, and conversion information of private computer or data warehouse into knowledge.

The Role of the CKO

- Excavating and Sharing of Knowledge
- Designing and Managing KMS Infrastructure
- Bridging Key Members of Organization Network
- Measuring Strategic Performance and Getting Feedback

◎ Reward System for Knowledge-created Organization

Performance-Oriented Pay System

- Officer training system reconfiguration with improve job performance
- Acknowledgment of reasonable discrimination and step-by-step introduction of civil servant annual salary system by capacity and performance
- Output and measurement of administrative services is prerequisite
- Incentives by means of an objective evaluation

Performance-Oriented Budget System

- This performance system basically evaluates how each department achieves their goals in accordance with fundamental goal, community condition indexes, objectives, and performance indicators.
- It measures each department's quality of service and productivity and provide bonus to the managers who excess their objectives with the incentives of within 10% of their pay.

◎ Personnel System for Knowledge-created Organization

Getting Rid of the Inner-Oriented Bureaucratic Mindset

- Government cannot respond effectively to the 21st Mega-trends of globalization and knowledge revolution unless government officials remove its inner-oriented bureaucratic mindset.
- Remove the barriers of the existing bureaucratic system, institutions, and culture.
- Remove sectionalism and bureaucratic inertia.

Professionalism

- Recruit fresh talented experts with professional knowledge and action power in the government agencies.
- Set-up the open personnel system.
- Reform the Senior Government Service Examination System.

Career Management

- Set-up the promotion path in a rational way. Institutionalize the long service system to work for a long time in the same or similar positions. To be a knowledge servant, or to be a real expert on his tasks, the public official should not turn over his position too frequently.
- Reform the current Generalist system and cultivate a T-shaped higher policy experts who has both general administrative abilities with professional special abilities.

◎ Work Process for Knowledge-created Organization

Definition

- The process to effectively manage organization's resources and knowledge.
- Creation and accumulation of knowledge and at the same time sharing within the organization in order to create new knowledge.

Contents

- Creation of Knowledge: Intellectualization phase of information for knowledge creation
- Accumulation of Knowledge: The phase which verifies classification and

enrollment of created knowledge

- Sharing of Knowledge: The phase where accumulated knowledge was spread and internalization through interaction between organizational members.
- Utilization of Knowledge: The phase where acquired knowledge applied an actual business through knowledge sharing work processes.
- Learning of Knowledge

◎ Organizational Culture for Knowledge-created Organization

Definition

- The entire of structure of consciousness, values and attitudes shared by members of a particular organization

Function

- Organization to provide organization identity as members
- Provide a collective commitment
- Stability improvement of organizational system
- Form of organization behavior

Knowledge Management and Organizational Culture: How to implement the organizational culture of knowledge-creation model for Knowledge government?

- Create knowledge-oriented organizational culture that highly appreciates the values of creative knowledge.
- Build trust and cooperative organizational culture.
- The perception about mistake must be changed. In the organization that does not allow any mistake, the bold, future-oriented, experimental attempts could not be tried. Mistake could be the source of new idea and inspiration; as long as an organization is learning from its failures or mistakes, there is no failed attempt (Marquardt & Reynolds, 1995: 101).

Key Question!

◎ After looking into the concepts of human-oriented knowledge management and technology-oriented knowledge management, explain the differences of two approaches.

◎ What is knowledge management system?

◎ Explain policy strategies for building of successful knowledge management system.

◎ What is the concept and role of knowledge manager?

◎ What is the ways to promote knowledge culture of government? Explain ways to achieve this open culture favorable for knowledge creation.

PART 5

THEORY & STRATEGY OF E-POLICY I: OVERALL REVIEW

In Part V, Theory and Strategy of E-Policy I, we will elucidate the overall review of E-Policy.

First, we will first examine the Policy-making Theory, and thereby the relationship between the e-Government and the Policy-making Theory in the Information Society.

Second, we will highlight the logic of information policy. Here, we will discuss about strategic information policy to enhance national competitiveness.

Chapter 14

E-GOVERNMENT AND POLICY-MAKING THEORY

The Smart e-Government will greatly enhance policy-making capacity by utilizing the Big Data and Sementic-based Algorism.

Objectives

The purpose of this chapter is to elucidate the relationship between e-Government and the Policy-making Theory in the Information Society.

First, it will highlight the point of contact between e-Government and Policy Science, and also the relationship between e-Government and Policy-making Theory.

Second, it will highlight the relationship between e-Government and the theory of Policy-making. In this section, it will discuss the roles and functions of e-Government in the policy process and then derive the proper policy-making model for e-Government.

Policy Science in Information Society: Analytical Framework

Think about the policy science in Information Society. What the Information Society and Policy Science have in common? How is e-Government related to the policy theory? For the framework for our discussion, Let's think about D. Easton's System Model in which e-Government is a government system where people's demand and support (as policy input) could be processed to policy outcome. In Industrial Society, it was a bureaucratic model that had held this position as a traditional governing model. But as Knowledge Society evolves, It is now e-Government model that holds the position of a government's policy-making model.

In policy science, government innovation can be realized by 1) Enhancing the Government's internal operations (internal efficiency); 2) Enhancing people's satisfaction outside the government from the public services (external democracy). Then, our focal question should be: Could e-Government contribute more to its internal efficiency and its external democracy than the existing government model of bureaucracy? This will be discussed as an important subject of section 4.

Figure 14-1 E-Government and Policy Science: Analytical Framework

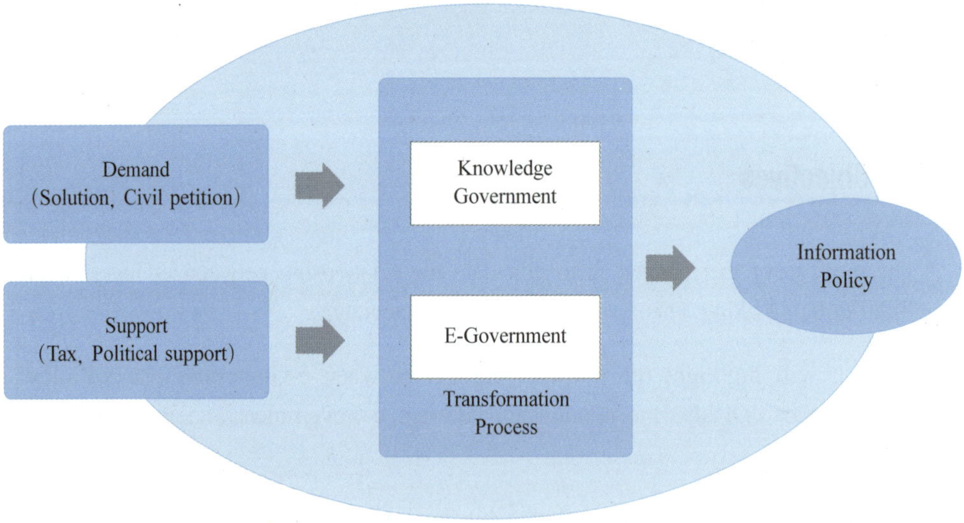

- Note:

E-Government and Policy Science: A Point of Contact
E-Government and Policy-making Model: Inside-Transformation Process
E-Government and the Logic of Information Policy: Outside-Information Policy

Government performance from the Policy Science perspective are related with, 1) Government's internal policy-making capacity (the issue of productivity and efficiency), and 2) Government's external process of democracy and transparency.

Therefore, the main issues concerning the relation between e-Government and Policy Theory can be reviewed, 1) How e-Government could enhance the policy-making capacity by utilizing the more and the better policy information?(the issue of e-Government and Policy-making), and 2) How e-Government can contribute to democracy, transparency, and reflexivity at national and social level? (the issue of e-Government and Information Policy)?

Thus, the perspective of this book, written in the purpose of broadening our understanding of Policy Science in Knowledge Society, is focused on two issues: 1) Policy-making models internally, 2) The logic of information policy externally (See Figure 14-1).

E-Government and Policy-Making Theory

E-Government and Policy Process

E-Government significantly contributes the rationality of policy process, i.e. agenda setting-policy making-policy implementation-policy evaluation, by using information technology and management science.

First, e-government helps to the quality of policy agenda-setting because information technologies allow handling a great amount of policy information within a short period of time. With the aid of interactive smart ICT devices, policy makers now can contact stakeholders more conveniently. It means the government is able to secure democracy and transparency of the policy process, while improving the effectiveness and efficiency of the internal operation.

Second, e-government helps to the quality of policy making because not only with the introduction of electronic approval in the process of policy-making but also with the introduction of decision-making techniques and scientific theory. Policy makers have more possibilities and opportunities to make an evidence-based decision making based on Big Data.

Third, e-government helps to the quality of policy implementation. The possibility of the successful implementation will be increased through the promotion of ICT communication with policy stakeholders and policy target group, thereby increasing policy compliance in

Figure 14-2 E-Government and Policy Process: Analytical Framework

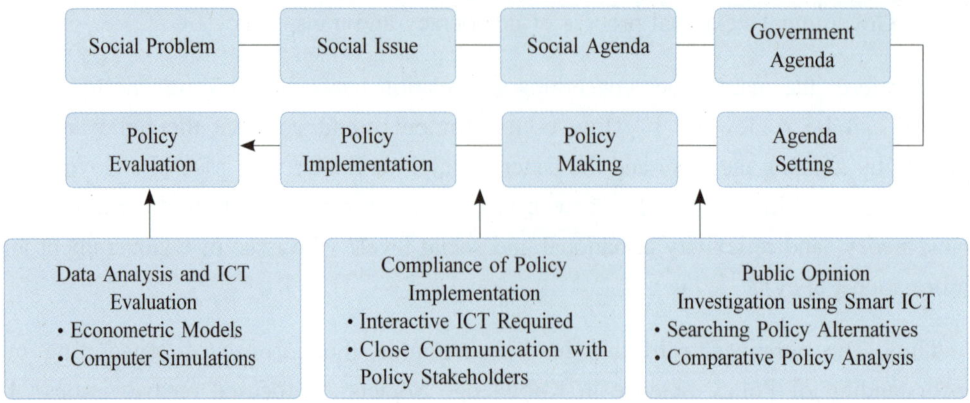

the policy implementation process.

Fourth, e-government helps to the quality of policy evaluation using econometric model or computer simulations, and the systematic policy analysis. The evaluation of policy is better conducted and can be more reasonable as information technology being combined with probability, statistics and linear programming theories.

Lastly, e-government helps to the quality of policy feedback because information technology provides more effective and transparent policy mechanism (See Figure 14-2).

The relationship between e-Government and policy process is explained in 〈Figure 14-2〉.

In short, the important issue is: how e-Government plays its roles related to policy decision-making in a more systematic and rational manner with an aids of smart ICT devices? For this purpose, let's not examine the theoretical models of decision-making in the following section.

Theoretical Model of Policy Decision-making

Firstly, let's review the policy decision-making models. The policy decision-making model has been developed greatly by behavioral science of H. Simon and his colleagues from the concept of bounded rationality and satisfaction model.

1) Rationality Model and Cognitive Model

Rationality model is a policy decision-making model which stresses the fact that people behave and make decisions based on their reason and rationality. The theory assumes humans as 'Homo Economicus' with subjective rationality and whose behavior is based on maximizing utility. It also assumes them as a decision-maker of omniscience based on objective rationality.

The rationality model assumes the following points:

First, decision-maker could clarify his goal or matter to be solved. Second, decision-maker could study every possible alternative in a wide range. Third, decision-maker could predict the whole result when the alternatives are carried out. Fourth, decision-maker could evaluate the alternatives so that he should know the priority of the criteria for the evaluation. Lastly, decision-maker could choose the best alternative based on the comprehensive analysis stated above.

Comparably, the cognitive model puts its emphasis on practical aspects. It explains that the cognitive ability of human is bounded so that the way of decision making asserted by rational theory is unfeasible. The theory has been theoretically developed through Simon and March's bounded rationality model and satisfaction model.

2) Personal Decision-making Theory and Collective Decision-making Theory

(1) Personal Decision-making Theory

Personal decision-making theory is a psychological decision-making theory that concentrates on how an individual makes a practical decision. Simon's process-theory is a typical example of it. According to Simon, the theory is divided into three steps: Intelligence, Design, and Choice. The first step is intelligence. For this, 'researching' and 'collecting' information is necessary when the decision-making is required. Next is design. Design means 'planning,' which is creating, developing and analyzing feasible alternatives and examining the feasibility and predictable challenges. The last step is choice. It means selecting the best feasible alternative among all alternatives.

In Simon's satisfaction model, he draws Administrative Man into comparison with Economic Man. The assumption of "Economic Man Model" is as follows:

① Organizational goals are known and there is no incongruity among these goals;

② The organization's decision-maker understands the problems and opportunities of the organization;

③ Grasping them accurately as well;

④ When preparing for capitalizing on opportunities or solving problems, the decision-maker fully understands every feasible alternative and the expectation effect of each;

⑤ The decision-maker has perfect knowledge of relevant situation factors;

⑥ Therefore, the decision-maker selects 'the best alternative';

⑦ The evaluation of the alternative is scientific and rational.

Observe the assumption of 'Administrative Human Model' which contrasts to 'Rational Human Model':

① You can find that the organizational goal is sometimes ambiguous and reciprocally conflictive;

② Occasionally a decision-maker does not understand the problems and opportunities of his organization;

③ Even when he recognizes them, they are often wrongly conceived;

④ Decision-making is based on a model;

⑤ Therefore it is common that 'the rationality' of decision-making applies to the most important part of the organization and the main data or variable is not captured in many cases;

⑥ Consequently, the knowledge that the decision-maker has is bounded and the selection of alternative is confined to 'the extent of being moderately satisfied' rather than being 'the best';

⑦ The evaluation of alternative is conducted not in a systematic way but just in general level, which means 'the rationality' of decision-maker is the bounded rationality 'limited' by many restriction factors.

(2) Collective Decision-Making Theory

The collective decision-making theory is focused on a process in which various people make a decision as a whole, therefore affecting one another. Typical examples are Simon and March's organization model and Cyert's corporate model. These two collective decision-making models explain all human behavior in terms of control by feedback and information, based on the Cybernetics theory. The major contents of collective decision-making model are as follows:

(A) Adaptive Decision-Making

The collective decision-making in an organization indicates that decision-making does not necessarily occur through the whole steps of rational decision-making, and neither premises the steps of goal and value that Rationality model premises. A company's decision-maker has interests in maintaining the important variables at a certain desirable level such as total sales or image of the company. The important variable that matters to decision-maker in operating this kind of automatic temperature device is 'Temperature'. It lifts lever to maintain the state safe when the device is out of normal state, which indicates the decision-making of an organization. In short, decision-making set in the organization model is a cognitive result when an organization attempts to adjust itself to a certain state.

(B) Avoiding Uncertainty

An organization adapts itself in trials and errors, through information gathered from feedback channels. The newly added information diminishes uncertainty of alternative result, and therefore, deals with problems that occur daily in the short term (not prevent the possibility of uncertainty in the long term, as Rational model predicts). The theory asserts that the organization adapts itself in trials and errors through the short-term process of response.

(C) Learning

Once the decision maker obtains a positive result by selecting an alternative, the learning process takes place (albeit slowly) and this learning dependency forms a pattern of decision-making, called SOPs, which does not change very often. The Rationality model asserted that causal learning occurs when the existing alternative and model are revised by newly added information. But actually, it is not like that. In reality, an organization changes its goals and center of attention through experiences and revising the procedures necessary to search, showing the adaptive decision-making pattern.

(3) Normative Model and Positive Model

Positive model is an empirical model whose goals are to describe, explain and predict phenomena in reality in scientific way, by the procedure of researching the causal relationship based on the principle of observability, objectivity, and reproducibility. In policy decision model, based on positive model, there are various kinds of statistical analysis and econometric models such as regression model, factor analysis, structural equation model (path analysis), and cost-benefit analysis.

On the other hand, normative model is designed to define what the desirable goal is and to find out what a policy should do for the future rather than analyzing phenomena in a scientific way.

E-Government and Policy-Making Model

George P. Huber (2001) classified the policy-making models associated with the e-Government and discusses how information technology and e-Government could contribute to each model as shown below.

1) Policy Decision-Making Model

(1) Rational Model

Rational model assumes that an organization reaches its best solution through rational and systematic analysis. This model is important as it serves an ideal type of the roadmap for organization.

(2) Political Competition Model

Political competition model argues that the decision-making of an organization is an outcome of the trial of strategies and tactics of a unit while getting advantageous selection for its sub-system. Policy competition model highlights that the participants of a policy-decision have respective goals and therefore puts a special attention on the power relationship in the analysis of decision making conducted in an organization.

(3) Program Model

Program model emphasizes the two factors that control the decision-making of an organization; they are program and programming. 'Program' means Standard Operation Procedures (SOP) and budget constraints which can affect decision-making within the organization. 'Programming,' another influential factor in the organizational decision-making, indicates some cognitive and motivational factors such as specialized education for decision makers.

The decision-making is influenced by various programs and programming inside an organization and therefore, program model argues that the decision making is relatively easy to be predicted because the programs of an organization can be easily changed.

(4) Policy Stream Model

Policy stream model has been first established by M. Cohen, J. March and J. Olsen as the name of 'Garbage Can Model,' and later developed by J. Kingdon as the name of Policy stream model. This model assumes that three policy streams, namely, problem, policy alternatives, and politics(participants and opportunities), flow independently and when a focusing event occurs, those three streams are 'coupled' and the policy window for decision making could be opened.

The model can be useful to explain the decision-making process under catastrophic situation and also powerful to explain that of organizations without hierarchy such as university organizations or a parliament with multiparty system. Representative examples are the process of Norwegian policy-decision studied by Olsen and J. Kingdon's study of the process of policy-decision in public health policy and transportation policy in the United States written in his famous book, 'Agendas, Alternatives and Public Policies'(1984).

(5) Evaluation and Implication

The four models above can be forceful to explain respectively in different aspects and dimensions of policy-decision, because policy-decision contains rational aspect, political aspect, predictable SOP aspects, and contingency and catastrophic aspect. Therefore, in designing and applying e-Government, and applying policy science techniques to policy-decision, it is desirable to consider the various aspects of decision-making process to offer the appropriate policy-decision information and support. For this purpose, we need to find out what is desirable information and support for policy-decision of each model because according to each model the specific role and support of e-Government would be different. Thus, we will examine the information and support necessary to each policy-decision model as the following section.

2) The Role of E-Government for Policy-Decision Support

(1) Rational Model

Rational model, though it has faced many criticisms, is still a very useful model as it guides us to a direction in policy-decision. The data necessary to this model can be arranged into three steps: Basic data, Elaborating data, and Performance data.

① *Basic Data*: What are the alternatives for policy-decision? What are the upcoming situation or conditions will it encounter? What are the evaluation criteria to be used for assessment of policy alternatives?

② *Elaborating Data*: What are the concrete possibilities of situation to occur in the near future? What would be the relative importance of various evaluation criteria?

③ *Performance Data*: How are the cost and benefits for different kinds of alternatives? How much would each alternative be feasible, that is, to what extent can the decision-maker pay for?

This model suggests the logical grounds that e-Government can help rational policy decision-making. The useful analytical techniques, associated with computer programming, could be utilized in this model, including regression analysis, factor analysis, path analysis(SEM model), B/C analysis and policy delphi techniques(Foresight methodologies) among others.

(2) Political Competition Model

The facts and data necessary for the model are as follows:

① Which groups are related to the current policy decision-making?

② What are the potential impacts that each group could potentially have?

③ What kind of cost or benefit associated with each alternative for each group?

④ What kind of influence does it have to these groups or competitors?

⑤ What kind of strategy the each competitor could choose and what are those consequencies from each selection?

It is true that the management techniques or statistical methodologies associated with the computer system of e-Government would be the most helpful for the rational model. However, e-Government could also help to analyze the political competition model if we are able to obtain the facts and data as described above. For example, computer simulation can be used to analyze the changes of outcome based on the incremental changes of the conditions or assumptions and Game theory can also be applied to analyze the situations of collective bargaining or negotiations.

(3) Program Model

Program model, as mentioned, highlights decision-making of organization as an outcome of 'program' and 'programming'. As this process of program and programming changes slowly, this model assumes that the process and outcome of organizational decision-making could be predicted by using the procedural data of the organization. Program such as SOPs strengthens a user's tendency to be attached to status-quo and make them reapply the same method which has been used to the similar problem of the past. E-Government has significance in the sense that it can help break down the 'path-dependency' (status-quo) phenomena because information system could help to find out new alternatives from the broader search activities by raising more fundamental question of the problem.

In order to break down the conservative phenomenon discussed in Satisfaction

Model or Organizational Model, it is required for an organization to have decisive and innovative policy design, disconnecting with the past, through vision, strategy and policy innovation. This is what is stressed out in Y. Dror's Meta-policy-making and the necessity of Societal Guidance System emphasized in A. Etzioni's Mixed Scanning Model.

Here, e-Government can contribute to identify the vision and strategy of the organization using brainstorming, policy delphi, and the scenario planning. It using the Smart and Social Network devices, could also contribute to enhance an interactive communication with the main policy-target groups when it derives the more desirable policy vision and future roadmap.

(4) Policy Stream Model

Policy stream model assumes that decision-making is made through the interaction among problem, solutions and opportunity to interact in the streams of problem, policy and politics. The issues needed for information support of e-Government are as follows:

① What are the problems that will arise in the future? When are the opportunities? And, in what way, will it occur?

② What are the solutions for them and how and when should they be arranged?

③ What kinds of decision-making opportunities are to be arranged and when?

As Policy Stream model focuses on the matters that are not easily predicted, what is required for the information support in this kind of decision-making is a process to be carried out in a dynamic and interactive way. The function required for e-Government is to provide information necessary to policy manager under the 'turbulence of vortex.' Under this dynamic and constantly interactive environment, policy analysis using decision-making tree, based on the computer simulation, is useful to analyze the 'problem' or 'solution'.

3) Summary and Implications

We have examined different policy decision models of organization such as Rational model, Political competition model, Program model, and Policy stream model. In each decision-making model, we also learned what would be the crucial information and what kind of policy support that e-Government could provide.

As e-Government is based on information system, it allows computer application for extensive comparative analysis of the policy alternatives. It helps systematic application and utilization of Big Data in the scientific policy-making process on which Rational model puts emphasis.

However, because policy-decision contains rational, political, predictable SOPs, and contingency and opportunity aspects, each policy-making model has different power of explanation in different context of decision. Although in different degree when applied, e-Government can also help to deal with these irrational factors, i.e. political factor, SOPs, and contingency and opportunity factor in the decision-making process.

Accordingly, to design and implement e-Government in the future, it is required to consider these various aspects of the policy decision-making processes and, therefore, to provide the appropriate support for the desirable decision-making system in the entire governance processes.

Key Point!

◎ Policy Science in Information Society: Analytical Framework

e-Government

- The governmental operating model that is the policy switch process from the input(demand and support of the people) to the output of policy.

The contact point of e-Government and Policy Science

- The e-Government can improve the ability of decision-making than the existing governance model.
- Also it can contribute to national innovation as a new management system of national governance.

e-Government and the Result of Government

- Views in the science of public administration
  - In internal aspect, it improves the government efficiency.
  - In external aspect, it improves the citizen satisfaction for the government.
- Views in the policy science
  - It strengthens the ability of decision-making by improving the quantity and quality of policy information.
  - At the national and societal levels of information policy, it contributes to achieve the efficiency, equity, democracy, and reflexivity of society.

◎ E-Government and Policy-Making Theory

E-Government and Policy Process

- Improving the rationality of policy-making through ICT and scientific management techniques.
  - It can handle much policy information economically → effectiveness, efficiency
  - It can reduce the time required to communicate among the policy target group → democracy, reflexivity

- Improving the opportunities and possibilities of the scientific decision-making
- Revitalizing the opportunities of communication between the policy target group in the policy implementation process → easy-to-secure adaption
- Being possible to compare/analyze systemically and to evaluate policy programs rationally.
- Providing the efficient and transparent policy mechanism in the policy feedback process

Theoretical Model of Policy Decision-making

- Rationality Model and Cognitive Model
  - Rational Model : All men decide their behavior and act based on logos and rationality.
  - Cognitive Model: It criticizes the rational model because men's cognitive capabilities are limited.

- Personal Decision-making Theory and Collective Decision-making Theory
  - Personal Decision-making Theory: It focuses how to men make their decision in reality.
  - Collective Decision-Making Theory: It focuses that members of an organization affect each other and decide their behavior as a whole → adaptive decision-making, uncertainty avoidance, and learning.
  - Normative Model and Positive Model: It focuses to study what is the desirable goal and how to do for this goal; the positive model focuses to describe, explain and predict the policy processes of the governance.

E-Government and Policy-Making Model

- Policy Decision-Making Model
  - Rational Model: It assumes that the organization goes through rational analytical and process and finally it can make the best rational decision.
  - Political Competition Model: It assumes that many participants who has different goal uses various strategies for achieving their purpose under the constraints of the power relationship
  - Program Model: It assumes that the decision-making in the organization is influenced and changed by various programs.

- Policy Stream Model: It assumes that three policy streams, namely, problem, policy alternatives, and politics(participants and opportunities), flow independently; and when a focus event occurs, those three streams are 'coupled' and the policy window for decision-making will be opened.

▸ The Role of e-Government for Policy-Decision Support

- Rational model: It provides the logical basis to help the rational decision-making.
- Political competition model: It helps the policy analysis and decision-making with consideration for political position.
- Program model: It helps to maintain the status quo or break the conservative situation by new, broad, and fundamental alternative search.
- Policy stream model: It provides the dynamic information to analyze the unpredictable cases.

Key Question!

◎ Discuss the contact point of e-Government and policy science.

◎ What is the contribution of e-Government in the policy processes?

◎ Explain the normative model and positive model of decision-making.

◎ Explain the Rational Model, Political Competition Model, Program Model, and Policy Stream Models.

Chapter 15

THE LOGIC OF INFORMATION POLICY

The vision of e-policy is to make a genuinely humane society by balancing between commercial interests and public values.

Objectives

This chapter will elucidate the logic of Information Policy and the strategic e-Policy approach to strengthen national competitiveness.

First, it will highlight the principles and the rationale of e-Policy by looking into the stimulation of social vitality, building human network and protection of public value, enhancing social equity and spiritual value of information policy.

Second, it will also discuss the significance and priorities of strategic e-Policy. It will further discuss strategic e-Policy model of high-tech industry by examining the critical factors to enhance national and business competitiveness in the global scale.

The Principle of E-Policy

In his book 'The Road Ahead,' Bill Gates mentioned:

> "*The information superhighway will transform the mentality of people. You will be able to take finance, law, even medical service without stepping outside of your house...the context of the education program we will get will also be awfully diverse...However it will take decades for these important changes to be real because most people have tendency to stick to what is familiar to them. So it is natural for them not to change the things that are familiar. But the new generation will bring about new value. Our children will not have aversion toward the notion that they work using this means of information communication technology in a distant place. They will take this new technology for granted like we do when using ours such as telephone or ball-pen*" *(Bill Gates, 1996:155~156).*

It is interesting to reflect Bill Gates' notion at the time that social change will proceed not abruptly but with social relationship or traditional form of life remains as information society arrives. It is rather a conservative opinion when considering the speed of the development of current ICT.

The vision of information society is to upgrade our lifestyle using the smart ICT devices while keeping our core traditional values. Would this be possible? What policy mindset is necessary for this to be realistic? What form of policy approaches could make a genuine civilized society? It is but natural for a policy-study-student to bear these questions.

The U.S. government has announced five principles on information policy which has been a helpful reference for making a principled information policy discussion. These principles are as follows:

① Promotion of Private Investment
② Promotion of Dynamic and Fair Market Competition
③ Assurance of a Flexible Laws & Regulations
④ Provide Wide & Open Information Access
⑤ Assurance of Universal Service

In conclusion, it is desirable to establish e-Strategy to maintain traditional values and minimizes the alienation of human being while increasing efficiency of e-Government. Meanwhile, it is also crucial not to suffocate private sector and governmental productivity, while paying closely attention not to alienate the majority of people in informatization process. As well as procedures of information, education and democratic

Figure 15-1 The Principle of E-Policy

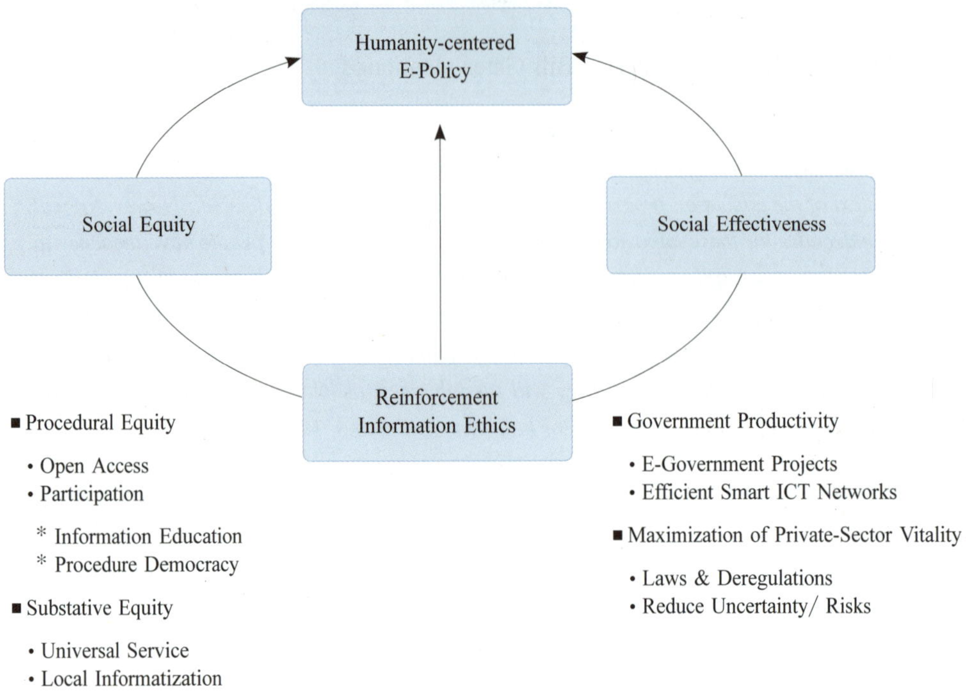

process maintained as a safe-valve. For this to be actualized, it is fundamentally important to cultivate the healthy civic culture and information ethics.

The Logic of E-Policy

Promotion of Economic Vitality

The sectors which are mostly considered to be enhanced by information technology are business, education, medical, and environment sector. It is expected that the technology will take a crucial role in enhancing creativity and efficiency being freed from time, space and organizational boundary restriction.

New smart digital technology will maximize 'synergy effect of national economy' by organically connect and integrate the resources scattered around the subunits of the society. In addition, the new interactive information communications technology will bring better medical benefits and revolutionary innovations in transferring methods in education field as well.

1) Information Technology and Investment

A corporate enterprise should enhance economic efficiency through investment of smart information technologies that customers want. This kind of investment can be activated when the government should do the leading role in setting up the strategic direction with the spirit of cooperative governance between the government and business.

2) Enhancing Private Creativity

The core of economic vitality is to maintain the value of private investment and creativity. If business is not confident about the future and its willingness to invest is discouraged, there will be no employment stability. Therefore, the government has to consider minimizing regulations that would obstruct private sector vitality in order to lessen future business uncertainties. For this, the government must foster transparent and accountable policies and must endeavor to promote private sector participation in governance. In this regard, the public and private sector need to consider actively of the possibility of becoming a partner to conduct pilot project or advanced information network projects(Fields, 1994).

3) Promoting Government Productivity

The role of government is important for the creation of successful supply and demand for network and information technology. The government productivity is a crucial element for efficient business activity. Accordingly, the government should make effort to build network of information system by itself so that the public service should be provided efficiently to the private sectors.

Conservation of Public Value

There is a fundamental difference of purpose between public, private, and non-governmental organizations. Private or business investment is based on commerciality, whereas public and non-governmental organization is based on public value. The government must consider both the vitality of private investment and the principles of public value. It is hard to hold technical issues in abeyance once they appear. Thus, in developing information policies in the context of information society, the following issues must be considered: Why we need build information network? What groups or organizations we need to connect, and why? In what context should we convey information policies? Above all, what kinds of information society should we develop?

1) Building Humane Network

Instead of being enthralled by technology that is nothing but complex, we need to build information society that meets citizen needs and that is genuinely necessary to human being (Menichelli and Blau, 1994). To promote humane network, the diversity of contents should be guaranteed. We need to listen to the people's voice that is not heard under the routine of commerciality and need to enhance accessibility of these people. For this, the fee of the Network must come to the level that people from all walks of life can use and participate(Branscomb, 1994). These efforts to widen 'public space' will be greatly helpful to develop a healthy civil community.

2) Protection of Public Value

Development in the communication technology brings about changes in the way of life. In the same manner, a change in the human relationship causes social change. These changes in the way of life will remotely isolate human being from the conventional practices.

In the 1970s, Marshall McLuhan has predicted an 'e-Global community' that is peaceful and harmonious as information society arrives. But looking into the current feature of information society, we can easily find our community being divided and fragmented. While people were able to make friends or communicate with others through Facebook in cyber space, the traditional sense of camaraderie is vanishing.

It is necessary to actively examine policies to discover valuable project that gears towards preservation of established cultural heritage. The preservation and maintenance of human values is essential to maintain the value of human life.

3) Guarantee of Social Diversity

The principles for democratic administration of Information Network should follow the clear path to respect of the freedom of expression and guarantee of diversity, which force the existing freedom of speech to be modified to this new media environment. Likewise, it is also a requisite to devise prevention mechanisms on invasion of privacy(Firestone and Kopp, 1994; Kapor, 1994).

Promotion of Social Equity

Human-centered information society must be open not only to upper classes that are technically outstanding and wealthy but also to the whole public. Whether being rich or poor, living in a city or country, or being old or young, it is our ideal that every human being has his or her own right to access to information society.

1) Realization of Universal Service

The advancement of information society is already offering infinite opportunities for the businessmen. However, although the quantity of information rises, and the network gets wide and open to more people, it is also inevitable true that the benefit doesn't goes to all the people. So we need to understand the notion of universal service based on this awareness.

Universal service indicates the policy choice that the lowest opportunity of politic, economic and society should be guaranteed to everyone. So it is the very concept of universal service to provide information resources with people of every age and walk of life at appropriate fee.

First, this concept should be reorganized from that of voice telephony centered into the one that includes interactive broadband e-Services. And related to this, it should be actively discussed about the issue of the duty of offering public service, funding plan, and subsidy system.

The government should pool the wisdom concerning the following issues:

What form of information and e-Program should be provided in inexpensive prices or for free? What is the proper price that will make everyone accessible? What kind of payment method should we choose? Who will preserve the shortcomings?

2) Guarantee of Open Access

Information and the accessibility to information are crucial factors in information society(Craig, 1979; Nimmo, 1985). Establishing favorable environment to access to network and transmission facility free from any distinction is essential for all information service providers. Furthermore, publicity creates social benefit through combination with accumulation of information and knowledge by connecting the various information network.

The Most Fundamental Issues: Issues of Spiritual Values

It has been illustrated that the gist turning point of utopianism and dystopianism in the fact-information society can be concluded as the matter of equality, universal services, professed access and participation(Bates, 1989:24). Our effort to establish civilized, humanity-based information society should focus more on construction of humane network, preservation of public values and social equity. But the backstay of all these political principles is the matter of information education and information ethics/culture.

1) Information Education

HRD issue is critical to build up an effective e-Government and national development. One should be able to cultivate intellectual capacity while enhancing the ability to creatively use the smart ICT. In fact, one of the critical success factors of Korean economic development was education. The passion and zeal of education to offer the best quality of education from the family perspectives were tremendous even with sacrificing of other factors.

2) Information Ethics and Information Culture

Information mindset and civic consciousness is critical to realize the trust and mature information society. The followings are the minimum issues to be considered:

The first one is a theft or an act of destruction in information society. By the invisible matrix of information, computer hackers who steal information commit a crime without any sense of guilt in the existing value. It means the destruction of humanity and it is a fundamental problem of information society.

The second one is the obscene information or undesirable information spreading indiscriminatingly on the net. It prevents healthy emotional development especially for the children. To solve these problems, the appropriate education for making healthy consciousness and self-awareness high of teenagers must be provided. Also information communication ethics of internet service providers must be established at the same time.

The third one is the issue of intellectual property right. The issues of content protection and intellectual property right are important as the information overflow and computerization make the reproduction and steal of information be easy. Without properly responding to these problems, information society can easily become a mimic society.

Conclusion: The Cultivation of a Spiritual Value and Civic Consciousness

The human-centered information society must be opened not only to the elite class but also to all the people. The government should approach to this matter with the standpoint of universal service, and not neglect to make an investment in both backwoods and rural district to prevent 'oversight of connection' when establishing info-communications infrastructure. When this policy based approach fails, the cultural, social and political impact on information-paupers will be tremendous.

In order to make the information society become civilized society, the cultivation of civic consciousness is the most fundamental. It is also important to note that the humane network that is based on the citizen need, not on the technological drive, must be constructed, and diversity of information content must be guaranteed.

The logic of e-policy, discussed up until now, is summarized as 〈Figure 15-2〉.

Figure 15-2 The Logic of E-Policy

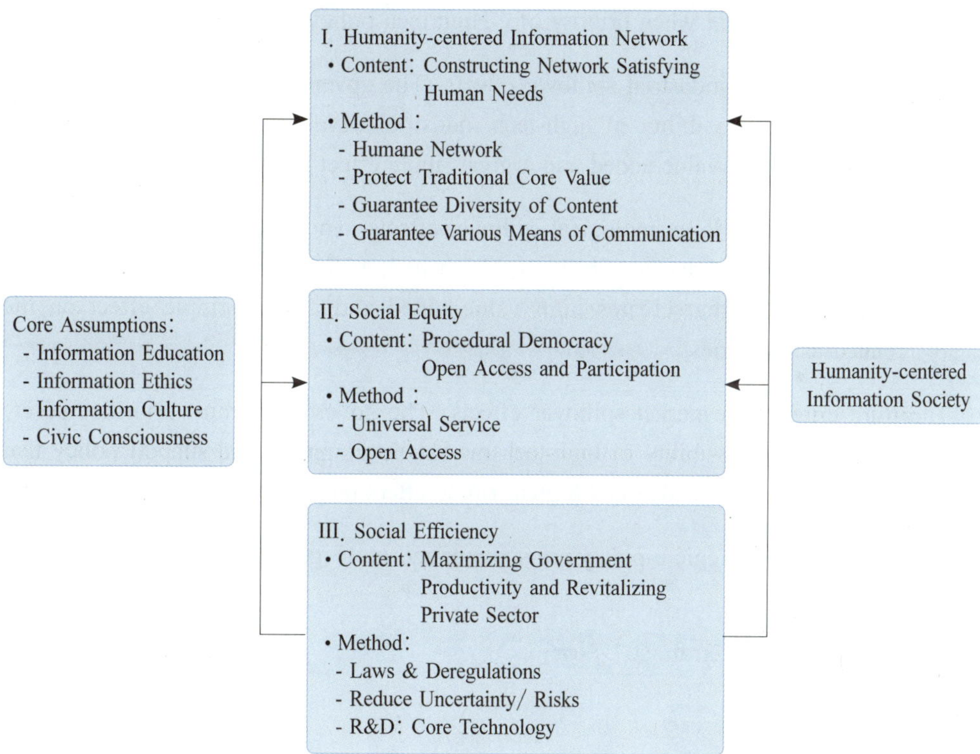

The Strategic Information Policy

In this section, we will discuss the strategic e-policy relating with strategic industrial policy, which belongs to the 'maximization of economic efficiency through e-Government,' under the logic of e-policy discussed above.

Strategic Elements of E-Policy

A strategy is an act of selecting a set of policies which would have the best effects. In the strategic standpoint of e-policy, it is important to prioritize policy items as the nation tends to always lack the financial resources. Therefore, we cannot overemphasize the importance of strategic thinking for efficient allocation of the limited national resources.

There are three criteria when priority of e-High tech policy should consider.

The first criterion is industrial spillover effects. The government must prioritize policy that involves possibility of high-tech industrial development and support policy that creates high value-added and a great ripple effect on the related industries.

The second criterion is technological spillover effects. The government must prioritize policy that involves possibility of high-tech technological development and support policy that creates high value-added and a great ripple effect on the related technologies.

The third criterion is market spillover effects. The government must prioritize policy that involves possibility of high-tech market development and support policy that creates high value-added and a great ripple effect on the related markets.

These criteria of strategic e-policy are summarized in 〈Figure 15-3〉.

Figure 15-3 Criteria of Strategic E-Policy

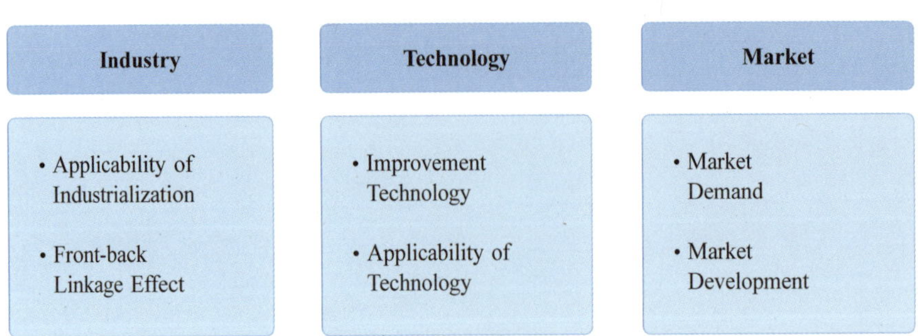

Figure 15-4 Cubic Effect Model of Strategic E-Policy

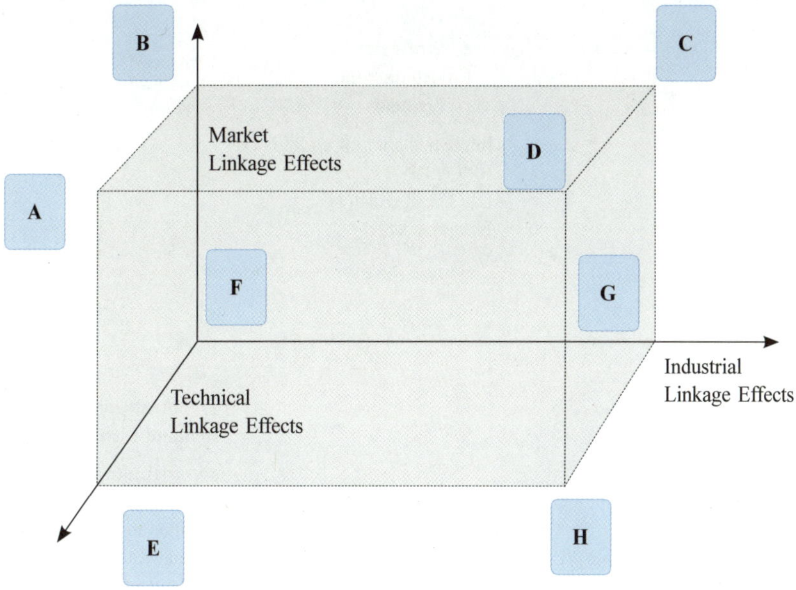

〈Figure 15-4〉 shows the three-dimensional cubic model of the three variables discussed above. In the figure, A～Hs illustrate the position of each policy element. The best position is D that all three axes are the highest position.

Strategic E-policy: Three dimensions

Considering the three criteria presented above, there is need to be analyzed in three dimensions: Supply side, Demand side, and Environment side.

In strategic supply-side, it needs to provide the supply by constructing the super-high speed information and communications infrastructure, core technology and professional HRD training.

In strategic demand-side, it needs to create the demand by constructing industrial information network, information education, and local informatization program.

In strategic environment-side, it needs to qualitatively upgrade e-Government strategy, and arrange the laws and regulatory frameworks of e-Government.

The relationship among these strategic elements is shown in 〈Figure 15-5〉.

Figure 15-5 Cubic Effect Model of Strategic E-Policy

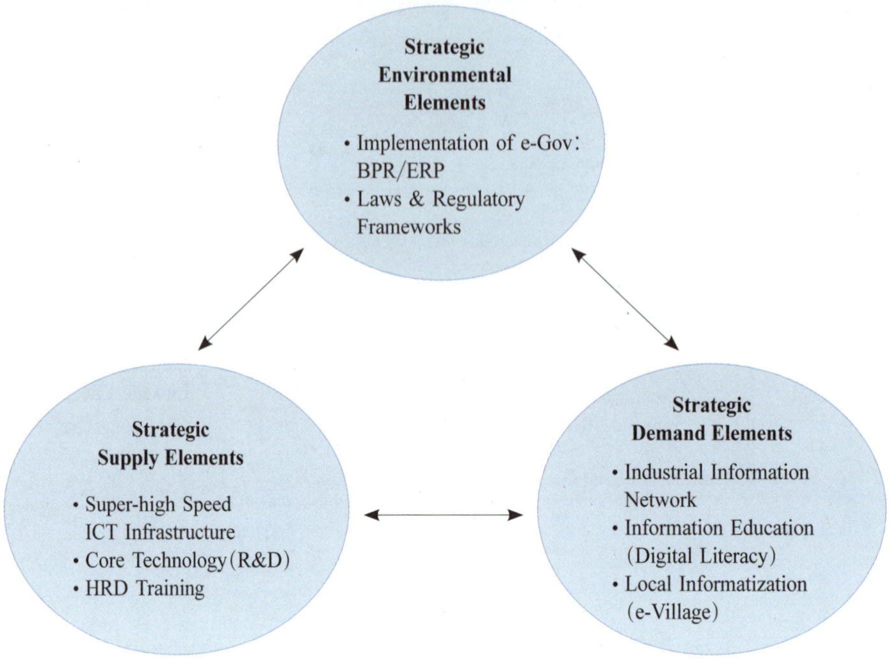

1) Strategic E-policy and National Competitiveness

The three dimensions of strategic e-policy are associated with the theory of national competitiveness.

〈Figure 15-6〉 shows the overall relationship between strategic e-policy and national competitiveness. By completing information infrastructure, it will contribute to enhance the business and industrial productivity, and eventually to the national competitiveness.

Based on the diamond theory of competitiveness of M. Porter, business activities, factor supplies, domestic demands, and the government productivity are selected as the fundamental components of national competitiveness.

KII(Korea Information Infrastructure), for the Korean case, made a significant contribution to increase business competitiveness, through industrial competitiveness, and eventually to the national competitiveness.

The figure illustrates the overall relationship of information infrastructure-based business competitiveness, industrial competitiveness, government productivity and national competitiveness.

Figure 15-6 Strategic E-Policy Elements

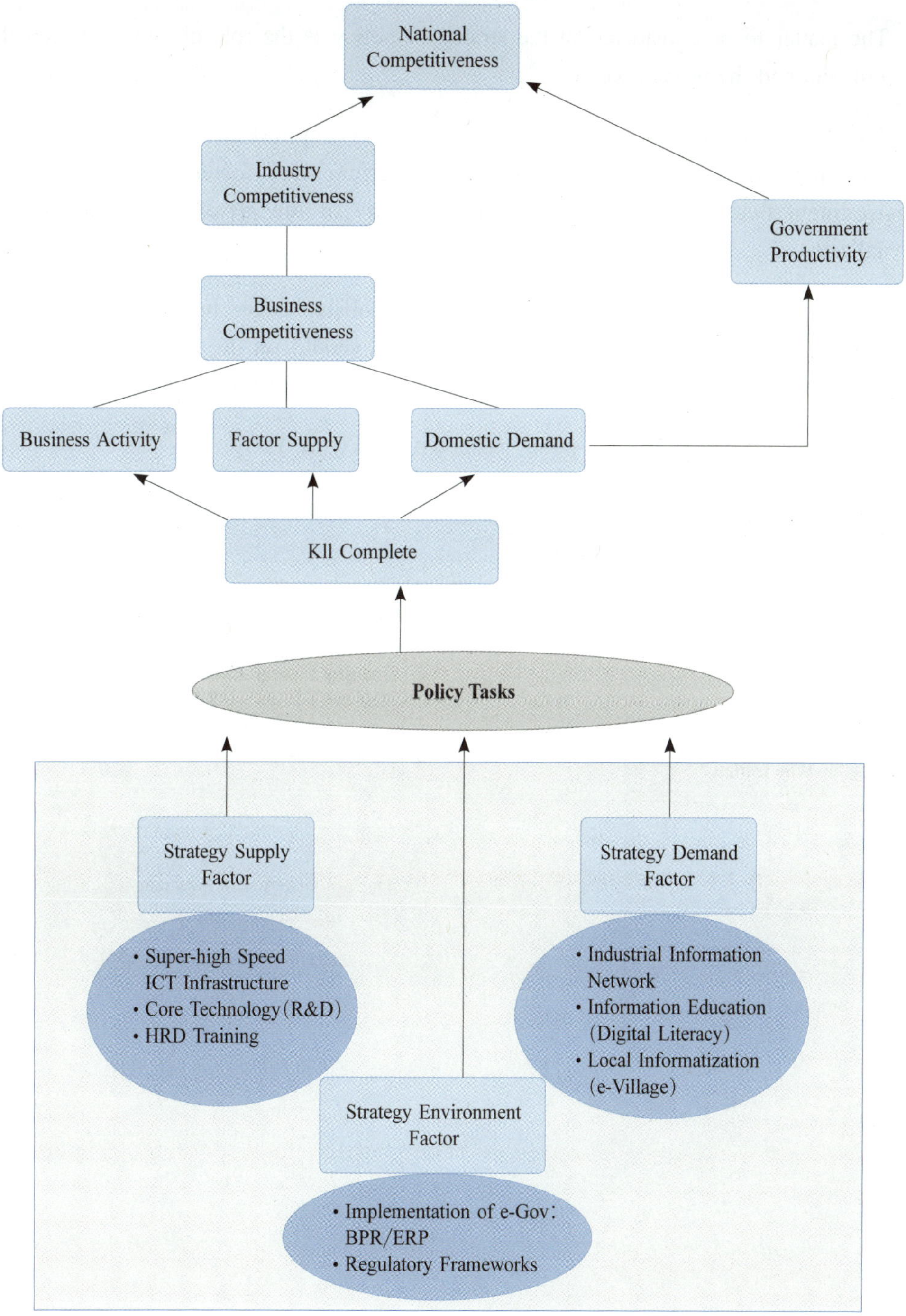

2) Framework of Strategic E-Policy: Government Leading & Private Support

The matter to be considered in the strategy e-policy is the role division between the government and the private sector.

The government should provide the necessary support to foster the strategic environment. It is very important for the government to foster strategic e-policy environment that led the autonomy and creativity of the private sector should be revitalized.

Government should first significantly remove obstacles for business activities by rearranging laws and regulation in the field. It also should set up the effective and fair competition rules that the major economic agents should observe in the market.

The framework of strategic e-policy is shown in ⟨Figure 15-7⟩.

Figure 15-7 Framework of Strategy E-Policy

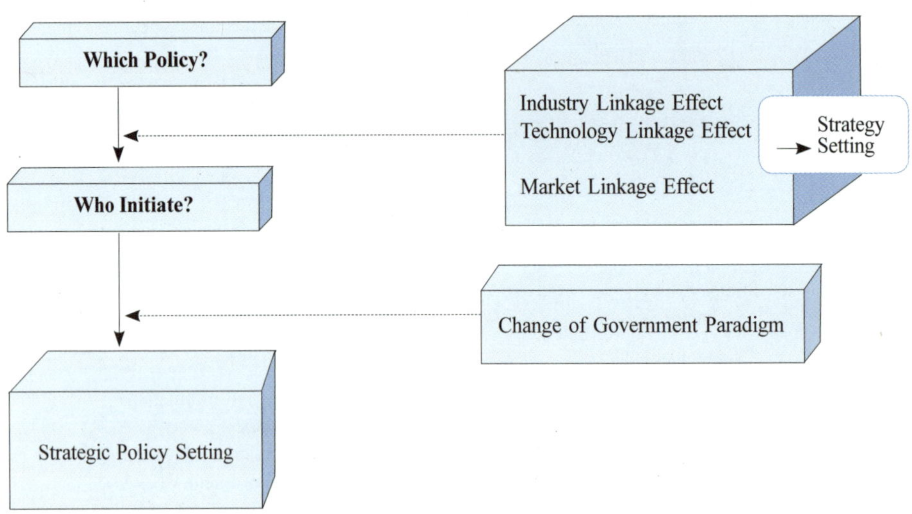

E-Policy Case

Successful Case of Cooperative Governance: Public-Private Partnership

▸ **Oulu Region in Finland**

Oulu, the central city in northern Finland, is called the Silicon Valley of the Artic. Success factors in Oulu as follows: 1) The local government played a leading role by selecting the Hi-tech research park and investing R&D to induce the Hi-tech Services; 2) The local universities took the important role by providing high competent human resources(HRD); and 3) Hi-tech companies actively participated and made a synergy effect for the research park.

▸ **Ireland National Digital Park**

The new industrial town in Ireland, CityWest of National Digital Park, established in 1999, has three factors of success. They are largely the same as the case of Finland and give us insightful lessons and implications. The successful factors are as follows: 1) The Irish government has an important role to provide the best support for the software companies leading to the level of world-class by lowering corporate tax; 2) Local colleges focused on HRD to provide the best human resources who is fluent in English; and 3) The successful public-private partnership between the local government and the local developing companies to vitalize the National Digital Park and provide the best business environment for the participated corporate.

Conclusion

In the 21st century, the key issues of competition, in the 21st century, are "overcoming time and space," through reinforcement of national competitiveness and improvement of the people's quality of life. The high speed information and communication will be a key means of a national strategy to become an advanced nation. It will upgrade the national intelligence level by organically integrating government, business, and people.

From strategic e-policy standpoint, it is important to consider the supply, demand, and environmental aspects of the national strategy. Government, for this purpose, should accelerate to realize the high-tech information community by rearranging law and regulatory framework for the e-Government.

To become the world first-class nation is not an easy task. Clear vision and paradigm change should be followed by the blue print and its action plan. Strong leadership and commitment should be supported by the people's awareness and civic consciousness. The prosperity of next generation and the opportunity of world business do not come automatically. The policy environment should be established to support business creativity and entrepreneurial innovation.

Without such a firm vision and policy strategy, "the future of the 21st century, and the realization of world-class country" is such a vacant dream.

Key Point!

◎ The Principle of E-Policy

- Promotion of Private Investment
- Promotion of Dynamic and Fair Competition
- Assurance of Flexible Law & Regulations
- Provide Wide & Open Access
- Assurance of Universal Service

◎ The Logic of E-Policy

- Promotion of Economic Vitality
  - Information Technology and Investment
  - Enhancing Private Creativity
  - Promoting Government Productivity

- Conservation of Public Value
  - Building Humane Network
  - Protection of Public Value
  - Guarantee of Social Diversity

- Promotion of Social Equity
  - Realization of Universal Service
  - Guarantee of Open Access

- The Most Fundamental Issues: Spiritual Values
  - Information Education
  - Information Ethics and Information Culture

◎ The Strategic Information Policy

▸ Strategic Elements of E-Policy

- Industrial spillover effects
- Technological spillover effects
- Market spillover effects

▸ Strategic E-policy: Three dimensions of Strategic E-Policy

- Supply-side, it needs to provide the supply by constructing the super-high speed information and communications infrastructure, core technology and professional HRD training.
- Demand-side, it needs to create the demand by constructing industrial information network, information education, and local informatization program.
- Environment-side, it needs to qualitatively upgrade e-Government strategy, and arrange the laws and regulatory frameworks of e-Government.

▸ Framework of Strategic E-Policy: Government Leading & Private Support

- The government should provide the necessary support to foster the strategic environment.
- Government should first significantly remove obstacles for business activities by rearranging laws and regulation in the field.

Key Question!

◎ What are the five fundament principles of information policy?

◎ What does the "constructing the humane network in the information society" mean, and how to achieve it?

◎ In the information society, many people predict that the gap of the haves and the have-nots will grow bigger. For solving this Digital Divide problem, what should be the government roles?

◎ What is the fundamental rights of citizen in connection with the application and selection of information?

◎ What does the "information ethics" means, and what are the issues about information ethics?

◎ Explain the three priority standards for e-industrial policy(industrial value, technology valuc, markct value).

◎ Explain what should be the government strategy for strategic industrial policy. And in this process, what are the role of government and private sector?

PART 6

THEORY & STRATEGY OF E-POLICY II: PARTICULARS OF SPECIFIC E-POLICY

In Part VI, Theory and Strategy of E-Policy II, we will elucidate the particulars of specific E-Policy.

First, we will examine the overview of e-Policy. Here, three dimensions of e-Policy will be elucidated along the line of three governance unit of analysis, i.e., state(government), market(enterprise), and civil society (NGO).

Second, following the overall scheme of e-Policy, the three dimensions of particular e-Policy will be discussed, i.e., productivity, democracy, and reflexivity. These include, national competitive dimension of e-Policy: productivity, market efficiency dimension of e-Policy: productivity, civil society dimension of e-Policy(I): democracy & transparency, civil society dimension of e-Policy(II): ethics & reflexivity, and as a final one, civil society dimension of e-Policy(III): equity.

Chapter 16

THE OVERALL SCHEME OF E-POLICY

The future e-Technology will greatly enhance brain power and innovation capacity.

- Alvin Toffler -

Objectives

The purpose of this chapter is to elucidate the overall scheme of e-policy. After the discussion of the three critical dimensions of e-Government, this chapter will focus on the overall blueprint, dimensions and elements of e-Policy.

First, it will discuss the analytical model of e-Policy based on the three governance unit of analysis, that is, state (government), market (enterprise), and civil society (NGO).

Second, it will highlight the concept of e-Government based on the three dimensions, that is, productivity, democracy, and reflexivity.

Third, it will examine the typology of e-Policy based on the three dimensions associated with the unit of analysis.

Overview: Analytical Model of E-Policy

Classifying e-Policy based on a workable and meaningful typology is very important as such categorization will facilitate clearer understanding of e-Government. In this regard, policy analysis need to be dealt with along the three levels of governance: state/government, market/enterprise, and civil society/NGO (see Figure 16-1).

E-Government as a mechanism of governance should consider on the following three critical areas:

The first domain that e-Government should focus on is the economic and administrative area that promotes economic and government productivity. The model of e-Government should center on strengthening national competitiveness by (1) Setting up an effective e-Government system within the government that maximizes government productivity and (2) Supporting a knowledge-based economy and high-tech industry that will enhance economic productivity.

The second domain that e-Government should focus on is the political area that promotes participation and accountability. The e-Government model should advance e-Democracy by way of (1) Promoting participatory governance that encourages the strengthening of

Figure 16-1 Analytical Framework of e-Policy: Governance as the Unit of Analysis

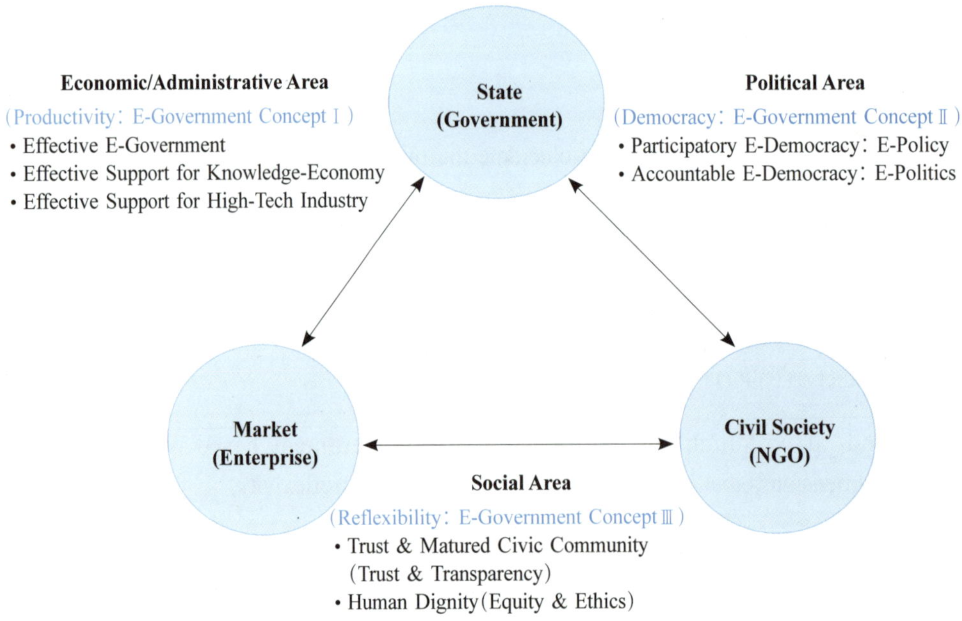

direct and representative democracy, and (2) Advancing accountability in governance.

The third domain that e-Government should focus on is the social area that promotes trust, transparency, equity and ethics. The e-Government system should advance and promote a healthy civic community by (1) Reaching a trustful, harmonious, and matured society by utilizing advance social communication approaches that easily encourage an active citizens participation (e.g., e-Forum that fosters trust and transparency), and (2) Advancing and nurturing human dignity and equality through humane e-Policies such as free access to public information, e-Education, and universal service to bridge the digital and information gap while guaranteeing e-Security.

Three Dimension of E-Government

The analytical framework of e-Policy as discussed above was framed in accordance with the three dimensional approaches of e-Government. This particular topic was emphasized and thoroughly discussed out in this book.

The first dimension of e-Government is **Productivity**. E-Government is to maximize productivity of government through ICT. It must support efficiency as well as business activities of the market. Under the Knowledge-based economy, government must be able to provide efficient services to the stakeholders (i.e., private sector, corporate, etc.) and/or customers to maximize their productivity, efficiency, autonomy, and creativity. To do this, it is mandatory for government to maximize productivity within the organization. Thus, digital neural network must be utilized and adopted effectively in the internal operation system of the government.

1) Democracy

The second dimension of e-Government is **Democracy**. E-Government has to realize e-Democracy through information technology. To do this, e-Government should encourage participatory e-Democracy (e-Policy) and promote accountability through e-Democracy (e-Politics). Democratic government needs to enhance e-Participation in the policy process and promote e-Politics through e-Voting or e-Legislation in the political process.

2) Reflexivity

The third dimension is **Reflexivity**. E-Government has to realize a healthy civic community through information technology. To do this, e-Government should achieve the trust, matured and integrated society through revitalizing the horizontal and vertical communication among the members of the community utilizing public space or e-Forum (trust and transparency). E-Government, at an individual level, should enhance human dignity through utilizing human-based e-policies such as open access, e-education and universal service to minimize digital gaps, while guaranteeing e-Security(equity and ethics).

Three Dimension of E-Policy

Dimensions of e-Policy may follow suit with the elements of e-Government: productivity, democracy, and reflexivity as well as its main actors or subjects (i.e., state/government, market/enterprise, and civil society/NGO). These important dimensions defines a clear delineation of specific policies that are necessary to advance meaningful change and benefits for the society.

1) Productivity(I)

The first dimension of e-Policy is the matter of productivity or efficiency at the government level. The government should effectively use e-policy as a strategic instrument for upgrading national competitiveness. These kinds of e-policies include the next-generation Broadband ICT Infrastructure Policy(Super-high Speed BcN Policy), Strategic Industrial Policy(High-tech Industrial Policy), Local Information Policy(e-Village Policy), and U-City Policy(Smart-City Policy).

2) Productivity(II)

The second dimension of e-Policy is related to Market (Enterprise). This dimension is also related with strengthening market efficiency in the private sector. These kinds of e-policies includes Electronic Commerce Policy, Standardization Policy, Intellectual Property Rights Protection Policy, Broadcasting and Communications Convergence Policy, Digital Content Policy, and Green Growth Policy (e-Green Policy).

3) Democracy and Reflexivity

The third dimension of e-Policy is related to Civil Society (NGO). This dimension is deeply related with the ideology of democracy, equity, and ethics in order to realize a trusted (trustful), matured, and harmonious society. These kinds of e-policies include

Figure 16-2 **Three Dimensions of E-Policy**

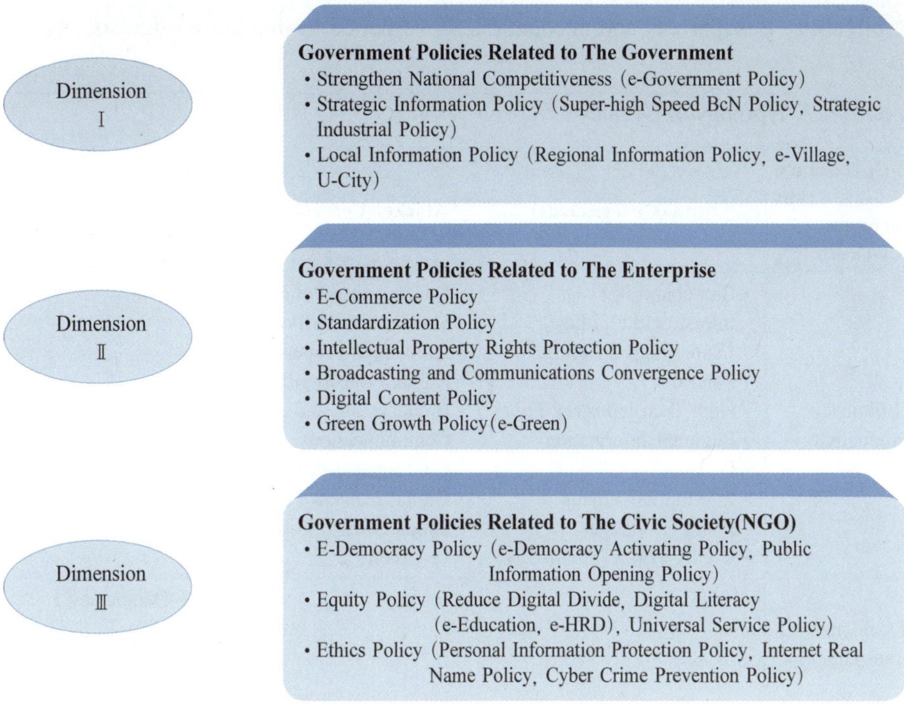

e-Democracy Policy, e-Voting, and Public Information Opening Policy (at the level of Democracy); Reduce Digital Divide, Digital Literacy (e-Education and e-HRD), and Universal Service Policy (at the level of Equity); Personal Information Protection Policy, Internet Real Name Policy, and Cyber Crime Prevention Policy (at the level of Ethics).

4) Summary and Conclusion: Typology of E-Policy

Based on the unit of analysis of state/government, market/enterprise, civil society/NGO and the policy ideology of efficiency, democracy, equity, and ethics, the following 〈Table 16-1〉 shows the typology of e-Policy to be adopted to each dimensions and policy actors.

One caveat is that, it is not possible to clearly classify the area and the dimension on a totally exclusive basis, because all policies are interlinked with each other. For example, efficiency and democracy are closely linked just like equity and ethics. Even though market's main concern is related with its efficiency and profits, it also has interests on transparency and ethics. Likewise, although civil society's main concern is related with its transparency and ethics, it also has interests on efficiency and democracy.

Nevertheless, it should be very useful to classify e-Policies along the governance unit of analysis, because it offers very useful information for strategic policy-making to realize more effective, transparent, and accountable governance in this knowledge society.

Table 16-1 Typology of E-Policy

Governance Unit / Governance Policy Unit	State(Government)	Market(Enterprise)	Civic Society(NGO)
Efficiency (Productivity)	• Broadband ICT Infrastructure Policy (Super-high Speed BcN Policy) • High-Tech Industrial Policy • Regional Information Policy • Information Village Policy(e-Village) • U-City Policy(Smart-City)	• E-Commerce Policy • Standardization Policy • Intellectual Property Rights Protection Policy • Broadcasting and Communications Convergence Policy • Digital Content Policy • Green Growth Policy (e-Green)	
Democracy (Transparency)			• E-Democracy • E-Voting • Public Information Opening Policy
Equity (Fairness)			• Reduce Digital Divide • Digital Literacy (e-Education & e-HRD) • Universal Service Policy
Ethics (Reflexivity)			• Personal Information Protection Policy • Internet Real Name Policy • Cyber Crime Prevention Policy

Key Point!

◎ Analytical Model of E-Policy

▸ The national government should focus on the three critical factors in its policy design and implementation:

- In the economic/administrative areas, e-Government should consider strengthening the national Competitiveness.
- In the political area, e-Government should advance e-Democracy.
- In the social area, e-Government should promote a healthy civic community .

◎ Three Dimension of E-Government

▸ Productivity

- Maximize the productivity within the government
- Utilize the digital network technology at the internal operating system

▸ Democracy

- Revitalize the e-democracy using the Smart ICT
- Improvement of transparency in the policy process and revitalize the civic participation

▸ Reflexivity

- Revitalize the vertical and horizontal communication using the Smart ICT
- Realize the trustful and matured civic community

◎ Three Dimension of E-Policy

▸ Productivity(I)

- The government should effectively use e-policy as a strategic instrument for upgrading national competitiveness.
- The next-generation Broadband ICT Infrastructure Policy(Super-high Speed BcN Policy), Strategic Industrial Policy(High-tech Industrial Policy), Local Information

Policy(E-Village Policy), and U-City Policy(Smart-City Policy).

▸ Productivity(II)

- This dimension is also related with strengthening market efficiency in the private sector.
- Electronic Commerce Policy, Standardization Policy, Intellectual Property Rights Protection Policy, Broadcasting and Communications Convergence Policy, Digital Content Policy, and Green Growth Policy(e-Green Policy).

▸ Democracy & Reflexivity

- This dimension is deeply related with the ideology of democracy, equity, and ethics to realize the trust, matured, and more integrated society.
- E-Democracy, e-Voting, and Public Information Opening Policy(at the level of Democracy); Reduce Digital Divide, Digital Literacy(e-Education and e-HRD), and Universal Service Policy(at the level of Equity); Personal Information Protection Policy, Internet Real Name Policy, and Cyber Crime Prevention Policy(at the level of Ethics).

Key Question!

◎ The most important dimensions of e-Government are the productivity, democracy, and reflexivity. Explain these three dimensions and its policy directions.

Chapter 17

INFORMATION POLICY DIMENSION OF NATIONAL COMPETITIVENESS: PRODUCTIVITY-DOMAIN POLICY

The goal of e-Government is to enhance national competitiveness and thereby promoting more efficient services to the people.

Objectives

The purpose of this chapter is to give understanding on e-Policy dimension in the national competitiveness standpoint. Discussion will center on the Super-high Speed BcN Policy, Strategic High-tech Industrial Policy, Local Information Policy, e-Village, and U-City policy.

First, this chapter will delve on the Super-high Speed BcN policy. It will highlight important issues in this recent development, its features, and the concept of high speed ICT infrastructure policy. The success, challenges, and strategies of Korea in the high speed ICT infrastructure will also be discussed.

Second, in the policy of Strategic High-tech Industrial Policy, it will discuss the concepts and features of the strategic high-tech industrial policy and the basic principles of strategic high-tech industrial policy. It will further discuss the lessons gained from the policy direction and strategy of the strategic high-tech industries in Korea.

Third, in the policy of Local Information, it will discuss the concept of local information. In addition, it will also discuss about the direction and strategy of the policy of local informatization.

Fourth, as recent trends of the policy, it will discuss the e-Village and u-City policy. In the e-Village policy, it will discuss the concept of e-Village and its operational performance. In the u-City policy, it will disucss the concept of u-City, and u-City as a national strategy.

High-Speed ICT Policy (BcN Policy)

Overview

The idea ultra-high speed communication system was touted by Pres. Clinton of the United States. It came out as an idea to enhance the education system of the American people regardless of its socio-economic status through ICT in the 21st century. The high tech ICT infrastructure creates new industry, services and products/applications. This phenomenon also leads to dramatic change in communication operators like TV, internet, and network and mobile industry.

In the context of super-high speed communication infrastructure policy, it is required to achieve a balance of both supply and demand side of information. Information transfer layer and information distribution layer, information application layer, and information society layer have the effect that triggers a series of correlated cross-circulation, and the rising mutual information supply and demand.

The Concept and Application Areas

1) Concept and Definition

The high-speed communication infrastructure refers to physical network that allows sending and receiving inexpensively, conveniently, anywhere and anytime with high speed required information for various types of voice, data, and video. Also, it means a new social overhead capital, including related laws surrounding environment information equipment, and software, social institutions, and culture.

Therefore, the concept of broadband high-speed communication infrastructure is a collective concept of a high-speed telecommunications network, the software and telecommunications equipment.

Figure 17-1 General Circulation Model of ICT Infrastructure

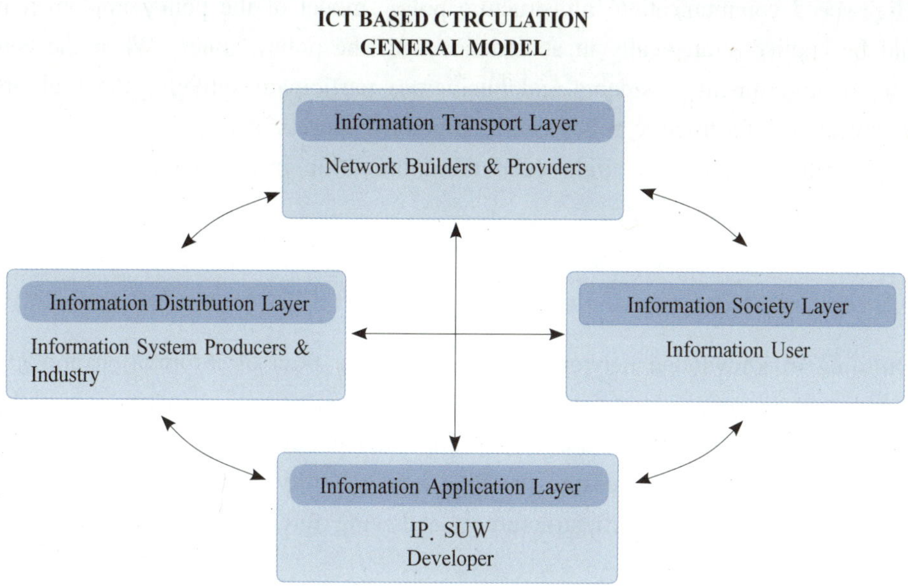

2) Policy Applications

Various applications of high-speed communication infrastructure may be viewed separately according to their fields (e.g., education, health care, government services, environment, library, and legal area).

First, in the education services, there are services like education information retrieval, virtual education, virtual or multimedia lectures, foreign language education services through interactive learning and using variety of online databases irrespective of time and distance.

Second, in the health care services, the new medical service includes telemedicine, medical information of emergency patients, blood distribution management, integrated services, outpatient appointments, supply and demand of medical resources and medical monitoring.

Third, in the government services, e-Government greatly improved the public services. As a result, the services provides some electronic identification, comprehensive information service of the city, copyright information service, patented technology information services, and comprehensive geographic information services.

Fourth, in the environment services, the new environment service includes disaster prevention, weather information services and environmental information services.

Fifth, services that are associated with the management of the book include digital library, electronic museum and cultural property information services. Services that are associated with the new areas of the law, is a tele-conference court.

Korean Model of Policy Mechanism: Successful Enforcement Strategy

High-speed communication infrastructure policy model of the policy implementation should be applied strategically in accordance with the policy issues. When the central and local government, residents and businesses participate actively, the high-speed communication infrastructure policy can be promoted successfully.

The strategic system of high-speed communication infrastructure policy can be described as in 〈Figure 17-2〉.

The Successful Factors of Korean High-Speed ICT Infrastructure Policy

Building of knowledge network that connects the flow of information and global knowledge is essential. In the vortex of infinite competition, construction of high-speed communication infrastructure is very important policy instrument to strengthen the national competitiveness, to ensure the long-term viability of the nation. In addition, high-speed communication infrastructure is a driving force for improving the overall quality of people's life.

Figure 17-2 High-Speed ICT Based Policy System

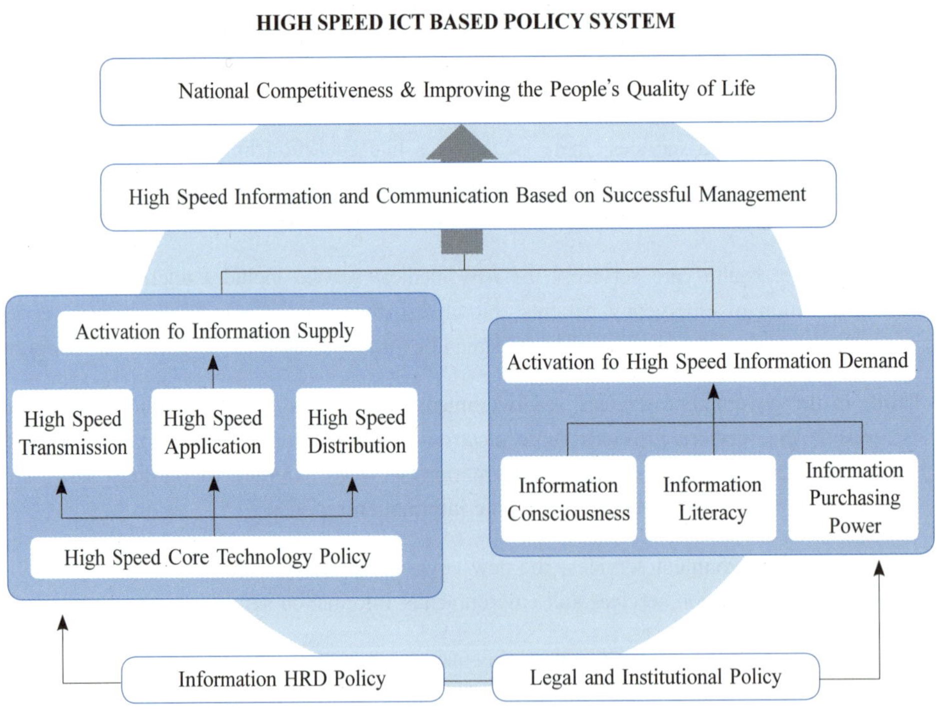

In order to promote the information society with the aim of building the internet infrastructure of the world's best; South Korea prepared in promoting information basic plan since June 1996. Then, divided into three stages until 2010, and presented the goals and its implementation plan of each stage.

Information environment changes to knowledge-based economy in 1999, thus emerged as a new concept in the field of Governance. The basic plan of information promotion was revised to accommodate the changed policy environment. The revised plan, called "Cyber Korea 21," was essentially to complete the high-speed ICT infrastructure by 2005 in the five years ahead of the original plan. Quite remarkably, as a matter of fact, the high-speed information network in December 2000, after 5 years from starting of the construction project of high-speed information network in 1996.

High-speed communication infrastructure project in South Korea was able to achieve within a quite short period of time as described above. Specifically, the following reasons are worth mentioning:

First, the establishment of a comprehensive and systematic information technology promotion system. That is, such as establishment of the Basic Law of Information Promotion(1995), Information Promotion Fund(1996), Information Technology Committee(1998), Information Strategy Meeting(1998) etc. to establish a national promotion system and ready for policy implementation.

Second, the vision of information that is appropriate to changing conditions. That is, based on the strong leadership and commitment of the president of Korea, such as the basic plan of information promotion, Cyber Korea 21, the government presented a vision and strategy, and has implemented it with a close cooperation with the private sectors.

Third, the construction of infrastructure through a nationwide automated telephone system and a national basic computing network built in the 1980s. The strategy was to make efforts to upgrade the existing network to the high-speed information network infrastructure.

Fourth, the government strategy of intensive leading investment to the strategic areas of high-speed Internet connection and CDMA, and thereby promoting a competitive environment to induce private investments.

Fifth, On the basis of cultural characteristics that is suitable for the internet, government and the private sector, through cooperative governance, encouraged the information demand by performing the project, such as all the people information technology education(10million people information education policy).

Recent Trend: BcN

1) Significance

Recently, high-speed ICT infrastructures are evolving to BcN, Broadband Convergence Network. The BcN is the Next Generation Intelligence Network, which enables the wide area multimedia services anytime and anywhere. It integrates the network of high-quality voices, data, and broadcasting information using the various connection networks of mobile and fixed lines.

2) Features

The key features of BcN are as follows:

First, integration of voice and data; fixed and mobile network; broadcasting and communication. Based on these integration, it is possible to transmit a multimedia service of clear voice, text message, and mobile image. It is also possible to provide a two-way interactive broadcasting service based on the next generation broadband network of FTTH, and beyond 4G.

Second, seamless connection of information is possible under the various network and media. Therefore, multi-functional devices can be commercialized.

Third, it is possible to provide a ubiquitous service based on the integrated network infrastructure.

Fourth, it is possible to ensure information security at all levels of network.

The ICT High-Tech Industrial Policy

Information Communication Technology is still the most important economic factor and has the highest impact among other technologies (see 〈Table 17-1〉). All technologies have no meaning without the ICT industry. ICT plays a role of vitamin of all the other technologies.

Table 17-1 Comparison of Economic Importance of Various Technologies

	ICT Technology	Space Technology	Atomic Energy Technology	Material Technology	Bio Technology
New Production/ Services	9	2	2	4	4
Cost Reduction	9	2	1	4	3
Technology Application	10	2	2	4	4
Social Acceptance	9	6	3	9	5
Business Profits	10	3	2	6	3
Employment	10	1	1	2	2

* Source: OECD(1998).

Policy Challenges and Strategic Direction

It is important to identify the new ICT paradigm in the knowledge-based economy and to provide the new government role model of ICT-related high-tech industrial policy

The policy direction and strategy can be discussed by these three categories:

① Change in the policy direction to the knowledge-based economy
② Policy for the creation, accumulation, and diffusion of knowledge
③ Policy of the supporting ICT for the knowledge based economy

1) Change in the Policy Direction to the Knowledge-Based Economy: Private Initiatives and Governmental Support

The paradigm of Korean ICT-related high-tech industrial policy has been changed by three developing stages. First stage was the government-driven strategies of 1980s in which government supported directly to the companies and industries. As it went through the early and mid-1990s, the paradigm of public-private partnership had emerged; at the time government functionally supported the industries as an indirect way. Finally, from the mid-1990s and on, the Korean industrial development was initiated by the Private entrepreneurship. At this time, it is characterized by the mode of de-regulation and efficiency (see 〈Figure 17-3〉).

People in this knowledge age pursue their own unique personality based on spiritual values and diversity. Change in the pursuance of value and social patterns, associated

Figure 17-3 Paradigm Change of High-Tech Industrial Policy

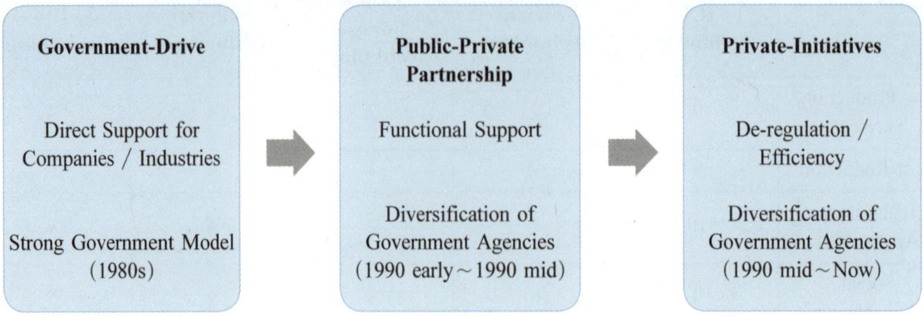

with the quick change of market trends, necessitates the role of government in the knowledge industry.

Strategic industrial Policy has to decide the issue of strategic selection and the strategic role of government: Which policy, who initiates, and select strategic policy. Government should select the strategy based on industrial, technological, and market spillover effects. And as for the intervention, there should be a precautious role of government because government intervention should not suffocate the vitality of private creativity and entrepreneurship(see 〈Figure 17-4〉.

Figure 17-4 Policy Strategy of ICT Industry Policy

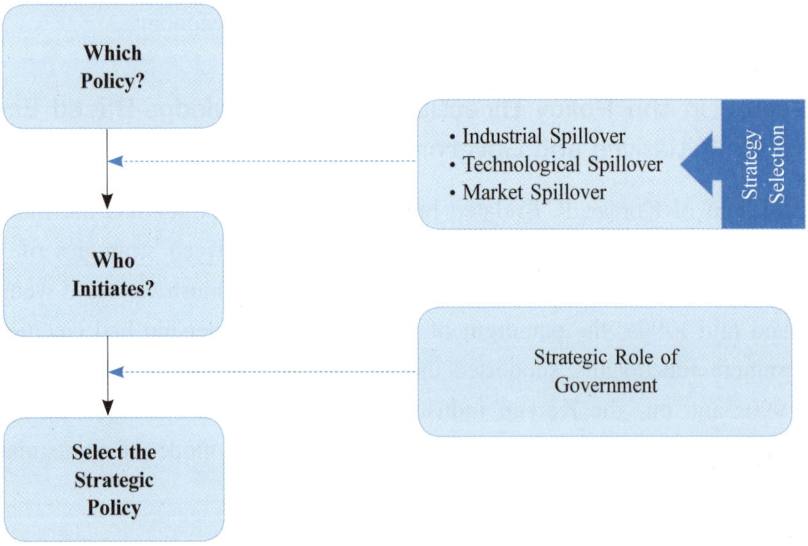

2) Creation, Accumulation, and Diffusion of Knowledge

In transition to a knowledge-based economy, the policy for the creation, accumulation and diffusion of knowledge should be carried out. Major policy challenges of ICT-related high-tech industrial policy are as follows:

① Knowledge creation accumulation and diffusion
② Role of government on knowledge-based economy
③ Knowledge-based economic infrastructure support

Figure 17-5 New Role Model of Government on Knowledge-Based Economy

Market	Government Role for Promotion Information Communication Industry (The ICT Industry Policy)	
Government Role for Promotion Information Communication Industry (The ICT Industry Policy)	Vitalization of Knowledge-Intensive Industries	• S/W, Digital Content, Internet Industry, Big Data Center, and GIS/GPS-Based Industry
	ICT Manpower	• ICT Skilled and Trained Workers • Information and Communication Education as Spread of Basic Knowledge
	Research and Development of ICT Accumulation	• Construction of a University-Centered Creative Technology Innovation System
Role of Government on Knowledge-Based Economy	Information Communication Policy and System Change	• Respect the Principles of a Market Economy and Induce Diffusion
A knowledge-Based Economic Infrastructure Support	ICT Construction	• Upgrading of the Network such as Building High-Speed Information Network
	Building a New Business Environment	• Creation New Environment Favorable for Information and Communication Venture Capital

3) Policy of the supporting ICT for the knowledge based economy

(1) Research and Development (R&D) of Information Communications Technology

In the knowledge-based economy, the most important resources are knowledge and information. Thus, in order to be well-established the knowledge-based economy, valuable knowledge and information should be developed.

(2) Information Communication Expert HRD Training

In the knowledge-based economy, the most important resource is manpower that embodies knowledge with the education system that can develop professional human resource of good quality. For this, policy for maximizing HRD incentives to the personnel should be promoted.

(3) Activating the Conditions of Knowledge-Intensive Industries

In the knowledge based economy, activation conditions should be made to support a strategic high-tech industries (i.e., software, digital content, internet, etc.).

(A) Software Industry

In order to gain a competitive edge in the software industry e-Government should create a system to encourage software industry. Domestic manufacturers should be encouraged to develop of high-quality software.

(B) Digital Content Industry

In order to vitalize the digital content industry, first of all, the laws and regulations related to the digital content must be enacted. Second, e-Government should establish the comprehensive formulation on digital content industry. Thirdly, the distribution of online content should be vitalized.

(C) Internet Industry

Since internet is growing as a media that offer multimedia information, development and support of internet contents industry should be accomplished. Also, technology that is related to internet such as high-speed networking technology, internet line managing technology, information processing and offering technology should be developed.

Summary and Conclusion

We have discussed so far and reviewed the core strategic challenges for the implementation of a knowledge-based economy in terms of policy direction, network, human resources, technology, and creative environment.

Strategy is a set of policy that should have a greatest ripple effect among the general policies. Thus policies that have a high priority and impact to a large group of people should be given the intensive support and significant attention. Among others, the following will discuss other important aspects that need to be considered:

First, the importance of spread and utilization of knowledge should be emphasized as it is the foundation of knowledge-based economy. To do this, the government should respect the principles of the market economy and change the policy direction that can support the market mechanism. Government will induce the spontaneous formation of the market and creative activity by offering social vision of knowledge based economy and maintaining the dynamism of the market economy. Similarly, by minimizing the proactive economic regulation will maintain the direction of the legal and regulatory regime by minimizing the possibility of an unfair deal that may occur.

Second, building of knowledge network to help connect the flow of global information and global knowledge is essential. It should be continued by investing in the advancement and efficiency of network.

Third, in the knowledge-based economy, the most important resource is knowledge and workforce that is embodied in the knowledge. Therefore, the education system to cultivate the high-quality professional staff should be encouraged.

Fourth, creation of knowledge and accumulation of technology through continuous research and development must be followed. Therefore, R&D policy is to maximize the utilization of the University's research resources and creative research development program. It is important to establish a strategic alliance among local governments, high-tech industries, and university and academic research institutions.

Finally, the software, digital content and internet-related industry should be strategically supported in the knowledge-based economy. Promoting conditions of these industries should be required; business environment should be established to foster the new venture capital.

Local Information Policy

Reality of Regional Society

Information society is expected to enhance the quality of human life, changes political, economic and social situation in a more beneficial direction. Also, it will bring the development of culture and the improvement of service. On the other hand, it is afraid that it may cause social inequalities due to the digital divide between the regional classes. The informatization level of the rural agricultural and fishing villages are very low compared with the urban city.

Informatization infrastructure of agricultural and fishing villages has not been established appropriately. The severe social problem is the gap between urban and rural in regard to IT and telecommunication facilities. E-Government should endeavor to improve the quality of life of rural residents by providing information communications technology and services of the information age.

Concept of Local Informatization

Local informatization has the fundamental purpose that mitigates regional information gap, to ensure equal access to information in a nationwide scale anywhere and establishes the urgent agenda that build the information communication system appropriate to local conditions and characteristics. Furthermore, balanced regional development should be carried out to revitalize the local economy and to improve the living environment of the local community.

Therefore, the local informatization means the information activities to solve the problems of information gap between the local area and urban area, or the regional and other regional areas(inter-regional problems) through the efforts of administrative, industrial, social, and cultural informatization. It also actively encourages the balanced development of the society by eliminating the gap between various environmental activities.

Significance

Local informatization is necessary to the resolution of regional information gap and promotes balanced national development. The purpose of the local informatization is to promote the strategic development of the region which includes:

① Equipped with up-to-date information media and network media which can produce, process, distribute the various required information for the region's administrative, social life, and the industrial activities.

② Utilize effectively for regional activities by systematizing information itself to the goals and characteristics of the area.

Balanced development of the country, as well as the justification itself to the development of the area should be made by the local informatization. The importance of local informatization can be summarized as follows:

1) Activating the Local Economy

Local informatization is important to vitalize the local economy. Current Information Technology is regarded as an important strategic resource in the industry. Industrial activities in each direction of informatization play an important role in order to survive in the fierce industrial competition.

2) Improve the Living Conditions of Local Residents

Local informatization makes the living standards of local residents comfort with richness in economic matters. Using advanced information systems, informatization will improve the quality of life for local residents by providing life information, resolving on living in metropolitan concentration, the possibility of telecommuting, and communication among family members, friends, and business partners is being strengthened by the Information Communication.

3) Improve Local Administrative Services

Local informatization improves the quality of administrative services for the local residents. It makes that processes like civil affairs promptly; conveniently, provide better data sharing and recognition of the regional development plan among the local residents. In addition, it also improves administrative services and can enhance the cohesiveness of the local community itself.

4) Unique Development Based on Regional or Local Circumstance

Local informatization helps to develop the unique geographical, social, economic, and cultural conditions that fit local characteristics and the local people's preferences.

Policy Strategies

Local informatization is a strategic concept for the balanced development of the country. The critical success factors of local informatization are the utilization and diffusion of information technology, information consciousness, the participation and interests of local residents, rather than just support of the central government.

In the more advanced local government era, the unique role of the local regions will be highlighted. The policy wisdom should be collected for the promotion of effective local informatization policy.

The local informatization policy strategies can be summarized as follows:

First, it must be founded on the creation of a balanced regional development through informatization and eliminating regional gap by establishing information communication infrastructure and resident's access to information.

Second, the private sector should be leading the local development to the direction of enhancing the autonomy of the local residents.

Finally, the regional-specific information must be obtained and the local informatization should be promoted by considering the unique characteristics of the local or regional circumstance.

Recent Development: E-Village

Definition

The policy of information network village is to construct various contents and internet use to increase opportunities for information access. Therefore, the "Information Network Village" is the village that contribute to make informatization a part of local residents life and increase their income. Furthermore, it helps to promote the formation of the healthy and vital local communities.

Background

Various information projects aiming to solve regional information gap have enjoyed remarkable success since the early 2000 in Korea. E-village project, aside from the 10 Million information education project, is one of the exemplar successful policy cases.

Operational Performance

The information network village aims to increase quality of life of local residents through the making of information technology a part of their daily routine. Also it contributes on the reinforcement of local competitiveness using e-Commerce for the sale of their special and locally made products. The information network villages started in 2001 and were increasing every year. In 2010, the total number of e-Villages has reached 363, thus it has increased by 1,400 percent compared with the first and is expected to increase every year.

Table 17-2 Operational Performance of E-Village

Classification		2006	2009	2013
Digital Divide	Local Information Education Outputs	19,726(people)	39,798(people)	15,527(people)
	Local Community Web-pages	548,707(cases)	3,545,447(cases)	1,071,869(cases)
Revitalization of Local Community	Online Members	28,473(people)	97,958(people)	18,424(people)
	Newly Established e-Communities	1,769(cases)	1,269(cases)	522(cases)
	Data / Message Uploaded to the e-Communities	148,788(cases)	269,036(cases)	227,477(cases)
Strengthening of Local Competitiveness (e-Commerce)	Sales of Local Special Products	2,356(millions)	8,986(millions)	3,975(millions)
	Revenues from Local Tourism	569(millions)	4,499(millions)	1,481(millions)
	Public Media Exposure	687(cases)	2,302(cases)	926(cases)

Promotion Strategies

To be a more successful project, the Ministry of Security and Public Administration, local governments and each village should continue to have a good partnership as a collaborative governance to establishe a better information network village.

U-City Policy

Definition

U-City is defined as a converged, integrated, intelligent, and innovative city by utilizing ubiquitous computing and the smart information communication technology (ICT). In other words, u-City is the future high-tech city based on the new ubiquitous technologies. Based on the ubiquitous sensors and network, the problems of metropolitan city like traffic, crime and disaster will be lessened dramatically aided by the integration of networks all over the city.

Features

U-City is based on strong ubiquitous computing technologies. It is distinguished from current and cyber city; stronger than current city, and more realistic than cyber city. The completely realized u-City collects and accumulates information and data, and provides solution itself through sensing or monitoring techniques. The communication between facilities, between facilities and human is possible. It is also possible that human can communicate, anywhere and at any time. In u-City, u-Government, u-Health Care, u-Education, and u-Life will be conveniently realized.

Promotion Status and Contents

U-City provides various u-Services based on ubiquitous computing technologies. Therefore it improves the quality of life of urban residents, creates new business opportunites to industry, and facilitates effective urban management and environmental conservation.

Policy Strategies

In Korea, various information businesses are successfully carried out since legislation of Framework Act on Informatization Promotion in 1996. As a result, quantitative outputs of e-Government performance were achieved quite remarkably, but the real effect of e-Government to the people is still falls short of people's expectations.

U-City policy should be promoted with the private or local initiatives with a central government support at the behind. And u-City project must be implemented with decentralized institutions instead of centralized authorities. While the R&D investment on the base u-telecommunication infrastructure must be performed centrally at governmental level, the specific plan and implementation about specific application services must be left to each departments or local governments.

Summary and Conclusion

Some of the key points and implications based on the discussion of this chapter are as follows:

- All technologies have no meaning without the ICT industry.
- We need the Local and e-Village Information Policies to reduce digital divide, boost local economies and improve local residents' quality of life.
- U-City project must be implemented with decentralized agencies instead of centralized system. Studies and R&D investments should be done by central governments and the implementation should be left to the local governments.

Key Point!

◎ High-Speed ICT Policy (BcN Policy)

▸ Concept and Definition

- Collective concept of a high-speed telecommunications network, the software and telecommunications equipment

▸ Applications

- Education services
- Health care services
- Government service
- Environment services
- Digital library, electronic museum and cultural property information services

▸ Recent Trend: BcN

- Significance
  - BcN is the Next Generation Intelligence Network, which enables the wide area multimedia services anytime and anywhere
- Features
  - Integration of voice and data; fixed and mobile network; broadcasting and communication
  - Seamless connection of information is possible under the various network and media
  - Ubiquitous service based on the integrated network infrastructure
  - Information security at all levels of network

◎ The ICT High-Tech Industrial Policy

▸ Policy Challenges and Strategic Direction

- Change in the Policy Direction to the Knowledge-Based Economy: Private Initiatives and Governmental Support

• Creation, Accumulation, and Diffusion of Knowledge
- Knowledge creation, accumulation, and diffusion
- Role of government for knowledge-based economy
- Knowledge-based economic infrastructure support

• Strategic Policy of the supporting ICT for the knowledge-based economy
- Research and Development (R&D)
- Information Communication Expert HRD Training
- Activating the Conditions of Knowledge-Intensive Industries

◎ Local Information Policy

▸ Concept of Local Informatization

• Local informatization has the fundamental purpose that mitigates regional information gap, to ensure equal access to information in a nationwide scale anywhere; and establishes the urgent agenda that build the information communication system appropriate to local conditions and characteristics.

• Local informatization means the information activities to solve the problems of information gap between the local area and urban area, or the regional and other regional areas(inter-regional problems) through the efforts of administrative, industrial, social, and cultural informatization.

▸ Significance

• Activating the Local Economy
• Improve the Living Conditions of Local Residents
• Improve Local Administrative Services
• Unique Development Based on Regional or Local Circumstance

▸ Policy Strategies:

• It must be founded on the creation of a balanced regional development through informatization and eliminating regional gap by establishing information communication infrastructure and resident's access to information.
• The private sector should be leading the local development to the direction of enhancing the autonomy of the local residents.
• The regional-specific information must be obtained and the local informatization

should be promoted by considering the unique characteristics of the local or regional circumstance.

▸ Recent Development: E-Village

◎ U-City Policy

▸ Definition

- U-City is defined as a converged, integrated, intelligent, and innovative city by utilizing ubiquitous computing and the Smart information communication technology (ICT).

▸ Features

- U-City is based on strong ubiquitous computing technologies. It is distinguished from current and cyber city; stronger than current city, and more realistic than cyber city. The completely realized u-City collects and accumulates information and data, and provides solution itself through sensing or monitoring techniques.

- The communication between facilities, between facilities and human is possible. It is also possible that human can communicate, anywhere and at any time. In u-City, u-Government, u-Health Care, u-Education, and u-Life will be conveniently realized.

▸ Policy Strategies:

- The private or local initiatives with a central government support at the behind.
- U-City project must be implemented with decentralized institutions instead of centralized authorities.
- The R&D investment on the base u-telecommunication infrastructure must be performed centrally at governmental level, the specific plan and implementation about specific application services must be left to each departments or local governments.

Key Question!

◎ What is the definition and application of super high-speed information communications infrastructure policy?

◎ What are the definition and characteristic of BcN?

◎ What are the direction and strategy of the ICT High-Tech Industrial Policy?

◎ What are the strategic policy directions for vitalizing local informatization?

◎ What are the definition and characteristics of u-City policy?

◎ What are the strategic policy directions for vitalizing the u-City policy?

Chapter 18

INFORMATION POLICY DIMENSION OF MARKET EFFICIENCY: PRODUCTIVITY-DOMAIN POLICY

The advent of e-Government and the Internet represent important opportunities for enhancing national competitiveness.

- UK Parliament

Objectives

The purpose of this chapter is to elucidate the e-policy dimension from its market efficiency standpoint. The discussion includes e-commerce policy, intellectual property rights protection, telecommunications standardization policy, broadcasting and communications convergence policy, digital content policy, and e-green policy.

First, in the policy of e-commerce, it will describe the recent problems, such as features and concept of e-commerce, and recently mobile payment policy through the use of smart phones. It will also discuss the lessons gained from the challenges and direction of e-commerce policy in Korea.

Second, in the protection of intellectual property rights policy, it will discuss the concepts and features of the intellectual property rights and the basic principles of intellectual property rights system. It will further discuss the lessons gained from the policy direction of the intellectual property rights system in Korea.

Third, in the standardization of information and communication policy, it will discuss the concept of standardization of information and communication. In addition, it will also discuss about the direction of the policy of standardization of information and communication.

Fourth, in the integration policy of broadcasting and communications, it will discuss the difference between broadcasting and communications. It will further discuss the policy strategies for the fusion of broadcasting and communications.

Fifth, as recent trends of the policy, it will discuss the digital content policy and Green growth policy. In the digital content policy, it will discuss the concept of digital content, digital content industry classification and its technical trends. In the Green growth policy, it will disucss the concept of Green growth, and Green growth as a national strategy.

E-Commerce Policy

The modern information age is an era that defines business through telegraph, telephone or mass communication, and internet network. There is no need to go through the usual adversities of direct and personal shopping because a convenient and easy online shopping is already available. This idea was a conception of the new idea called e-Commerce. However, though e-Commerce has brought many benefits it carries some unavoidable harm that needs to be minimized through policy interventions and initiatives. Thus, these policy issues and directions has to be developed and evaluated to maintain the positive attributes of e-Commerce and lessen the negative effects if possible.

The Concept of e-Commerce

The term e-Commerce is difficult to give a uniform and globally acceptable definition. From a limited point of view, e-Commerce is defined as, the "conduct of transactions using electronic means carried out in cyberspace." While in the broad sense, e-Commerce it is defined as:

"*The exchange of information needed for commercial transactions by electronic technology, including marketing, advertising, procurement, services, production, transportation, administration, finance, and purchase transactions conducted under an integrated automated information system environment between Government and Business*

(G2B), or Business and Business (B2B). In other words, e-Commerce may be defined as the exchange of information required for online transactions."

The biggest advantage of e-Commerce is that there are no time and space constraints, lessening the trouble of going to the store and pay by credit card. In addition, without any cost of rent of buildings and distribution costs, this has been likened to advance gold fishing in terms of the whole world Internet subscribers as potential customers.

Characteristics of e-Commerce

The characteristics of e-Commerce are as follows:

Firstly, it is a simplification of the distribution process. In e-Commerce the middle of the distribution process is omitted as transactions are connected directly to buyers and sellers through the network.

Secondly, it is possible to conduct commerce in 24 hours without being bound by time and space, widening the activities of businesses and consumers.

Thirdly, it is possible to provide a platform that allows 1:1 marketing resuting in a more efficient business management.

Fourthly, in e-Commerce, traditional physical space is no longer required. Instead, provision of information, promotion of products, marketing is now available through the internet.

Fifth, it became possible to quickly respond to the needs of the customer. In e-Commerce, it has become possible for real-time service to offer through the internet.

Sixth, it does not require huge capital to purchase land and buildings as is required in existing businesses.

E-Commerce in Korea

From the start of full-fledged e-Commerce from an Internet shopping mall opened in 1996, Korean e-Commerce has increased dramatically(see Table below).

Table 18-1 Domestic State of the Internet Commerce

Shopping Mall	Content	Annual Sales (2010baseyear)	URL
Auction	Korea's first Internet auction site, starting with the immediate purchase as well as the current auction.	2,674 billion won	http://www.auction.co.kr
Interpark INT	Korea's first Internet shopping mall with unique technological skills and strong brand power a rich experience of 12 years, It is a leader in the domestic e-commerce market, the growth in specialty distribution companies	3,745 billion won	http://www.interpark.com
Lotte dot-com	E-business company provides a comprehensive Internet shopping services that are differentiated by combining the know-how of e-commerce and a wealth of real distribution network Lotte.	1,350 billion won	http://www.lotte.com
D&shop	Started as an Internet shopping business of Daum Communication, and sustained rapid growth	184 billion won	http://www.dnshop.com

* Source: Data Analysis, Retrieval and Transfer System

Policy Strategy of e-Commerce

1) Government's Vision and Role

Because of the broad nature of information technology, there are many things that need to be established in order to facilitate electronic commerce. Firstly, it is necessary to provide a clear vision for the role of government in e-commerce. In addition, the leading role of government in setting up of e-commerce within public procurement sector is required. Public sector procurement and Electronic document interchange (EDI) of the different Ministries have significant impact government's stakeholders in e-Commerce such as, transporters, public enterprises, and private enterprises.

2) Activation of Electronic Documents

The current law such as the civil law or commercial law does not take into account the electronic document, it is necessary to research how business processing and legal action can be done using the electronic document.

3) Market and Industrial Development for e-Commerce

For the advancement e-Commerce, long-term problems should also be considered, such as issues that has something to do with software and hardware, such as the interoperabilty of e-Commerce platforms.

4) Strengthen International Cooperation

In response to the worldwide incorporation and legislation of e-Commerce, it is necessary to promote harmonization of domestic commercial laws with the internationally settled principles of trade transactions. This requires an adoption or customization of international law on e-Commerce into the domestic or muncipal laws. In addition, e-Commerce involves internet technology that leads to broader economic activity and borderless business deal which requires international unification and bringing together related laws and regulations.

Recent Trends: Wireless e-Commerce and Mobile Payment

1) The Concept of Wireless e-Commerce (Mobile Commerce)

Wireless e-Commerce or mobile commerce (m-Commerce) is business dealing at the point of need, anywhere, anytime, based on wireless terminals and mobile communication network technology. This includes paid commerce such as those that appears in B2B or B2C transactions, providing information, or entertainment and games through wireless devices such as mobile phone (hand-held phone, smart phones), palm computers, PDA, laptops, or vehicle-mounted interfaces.

2) Smartphone and e-Commerce

(1) Significance and Background

Recently, the "impact of iPhone" or the so-called Smart phones (Android phones) have brought surmountable development in the information and communication technology. Surpringsingly, despite the high price per unit it gained popularity, thus saturated all over domestic and international market with subscribers from all walks of life. In Korea, to maximize the mobile platform, financial institutions developed business systems that use smartphones such as mobile banking; development of business support systems using smartphone, and other smartphone applications providing customer-oriented services, etc.

(2) Prospects and Challenges

Mobile banking is being transformed into smartphone banking wherein services will become more diverse and accessible right in the hand of every citizen. However, one of the challenges that necessitate scrutiny is the setting up of a mechanism that lays out the payment process. The technical as well as the legal components of the payment system must be in place to ensure stability and security of the transaction.

(3) Policy Directions

The future of smartphone banking system requires various legislations that will clearly define its principles and mechanism. The following factors have to be considered:

(A) Inhancement of Payment System's Security and Reliability

The all-out adoption of electronic financial transactions necessitates several legal infrastructures. Among others, these are payment-related information systems and expansion of backup capacity, strengthen the participation requirements of the payment system participant, and strengthen the mobile payment security.

(B) Legal Stability of the Payment System

In order to ensure the stability of the payment system the legal issues surrounding it should be clarified in accordance with the settled principles of law.

(C) Internationalization of Financial System

As a financial hub in Northeast Asia, Korea is promoting the importance of building an efficient and reliable payment system, enough to efficiently manage the risks that threaten the stability and integrity of the current payment systems. To this effect, there is a need to continuously discuss coordination and conformity of financial system among nation states in order to resolve exisiting and future legal payment issues, and take the lead role on developing a reliable mobile payment environment.

Summary and Conclusions

E-Commerce has many advantages in today's modern society. However, the disadvantages cannot be overlooked. Therefore, our challenge is to maximize the benefits and minimize the disadvantages of e-Commerce. Furthermore, e-Commerce is from domestic transactions to transactions between countries, and it is necessary to narrow down the institutional differences among countries.

Protection of Intellectual Property Rights

Concepts

Intellectual property rights include all rights arising from the industrial, scientific, literary or artistic fields of intellectual activity, such as the literary, artistic and scientific works, performers, demonstrations, and music and broadcasting. Especially relating with information technology, the policy issues of intellectual property rights specially concerned with copyright industries, high-tech industries, intellectual property, copyrights and industrial property rights.

Features

Intellectual property rights are intangible and spiritual goods, and therefore their nature is therefore very ideological and abstract. The creator of intellectual property must enjoy exclusive rights and competitive advantage which can be accounted by his work. Intellectual property is a mental creation based on the very strong personal elements as industrial property or copyright is the subject of the invention.

Basic Principle

The primary purpose of the intellectual property system is to promote the development of human intellectual creation to stimulate creative activity. The author, through efforts to compensate by all members of the community who benefit from his/her work should be able to enjoy its benefits. In other words, the rights of the person who created the intellectual and artistic creations are protected within regular limit, and promote the common good in general.

Policy Strategy

There is a need to create intellectual property policy.

First, government should establish a system that can manage all intellectual property to promote intellectual property policies.

Second, government should provide legal provisions to systematically protect from intellectual property fringement.

Third, government should cultivate the professional expertises on whether it is about legal issues or technical issues. Also it should invest R&D about protection and nurturing about intellectual property rights.

Finally, there is a need to split the role of the companies and universities and research institutes for a synergistic effect among the powerhouses of intellectual property.

Standardization Policy

Concept of Standardization

Information Telecommunication Standardization is a procedure or activity aimed at establishing an information communication protocol. In other words, it is an agreed protocol that is necessary for the interoperability of the various IT systems.

Information Telecommunication Standard means a selection of a discussion method that will enable sending and receiving information between devices in the same way and within similar timeframe. Information Telecommunication Standardization is the procedures required to make this selection.

The Basic Principle

The two most fundamental philosophical bases are efficiency and democracy. Effciency emphasizes on the efficient utilization of human and physical resources and democracy emphasizes on transparency and fairness of participation. Both are the basic principles to control the entire process of the information communication standardization and the basic fundamental principles to effectively achieve the purpose of standardization.

Step-by-Step Roadmap

Recently, Korea established "Information Communication Core Technology Standardization Roadmap Version 2010" that proposed strategy for standardization for Korea. It identifies 37 core information communication technologies that are required in promoting international standardization based on technological environment analysis both domestic and abroad and within public and private sector.

Necessity of Standardization

1) Economic Development

The standards play a crucial role for leverage that will increase international competitiveness and development of the domestic industry. Standardization encourages broader market participation of new operators and can facilitate an appropriate competitive market centered environment.

2) Technology Development

The standards play a crucial role for leverage that will increase technological development. Advanced technologies can be introduced at an early stage through participation in international standardization activities. Duplicate investment is avoided and development of related industries can be supported through research and development of the leading standards and their timely application.

3) Consumer Protection

The standards play a crucial role for leverage that will increase consumer protection. Standardization is able to lead to a cheaper and more suitable products as through standardization production cost savings and promotion of competition can be achieved.

4) Types of Standards

Industry standards are divided into de jure standard and de facto standard. De jure standard is the standard certification by the public organizations. The de facto standard is a posing standard as a result of market competition.

Figure 18-1 Change of Standardization Paradigm

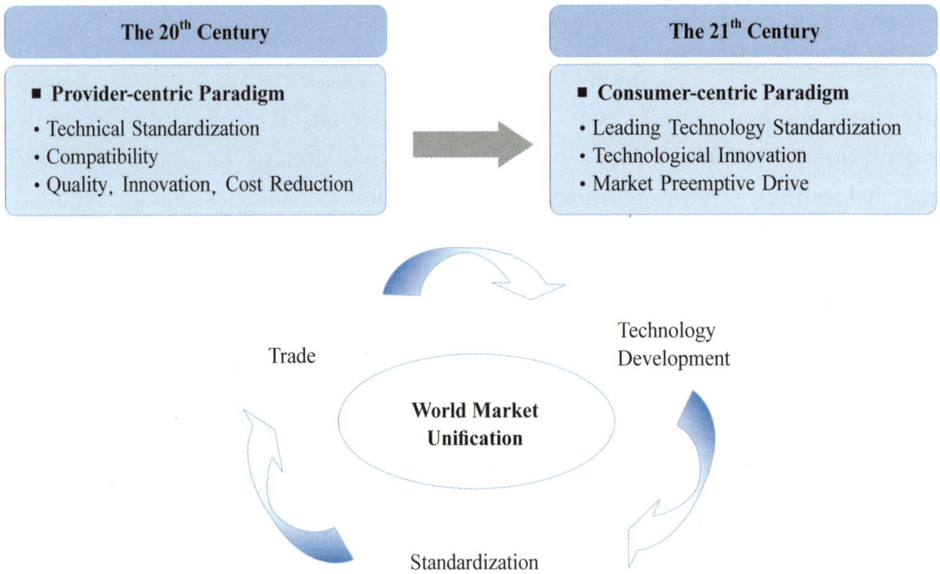

Policy Strategies

1) General Policy Direction

Standardization must be a private sector driven and market oriented process such that users' needs are reflected. For this, the government must provide relevant support and a clear implementing rules and guidelines.

2) Role of Government

(1) Standardization Support of the Private Sector

The first role of government is to support standardization activities of the private sector. For this, the government must set conditions to compete fairly between private enterprises and a level playing field, and must keep a close watch on this.

(2) Professional Manpower Training for Standardization

The government must provide various supports to train professional manpower for standardization. Remember, standardization requires a sharp skill and expertise that involves both the technical understanding and legal expertise. The latter is required for coordination and harmonization of existing domestic and international standardization laws.

(3) Support of Research and Development for Standard Technology

The government must provide support for research and developments of technology related to standardization and an interoperability environment, and establish a strong foundational structure for standards certification.

Summary and Conclusion

In the 21st century, the importance of international standards is growing bigger and bigger because the whole word have been integrated in the cyberspace through ICT. Therefore, success and failure of industry depends on the rate of adaptation to this environment. In particular, Korea ICT industry is rated as more competitive than other industries, but with traditional approach to intellectual property rights, the leverage enjoyed by the domestic industry will be muted. Therefore we must participate actively in the establishment of international industry standards and utilize intellectual property rights efficiently, avoid problems to do with monopoly and establish strategies to maintain market leadership.

Broadcasting and Communication Convergence Policy

Broadcasting sector and the telecommunications sector were converged as the development of information technology and the distinction of the network and services is getting faint. Convergence refers to a phenomenon that is going to integrate industry structure and regulatory regimes.

The Concept of Convergence

For the convergence of broadcasting and communication, is usually separated into three areas of convergence: convergence of networks, services, and enterprises in accordance with the guidelines of the OECD (see Table 18-2).

Table 18-2 Convergence of Broadcasting & Communication

Level	Broadcasting	Convergence	Communication
Network	□ Ground, Satellite □ Microwave □ Video/Sales	□ Network Sharing □ Network Integration □ Video Digital Terminal	□ Copper Wire, Optical Fiber □ Cable, Satellite □ Microwave
Service	□ Transfer Radio/TV Programming (1 to Multi)	□ Video conference, VDT □ Narrow-Broadcasting □ Broadcasting Data □ Interactive Services	□ Voice, Data □ Image (1 to 1)
Enterprise	□ Hardware Production Service Area	□ Interchagiable	□ Hardware Production Service Area

* Source: OECD(1992:13)

1) Convergence of Net (or Network)

It indicates the distinction between broadcasting networks and communication networks become blurred. Broadcast signals are sent not only through broadcasting networks, but also sent via communication networks. On the other hand, communication is transmitted via communication-network as well as broadcast-network. In addition, the hardware as well as software is independent of the data that is passed through the network, such as voice, video, and the exchange of digitized information. It does not distinguish the type of information being processed.

2) Convergence of Services

It indicates the distinction between broadcasting services and communication services become blurred. The impact brings the convergence of services, results to:

First, the emergence of new services brings the fierce competition between existing services and new services, and also increases the competition in the existing market itself with the emergence of new competitors.

Second, the emergence of new services is not defined within the framework of the existing legal framework, and because of ambiguous law that applies to the new services, establishing the difference between applications of new services versus existing services within the existing legal and institutional framework creates a regulatory confusion.

3) Convergence of Enterprise

It indicates the distinction between broadcasting enterprises and communication enterprises become blurred. It means that broadcasting and communication business operators can advance their business interest within each others domains. This happens because the convergence of technology previously used by broadcast and communication operators has already taken place. Also, the operators were engaged in business may advance to other fields. The covergence of these companies makes competition fierce between those companies. Each company tries to avoid competition and tends to increase the size of collaboration through strategic alliances or through merge.

Thus, due to the convergence of broadcasting and telecommunications markets, the market is becoming much larger and the existing legal framework is changing and adapting to the environmental challenges and legal controversies. Ultimately, this broadcasting and communication convergence phenomenon gives a great impact on the entire national economy and people's quality of life.

Policy Issues

1) The Nature of the Convergence

The nature of actual convergence can be divided into two aspects: (1) The evolution of the broadcasting service and (2) Expanding the communication operatons.

First, the evolution of the broadcasting service. It is possible that services that are provided by the broadcasting service, through broadcasting digitization, are extended to a variety of advanced and interactive data broadcasting services.

Second, the business expansion of communication operators. The expansion phenomena and discussion of the convergence between the broadcast-network and the communication-network facilitate the provision of broadcasting services by communication-operators, the desire for business diversification of these operators' acts as a strong drive to promote the broadcast communication convergence.

2) Policy Recommendations

(1) Redefine the Criteria for Classification of Broadcasting and Telecommunications

According to the accelerated advances in convergence of broadcast and communication characteristics, it is pointless to distinguish between broadcast-networks and communication-networks. It is desirable to see that bi-directional which is presented by the characteristics of the broadcast communication convergence is added to the sub-concept of broadcasting or that form of broadcasting concept was expanding due to the development of digital technology.

(2) Implications of Convergence Phenomena and Regulatory Policy

The new multimedia environment and the audience need to be considered. The raising prospects on the social impact of broadcasting will be further expanded with the use of broadcasting networks because it is capable of overcoming the limitation of time and space. Also, there is a need to identify the convergence of broadcast and communication in the social and cultural contexts rather than too much technology-driven approach to technological determinism. Technology is just the development of common carrier and what is more important is a content which has a variety of social and cultural influences.

Recent Trends

Digital Content Industry Policy

1) Concept

Digitalization of content means the transformation to digital form of information, including, cultural and creative work, among others that formally existed in analog form.

Digital content include a wide range of fields, such as visual media (publication, movie, broadcast, picture, etc.), auditory media (music, radio etc), and the interactive form (game or database, etc.).

2) Significance

As all the new digital media, especially IMT-2000, satellite broadcasting etc., convergence on internet and digital contents has emerged as the key element that influences national development. The optimal growth opportunity of the digital contents industry is coming as an extension of the window with the emergence of new networks and media as well as the advancement of broadband and mobile network. As a result, digital content has emerged as a key success factor to dominate the acceptance and expansion of new network market. It also creates new value-added services for global business market.

3) The Policy Promotion System

In Korea, Digital Content Industry Development Policy has been promoted as the center of Korea Broadcasting and Communication Commission and the Ministry of Culture and Tourism. The Korea Broadcasting and Communication Commission have promoted the digital content industry as a new industry converged with digital information technology. The Ministry of Culture and Tourism has pursued a content industry development policy in the field of cultural content. Above this, the Ministry of Industry and Trade etc. have promoted it as part of related industry development, not independent industry promotion.

The Green Growth Policy

1) Concept

Green growth means the harmonious and balanced growth of the economy and the environment. The concept of green growth can be linked to three areas:

First, it means the virtuous cycle of the environment and the economy. Through the transition of growth pattern and economic structure, it can maximize the synergy effectiveness of the pillars of the environment and the economy.

Second, the green revolution will improves people's quality of life. It means the culture of green life and is the practiced planning and consumption base of any industry in all of our lives. Also, it encourages the use of green transportation such as buses, subways, bike etc., and promotes transportation efficiency improvement based on Intelligent

Figure 18-2 Green Growth Paradigm

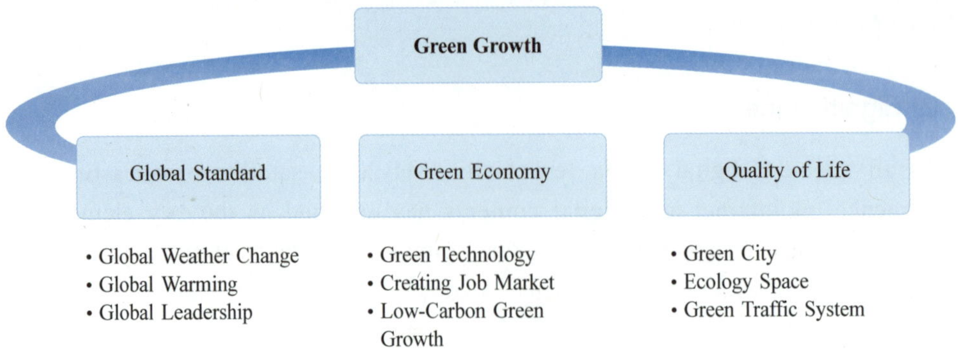

Transportation Systems.

Lastly, it means to establishment of national standard that meet international expectations. This takes advantage of green growth as a new momentum of national development in the active response to the recent world trends of global climate change.

2) The Importance of Green Growth

The importance of green growth is in line with the global important issues. In the context of this book, green growth is perceived to be an important strategic mechanism that may address prevailing and disastrous natural catastrophes.

First, there is a deepening environmental crisis caused by global warming. Global warming has been functioning as a threat to the survival of mankind. The economic losses due to climate change are in the range of 5 to 20% of global GDP each year. Like other countries, Korea is vulnerable to global warming which has a direct impact on its economy.

Second, there is serious energy crisis. Energy and resource are in danger of being exhausted and may be depleted around the world. Worldwide economic growth and increased economic demands tend to intensify the imbalance of demand and supply of energy. Fossil-fuel-based energy consumption structure has been accelerating the depletion of natural resources. Due to the excessive use of fossil fuels, greenhouse gas emissions are increasing rapidly.

Third, there is the need for the creation of a new source of green energy. Concern for green growth in developed countries is spreading as they struggle to overcome economic crisis and ncreasing energy independence. The strategic movement that

Figure 18-3 Vision & Strategy of Green Growth

the green industry and green market is used as a new national growth engine is increasing.

Lastly, there is the need for the transition to a new paradigm. In the face of the limitations of conventional economic growth paradigm, due to the intensified global competition, it is difficult to sustain the current high levels of competitiveness, unless the existing revenue model is to be changed. Given the environment and carbon regulation, fossil fuel dependency structure has inevitably negatively impacted on the economy, society, and the national environment.

3) Green Growth as a National Strategy

According to the ninth article of the Korean basic law of low-carbon-green-growth, the national strategy is to establish and enforce low carbon green growth of the nation. It includes policy objectives, implementing strategy, and major task. It is the top national plan related with low carbon green growth as a national strategy. It can be national participatory plan to present the basic direction of national policy for low carbon green growth and to embody action plans such as annual achievement goal, investment plan, and principal agent, etc.

The green growth policy directions consists of 1) Effective reduction of greenhouse gas emissions, 2) De-oil/energy-independence reinforcement, 3) Climate change adaptation capacity building, 4) Green technology development and growth power, 5) The greening of industry and green industry development, 6) The advancement of industrial structure, 7) Green economy foundation construction, 8) Green Land/ Transportation development, 9) Green revolution in lifestyle, 10) Global cooperation on green growth.

Key Point!

◎ E-Commerce Policy

The concept of e-Commerce

- Conduct of transactions using electronic means carried out in cyberspace
- There are no time and space constraints, lessening the trouble of going to the store and pay by credit card.

Characteristics of e-Commerce

- It is possible to conduct commerce in 24 hours without being bound by time and space, widening the activities of businesses and consumers.
- It is possible to provide a platform that allows 1:1 marketing resulting in a more efficient business management.
- In e-Commerce, traditional physical space is no longer required. Instead, provision of information, promotion of products, marketing is now available through the internet.
- It became possible to quickly respond to the needs of the customer.
- It does not require huge capital to purchase land and buildings as is required in existing businesses.

Policy Strategy:

- Government's Vision and Role
  - Clear vision for the role of government in e-commerce
  - Leading role of government in setting up of e-commerce within public procurement sector is required.
- Activation of Electronic Documents
- Market and Industrial Development for e-Commerce
- Strengthen International Cooperation

Recent Trends: Wireless e-Commerce and Mobile Payment

◎ Protection of Intellectual Property Rights

Concepts

- Intellectual property rights include all rights arising from the industrial, scientific, literary or artistic fields of intellectual activity, such as the literary, artistic and scientific works, performers, demonstrations, and music and broadcasting.

Features

- Intangible and spiritual goods
- Ideological and abstract

Policy Strategy:

- Government should establish a system that can manage all intellectual property to promote intellectual property policies.
- Government should provide legal provisions to systematically protect from intellectual property infringement.
- Government should cultivate the professional expertise on whether it is about legal issues or technical issues. Also it should invest R&D about protection and nurturing about intellectual property rights.
- There is a need to split the role of the companies and universities and research institutes for a synergistic effect among the powerhouses of intellectual property.

◎ Standardization Policy

Concept of Standardization

- A selection of a discussion method that will enable sending and receiving information between devices in the same way and within similar timeframe.

Necessity of Standardization

- Economic Development
- Technology Development
- Consumer Protection

Policy Strategies:

▸ General Policy Direction

- Standardization must be a private sector driven and market oriented process such that users' needs are reflected. For this, the government must provide relevant support and a clear implementing rules and guidelines.

▸ Role of Government

- Standardization Support of the Private Sector
- Professional Manpower HRD Training for Standardization
- Support of R&D for Standard Technology

◎ Broadcasting and Communication Convergence Policy

The Concept of Convergence

▸ Convergence of Net (or Network)

- It indicates the distinction between broadcasting networks and communication networks become blurred.

▸ Convergence of Services

- It indicates the distinction between broadcasting services and communication services become blurred.

▸ Convergence of Enterprise

- It indicates the distinction between broadcasting enterprises and communication enterprises become blurred.

Policy Issues

▸ The Nature of the Convergence

- The evolution of the broadcasting service
- The business expansion of communication operators

▸ Policy Recommendations

- Redefine the Criteria for Classification of Broadcasting and Telecommunications
- Implications of Convergence Phenomena and Regulatory Policy

◎ Recent Trends

Digital Content Industry Policy

- Concept: Digitalization of content means the transformation to digital form of information, including, cultural and creative work, among others that formally existed in analogue form.
- Significance: Digital content has emerged as a key success factor to dominate the acceptance and expansion of new network market. It also creates new value-added services for global business market.

The Green Growth Policy

- Concept
  - Green growth means the harmonious and balanced growth of the economy and the environment.
  - It means the virtuous cycle of the environment and the economy.
  - It means the culture of green life and is the practiced planning and consumption base of any industry in all of our lives.
  - It means the establishment of national standard that meet international expectations.
- Significance
  - There is a deepening environmental crisis caused by global warming.
  - There is serious energy crisis. Energy and resource are in danger of being exhausted and may be depleted around the world.
  - There is the need for the creation of a new source of green energy.
  - There is the need for the transition to a new paradigm.
- Green Growth as a National Strategy
  - Effective reduction of greenhouse gas emissions
  - De-oil/energy-independence reinforcement
  - Climate change adaptation capacity building
  - Green technology development and growth power
  - The greening of industry and green industry development
  - The advancement of industrial structure
  - Green economy foundation construction
  - Green Land/Transportation development
  - Green revolution in lifestyle
  - Global cooperation on green growth

Key Question!

◎ Discuss the concept of e-commerce and its perspective. Let's sum up each concept.

◎ What are the characteristics of e-Commerce?

◎ What is the policy direction and policy challenges of e-Commerce?

◎ What are the characteristics of intellectual property?

◎ What is the concept of standardizing information and communication?

◎ Explain the difference between broadcasting and communication based on its concept, objectives, and characteristics.

◎ What is digital content industry? What is its importance?

◎ What is green growth? What is its importance?

◎ What are the policy strategies for green growth?

Chapter 19

CIVIL SOCIETY DIMENSION OF E-POLICY(I): DEMOCRACY AND TRANSPARENCY

The advent of smart information technology will tremendously facilitate the process of e-voting and e-policy.

Objectives

The purpose of this chapter is to bring understanding on e-Policy in the civil society's standpoint of democracy and transparency. The discussion will center on these two important aspects together with some policy ideas associated with each of them. Specifically, the aspect of civic consciousness and political participation will be tackled to give a clearer understanding on the civil society dimension of e-Policy and the policy ideas associate with democracy and transparency.

First, it will discuss the issue of civic consciousness and political participation, and the problem of the ever increasing social surveillance for the precondition for democracy and transparency.

Second, it will discuss the specific policy relating with these dimensions that includes e-democracy, e-voting, and public information opening policy. The concept, issues, strategy, and the future direction will also be discussed.

Issues & Arguments

Civic Consciousness and Political Participation

The continuous advancement of information technology opened various venues for people's engagement and political participation. There are identified social platforms that allows citizens to freely participate in the policy-making and efficient political exercises. These mechanisms may have strengthened the democratic values but must be amplified by civic consciousness, awareness about one's society. Thus, we must always call for civility, objectivity and political maturity in order to translate information technology into a meaningful mechanism for democracy. Without such, wemay expect another chaotic society that lawlessness and disorder is prevalent.

Maximizing the benefits brought by the advancement of information technology shouldgive a balanced improvement or boost on political bureaucratic system and the democratic values for the citizens. Gandy (1989: 61-67) pointed out the risk of strengthening of political bureaucratic system rather than invigorating civil and democratic rights of the citizens. This could further be interpreted as the takeover of the government stepping on some inherent rights afforded to citizen such as freedom of expression and access to lawful goods available for the citizen. H. Schiller (1988) also noted the risk of mass democracy or mobocracy through ICT wherein people may follow certain political opinion without critical thinking and was solely driven by emotional burst. Some self-motivated politicians could easily use social network services (SNS) such as Twitter or Facebook to instigate political issues and maneuverpeople's opinion towards a certain point (Kellner, 1990).

Political debates on the online network become easily polarized into two extreme positions and tend to become quickly aggravated with a malicious banter or jeering, insulting words or curses without serious deliberating on a substantive aspect of the issue (Clifford Stroll, 1996: 30).

The Expanded of Social Surveillance

The extraordinary advancement of information society has resulted to an expanded and sophisticated surveillance system. The creation of social network services such as Face book, Twitter, Instagram photo stream wherein it allows others to freely view all available details about the account users.

The concept of e-Government is not always conclusive and affirmative, there are alsospots of vagueness and imperfections. One of the primary requisite for the establishment of e-Government infrastructure is a comprehensive national database that bears necessary information about the citizen. In the process, it calls for the surrender of personal information to the disposition of the government which apparently put an issue on 'privacy' and possible leakage of personal information.

The government through legal means may gain access to all personal information of its citizen such as names, birthdays, address, educational attainment, economic status, mental or medical information, and etc. The extent of information they can acquire and access is beyond our imagination. We should be reminded that except for the government's legal authority to obtain those information, there are other private entities such as bank, hospital, websites, or social media networks that for purposes of effective delivery of their services, citizens may unconsciously or voluntarily submitted information about themselves. For example, Facebook company have been doing the so-called dataveillance (Clarke, 1991) or actuarial surveillance (Philips, 2010) which refers to the collection and storage of personal information of their account users.

Now along this background where there is fear of intrusion to each individuality, the challenge will be on how we can address the issues of e-Government through e-Policy to make our society more trustful, mature in order to realize a brighter and a genuine humane society.

E-Democracy

Emergence of e-Democracy

e-Democracy can be divided into two important aspects: supply side and demand side.

1) Supply Side: The Development of Information Technology

The political process is influenced by the actors' approach of democratic engagement.People may participate in the political exercises by direct means through voting or Referendum; or may actively play role in the political process through ICT. This kind of democratic engagement gave birth to a new model of democracy, e-Democracy.

The development of an interactive smart information technology opened a new platform for the citizen to directly participate in the voting and the policy decision-making process. Through internet technology, a virtual and fast interaction between political candidates and the voters is made easy. People are informed of the platforms of a particular candidate that is made available online, may participate on online political surveys, and experience a hassle-free voting process.

The great opportunity for the expansion and exercise of democratic ideals were made possible through the emergence of the e-Democracy values. The integration and wise use of ICT in this domain enhanced the interaction of the political bureaucratic system with the stakeholders and contributed for the further engagement to democraticsociety of the citizens.

2) Demand Side: Social Necessity

Bringing meaningful changes in the government system cannot only be satisfied by the adoption of modern and applicable framework of governance. For example, the NPM that adopted the concept of market-based reforms or a business like governance is deemed to be insufficient mechanism to encourage and strengthen democracy.

The notion of 'active citizenship' should come to play. It means an integrated and inclusive governance approach that encourages citizens' direct participation in public governance. Direct participation has already been expanded and redefined from being limited physical engagement to an objective and practical democratic engagement through technological means.

These shift of social and democratic paradigm necessitates a clear vision of direct democracy anchored on the concept and model of e-Democracy.

Features of e-Democracy

The features of e-Democracy are as follows:

1) **Interactivity.** The significant changes in information technology brought us the feature of 'interactive communication. It can increase the density of social network that can lead to the activation of e-Communities. Online interactions may increase connected communications between individuals and groups that couldn't interact in the past due to technical limitations.

2) **Accessibility.** Accessibility is an important mechanism and means to achieve e-Democracy. The degree of accessibility can be measured and achieved through the development of the smart information technology and diversified channels.

They induce accessibility and active participation of the citizens. The individuals or groups can influence the decision-making process through a variety of accessible channels.

3) **Usefulness of Information.** The new smart information technology has the ability to communicate a variety of large amounts of information at high speed, without time and space constraints. The usefulness of information technology provides quality information to citizens, and accordingly, citizen who provide such information will have the ability to discuss or decide policy in the public space.

Vision for e-Democracy

The visions for e-Democracy are as follows:

1) **Complementary.** The Representative Democracy Perspective. The perspective contends that the discussion of e-Democracy began with the intention to compensate the shortcomings of representative democracy. It doesn't want to implement a direct democracy but rather representative democracy. Thus, it has given greater attention to the information channels for the expansion of information through communication technologies.

2) **Realization.** The Direct Democracy Perspective. e-Democracy realizes the participation of citizens in the policy process by using internet policy mechanisms to further the realization of direct democracy.

3) **Integrated Perspective.** It is desirable to understand and adopt and integrated perspective rather than exclusive classification of direct democracy and representative democracy. It can give variation on the contribution of e-Democracy depending on the level of development implementation of information technology and the degree of maturity of the civil society.

Advantages and Disadvantages of e-Democracy

The benefits of e-Democracy are as follows:

1) Fast communication
2) Increasing citizens' participation
3) Direct participation in the political process
4) Ease of access to information
5) Ensuring transparency of the political process

The disadvantages of e-Democracy are as follows:

1) Overload and inaccuracy of information
2) Limited participation of the citizen
3) The representation problem
4) The risk of e-Totalitarianism
5) Digital divide and inequality

E-Voting

Meaning of E-Voting

E-Voting emphasizes e-Government services by promoting computerization of election processes and providing convenient political exercise to the public. Therefore, e-Voting must be recognized as a mechanism to strengthen and enhance democratic participation, cost-cutting, and improvement of citizen's satisfaction.

Figure 19-1 Construction of e-Democracy

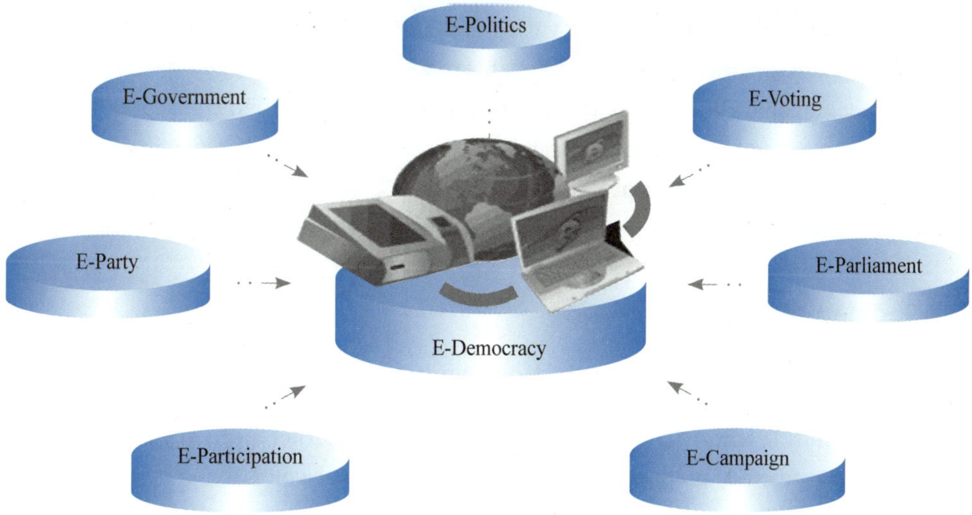

* Source: http://www.e-voting.go.kr

Types of E-Voting

The following are the different types of e-Voting:

1) **Electronic Reader.** Voters check a desired candidate on the ballot and then computer do the analysis and transmission of the result.

2) **Digital Records.** Voters use computer terminal instead of a ballot. All lists of candidates are flashed in the computer screen, voters may just touch their desired candidates' name, and then automatic transmission and counting are initiated. In this type, cheating or mistake due to ballot tampering can be reduced and votes are easily accounted and declared.

3) **Internet Poll.** As the name suggest, it is done through internet. Votes are cast at any given location or at the convenience of the voter unlike the other types that there is a determined place for voting.

Ubiquitous Voting

Ubiquitous Voting means that voters can vote freely in the wire-wireless network environment without any limitation of time and place. It includes the internet poll through electronic voting and electronic certification through touch screen. Furthermore, with various smart media such as notebook, PDA, wire telephone, Smart phone, Smart TV, it provides a convenient and transparent voting environment to voters and candidates, and provides maximized efficiency for those who manages the election process.

Developmental Stage of e-Voting

The stages for Ubiquitous Voting of Korea are as follows:

Stage 1. Pilot Testing. The necessary e-Voting or internet poll infrastructures are constructed, prepared, and examined with actual voters.

Stage 2. Electronic Voting. A consolidated and screened database of voters list was built, connected through electronic network, and accessed at each polling place.

Stage 3. Ubiquitous Voting (u-Voting). All necessary infrastructure were completed,

Figure 19-2 The Stage of e-Voting Development

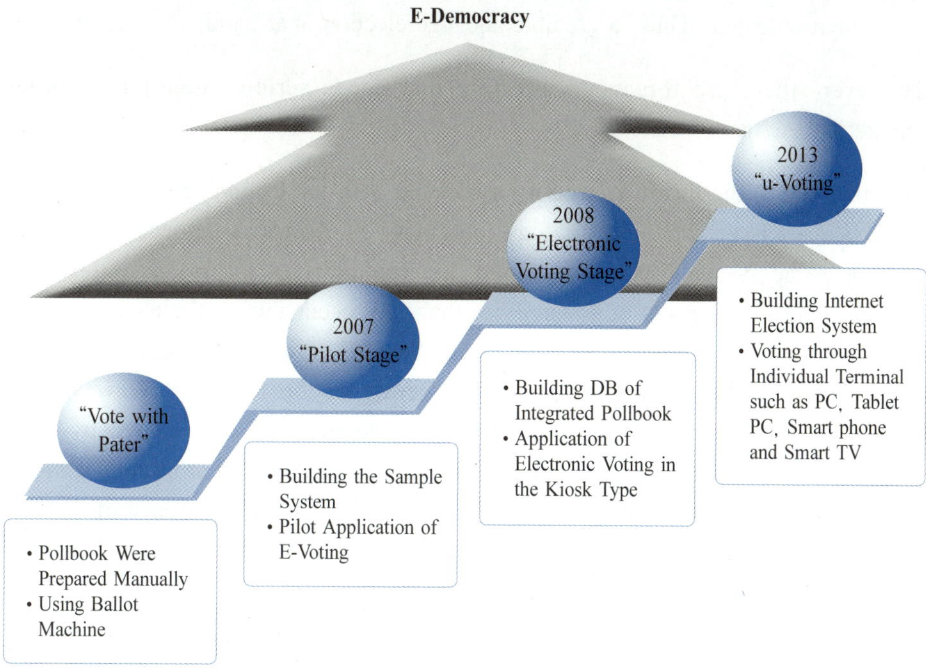

* Source: Revised from Seon-Gyu Go (2006: 38)

casting of votes through individual terminal such as PC, Tablet PC, Smart phone, SMART TV, and other smart digital device. (see the Figure 19-2).

Positive Effects and Threats of E-Voting

The expected positive effects of e-Voting are as follows:

First, computerization of electoral process addresses the issues of direct and representative democracy. Undeniably, e-Voting increases citizen's participation in public governance, thus boost the essence of direct democracy. Along with this, since e-Voting allows online voting, a mechanism that encourages wide participation of legal voters from all walks of life or regardless of its demographic level, the problem of representative democracy can be solved.

Second, economy and efficiency of electoral process can be improved. The computerization of the whole process allows it to managed, controlled, and secured in a manner different to that of the traditional paper-based elections. The installation and completion of the facilities may, at first, be costly but the long-term economic effect will not be as taxing as the traditional electoral approach. Efficiency is ensured and a fast transmission and counting of results will be unprecedented. Thus, a credible and free election is at hand.

However, there are threats to e-Voting that needs serious attention in order to maximize its benefits.

The first one is the threat to security associated with the technology. This has always been an issue when technology, internet, or electrical devices are involved. Once the system was compromised, the credibility of the results is just a fraud at all. There are lots of possibilities that may occur during the election time that may ruin the whole process such as hacking, power shortage, defects in the equipment, and other unexpected tampering of the facilities. However, these possible problems or shortcomings are curable and can be countered by different defense mechanisms. Thus, an e-Voting Security System must be fully established and regularly reviewed and updated to cope for possible occurrence of threats and challenges.

The second one is the cultural limitation because of digital divide. This issue may further expand the problem of alienation due to the incapacity of using the technology. Thus, it may discourage potential voters to participate in the elections.

The third one is an economic limitation due to the high-cost of installing and acquiring facilities necessary for setting-up the whole e-Voting infrastructure. A country must be ready for this challenge and adopt an approach that may encourage partnership or any applicable funding scheme. Indeed, development is not free.

Public Information Opening Policy

Concept

Access to public information policy is an open system that allows individual to view and copy public information. This is an important element in the realization of the modern democratic governance that contemplates transparency in public governance and recognition of people's right to information.

Such respect and acknowledgement of this human right should be appreciated. This will increase citizen's trust and satisfaction because they were being freed from the standard procedures in acquiring documents or information. Along this background, the government's vision for a trustful and mature society will be realized.

Positive and Adverse Effects

The positive effects of Public information opening policy are as follows:

1) Protection of People's Right to Know

Free access to public information is tantamount to respect of citizen's 'right to know.' The 'right to know' may not be an absolute right, but is an important constitutional right that encourages individual to boost self-realization.

2) Accessible and Useful Information for the Citizens

Access to public information will allow citizens to utilize vast and diverse information for whatever legal purpose it may serve them. Government agencies have collected and accumulated vast information while in the performance of their functions and duties.

3) Prerequisite to Democracy

An informed citizen is a basic quality to build civic consciousness and workable democracy. How the government is being run, its issues and challenges must be known to the public so that they can effectively and efficiently participate in building the country through participatory governance.

4) Ensuring Trustful Governance

Transparency of government is fostering citizen's trust to public governance. Opening the public information to the public will remove any doubt in the affairs of the government, thus will be dignified as fair, fraudulent-free, and uncorrupted governance.

The negative effects of Public information opening policy are as follows:

1) State secret or personal information may be compromised.

2) For company disclosures, company secrets may be exploited.

3) Additional administrative burden such as staffing, installation mechanisms, and additional required documents for authorizing access for the information.

4) Skills and knowledge gap may cause another social equity issue in the accessing public information.

Strategies for Public Information Opening

Here are some ways on how to promote public information opening.

1) Basic Direction

The existing access to administrative information are based and limited to individual request. This is the so-called passive access to public information. It is, however, limited to the information that are ready and classified as information for the public. In order to significantly expand access to public information, there should be an effort to move towards systematic information management and adopt a web-based one click system.

2) Strategy

(1) Determination whether or not a Document's Opening is Permissible at the Production Stage

Access to a public document should be determined in its production stage. An explicit legal criteria should be established as a guideline for marking whether or a not such document should be classified as public or confidential..

(2) Improve Management System of Confidential Document

Rules on confidential documents should follow a strict classification based on existing law, rules or regulations, or executive order. The strict "security matter test" should be applied for classification. Basically, this test contemplates that information that may affect national security should be kept confidential. However, such confidentiality is not perpetual, it should be for a determined period of time when the threat is no longer present.

(3) Competency and Awareness Building for the Civil Servants

It is necessary for civil servants to have the proper understanding and knowledge about information opening. Necessary Human Resource Development (HRD) interventions such as training for managers and education programs that will enhance the competencies and capacities of government employees on information opening must be initiated.

Summary and Conclusion

Because of the development of information and communication technology, people can have an easy access to information. Improved information access provides a solution to the problem of corruption caused by lack of information. The possibilities of information and communication technology may be endless. To realize these possibilities, there is a need for a strong leadership and policy commitment on the part of government.

If people and their government are to be able to share more information by more actively using the new smart ICTs such as the internet, Smart phones, SMART TV, and other channels, a considerable extent of corruption due to information deficiency will be solved.

Key Point!

◎ Issues & Debates of the Democratic Dimension

- Civic Consciousness & Political Participation
- The Enlargement of Social Surveillance

◎ e-Democracy

- Emergence of e-Democracy
  - Supply Side: The Development of Information Technology
  - Demand Side: Social Necessity

- Features of e-Democracy
  - Interactivity, accessibility and usefulness of information

- Vision for e-Democracy
  - Complementary.
  - Realization
  - Integrated Perspective

- Advantages and Disadvantages of e-Democracy
  - The benefits of e-Democracy
    - Fast communication
    - Increasing citizens' participation
    - Direct participation in the political process
    - Ease of access to information
    - Ensuring transparency of the political process

  - The disadvantages of e-Democracy
    - Overload and inaccuracy of information
    - Limited participation of the citizen
    - The representation problem
    - The risk of e-Totalitarianism
    - Digital divide and inequality

◎ E-Voting

▸ Meaning of E-Voting

- E-Voting emphasizes e-Government services by promoting electronization of election processes and providing convenient election services to the public. Therefore, e-Voting must be recognized as a process to improve citizen satisfaction and upgrade democracy as well as cost cutting and information offering.

▸ Type of E-Voting

- Electronic reader type
- Digital records type
- Internet poll type

▸ Developmental Stages of E-Voting in Korea

- Pilot application stage
- Electronic voting stage
- Ubiquitous voting stage (u-Voting)

▸ Positive Effects and Adverse Effects of E-Voting

- Positive expected effects of e-voting: an expanding range of direct democracy through increasing participation of resident.
- Adverse effects of electronic voting: security issues, coming from a dysfunctional cultural aspects, economic aspects of the dysfunction.

◎ Public Information Opening Policy

▸ Concept

- Public information opening policy is an open system that allows to view and copy public information by anyone. It is very important to realize the modern democratic governance.

▸ Positive Effects

- Protect people's right to know
- Easy to use information for citizens
- Prerequisite to the existence of democracy
- Ensure trust to governance

▸ Adverse Effects

- State secret or personal information may be compromised.
- For the purpose of disclosure, the secrets of rival companies can be exploited.
- Administrative burden can be increased such as on the additional list of required documents for opening of information, and installation of the task force and staffing.
- Variations between people's capability to access to information can cause social equity problem.

▸ Policy Strategies for Public Information Opening

- Determination whether or not a Document's Opening is Permissible at the Production Stage
- Improve Management System of Confidential Document
- Awareness-Raising of Civil Servants

Key Question!

◎ Think about democratic issues of information policy.

◎ What is the concept and the function of e-Democracy?

◎ Let's discuss the different perspectives on e-Democracy.

◎ Think about the concept and significance e-Voting.

◎ What is the positive and negative aspects of e-Voting?

◎ What are the policy strategies for public information opening?

Chapter 20

CIVIL SOCIETY DIMENSION OF E-POLICY (II): EQUITY DOMAIN

The promise of an information-rich society, supported by the smart e-technologies might be very compelling but disappointingly elusive to balance commercial markets and public interest.

- Lewis M. Branscomb

Objectives

The purpose of this chapter is to understand e-Policy from the civil society's standpoint of equity. In the information society, no one should be left behind. Everybody in it should be connected regardless of status in life, age, or other demographic levels, physical condition, or geographic origin. Thus, balance between the economic and commercial interest attached to information technology and its integration to public governance must display balance with the public interest.

Even in the advent of the introduction of e-Government, access to services has been limited for the middle level earners and rich families because of the insurmountable cost of technology. In this context, e-Policy has to address and ensure equitable distribution of technology, skills, and/or needed resources for full enjoyment of the benefits of information technology. It may include the realization of a universal and open access service; addressing the issue of information gap, and international information policy.

First, specific issues of information gap or the so called digital divide will closely be discussed. How was it manifested in the information society? What are the theoretical foundations that can help identify strategies to solve such phenomenon? Digital divide continuously challenges the equitability and accessibility of information society.

Second, approaches such as universal service delivery, policies and strategies that can possibly lessen the digital divide, if not to totally close the gap will be taken up.

Third, the book will look into the aspects of International Information Policy, its role in solving the problem of digital divide, and bring the issue this information gap in the international arena under the principle of coexistence and co-prosperity of world information society.

Information Gap

Concept of Information Gap

Information gap refers to the phenomenon wherein access and use of information does not progress on the same level among various social groups. Traditionally, information gap denotes the absence or lack of access to computer or useful technology that allows processing of information at home in contrast with those who could not. However, this definition may no longer provide an encompassing characterization of information gap in the present society. The concept of digital divide is sometimes confused with information gap.

Theories of Information Gap

1) Information Diffusion Theory: Shrinking Information Gap

The propagation of information technology and its role in the development of the society has been anticipated (see Negroponte, 1995). The swift change from the industrial age to information age has brought a significant change in human's life. Manual and mass production of goods, though are still relevant and necessary were slowly transformed through high-tech mechanisms and mass production; ICT became an indispensable element of governance; and information turned into a subject of commerce. Naisbitt (1982) stressed that we are already living in an era where economy is based on the creation and distribution of information while Toffler (1990) pointed out the imminent changes on power relations of the society due to this development.

2) Digital Divide Gap Theories: Widening Gap of the Digital Divide

As pointed out in the Information Diffusion theory, there is a widespread distribution of information technology in commerce, governance, and the whole society. Along this tenor, Digital Divide theory argues that such influence of information technology in public governance, business, and citizen's interaction is moving towards a peak of considerable strength and power. We may just think how ICT holds information like what Google has in its disposition. Google company have control on various information all over the world, just a click in their search engine of whatever information you need and there you have it. Indeed, information is power. However, who controls, has the easy access, means, skills and knowledge is the determining factor to claim power over it.

Digital Divide theory contends inequality in the access, use, and gap on skills and knowledge to effectively utilize ICT. Apparently, there is a wide difference among various groups of individuals within a nation and among nations as well. This dilemma may further complicate the already serious and deepening disparity between the rich and the poor (Haywood, 1998) not only within a specific country but also among nations.

The widening degree of information gap and digital divide can be attributed from the rapid development of the so called 'new media' or digital media. If we are going to look into the nature of analog or antiquated media devices such as analog TV, telephone, and radio, the quality of service provided are the same despite differences in size and cost. In some sense, there is a manifest lazy improvements or upgrades of this 'old media' that translates static and no vital developments. On the otherhand, the emergence of smart digital media such as android or smart phones, digital media players like smart TV media player, personal computers, laptops, etc. are out of the market in volume packed with various applications and up-to-date software. However, one of the features of this 'new media' is the unprecedented outflow of updates if not, new application or software that offers more superior services compared with the previous one. This phenomenon is a potential factor that causes serious deepening of information and digital divide because it limits the access and use of new technology.

Figure 20-1 Internet Penetration and Layered Model

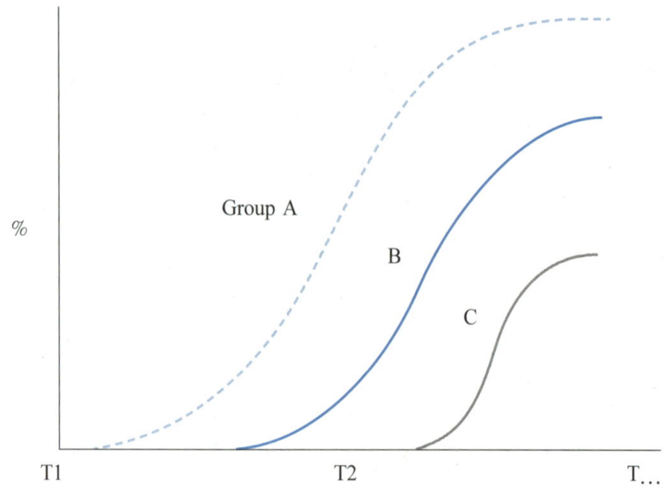

① Group A: Early adopters
② Group B: Mid-term adopters
③ Group C: The End-term adopters

The Figure above describes that groups B and C may still do not have access to information overtime.

3) Information Gap Realism Theory

The information Gap Realism theory focuses on bridging the information gap within a nation and between nations through local and international policy interventions. The acknowledgement of this societal impasse calls for a unified effort of information professionals, the public and private sector, and stakeholders in drawing a meaningful policy that is directed on settling the issue of information gap. This is by nature an integrated policy initiatives that emanates from the local level and a collaborative international policy drive geared towards weeding out information divide.

Policy Strategies

Here are some policy strategies that can be considered in addressing information and digital divide: 1) Support and supply relevant and needed technologies for the information disadvantaged group; 2) Continuous ICT education among all demographic levels in order to improve digital literacy; 3) Enactment of regional information policy to address geographical differences with regards to ICT use and accessibility; and 4) Construction of information facilities to be made available for the disadvantaged group.

One of the concrete and perfect policy initiative that reflects this is the e-Village of South Korea.

Since the 2000s, the development of information and communication technology (ICT) has given rise to the emergence of a social issue that intensified the polarization among regions and classes. In Korea, this phenomenon didn't escape the attention of the citizen and the government. Also, there has been an enormous expectation that ICT can do something for far-flung regions to revive its local economy. Accordingly, being convinced of polarization problem caused by gap of information technology, the government began to establish and showcase e-Village throughout the nation to decrease the digital gap between farming, fishing villages and urban areas. They provided IT infrastructure to designated villages such as internet and computer hardware, built village information center, distributed free PC to households, offered IT training and computer classes for the residents, developed information contents, established an operation system, and helped in the business model development and marketing.

Conceptually, e-Village is defined as a strategy designed to reduce the digital divide between rural and urban regions by increasing availability of IT services and to raise the income level of local residents through e-Commerce, which eventually leads to the improvement of the quality of life in rural communities.

The establishment of e-Village has the following objectives:

1) It aimed at building broadband internet infrastructure in agriculture/fishing villages, remote areas and other sites alienated from the information revolution in order to bridge information gap;
2) It aimed to create information content including online marketplace for local products to general practical benefits and rejuvenate local economics for balanced national development; and
3) It aimed to enable local residents to have easier access to information via the internet in daily life.

In Korea, the government followed a strategy that leads to the establishment of e-Village. First, it formulated an "e-Village Planning Group" consists of representatives from the government as well as private sector. Second, the central government organizations and local governments (Province, Municipality, City and District) took different roles. Third, active engagement of local residents was emphasized. Lastly, pilot e-Village sites were selected for even representation of urban areas, agricultural/fishing villages and mountainous villages.

Problems of Digital Divide

Although there is an optimistic development brought by informatization in the society, the problem of information gap and digital divide is always at issue. The socio-economic gap in the industrial society that is determined through control and access of wealth and income has already put the society in an abject disparity between members of the society. This dilemma is being complicated and expanded in the information society through information gap and digital divide. The absence or limited access, use, or capacity to utilize ICT for meaningful means is tantamount to information access inequality in the information society. Logically, this problem absolutely intensifies socio-economic gap between the rich and poor; and will surely impede the flourishing of democratic values and the building of a humane information society.

Summary and Conclusion

Information gap and digital divide is a two-level dilemma in the information society. The Information gap refers to the comprehensive inequality of access, use, absence or lack of skill, knowledge, and capability to translate acquired information to advance individual and societal development; whereas digital divide denotes lack or limited access to ICT and basic skills or knowledge required for the use of technology. Apparently, addressing the issues through policy initiatives that falls in gamut of information gap will accordingly cure the issues under digital divide. In short, bridging the information gap will slay naturally this digital divide.

Among the acceptable policy strategy that can address the issue of information gap and digital divide is through 'Universal Service.' This requires the promotion of equal access, participation in information network, and continuous education for the disadvantaged group to effectively utilize ICT. It also promote access and use of information and communication services in affordable price anytime and anywhere.

Universal Service

Concept

'Universal Service' refers to the delivery of basic information and communication services at just, reasonable, and affordable cost, anywhere, and anytime to every member of the society regardless of demographic level and geographical location.

Strategy

For the advancement of 'Universal Service' of information and communication services, the following policy issues are required to consider: 1) Accessibility, 2) Applicability, 3) Just and affordable rates, and 4) Training and development for the people. Along with the basic and fundamental policy issues, there is a need to look into the following crucial factors to effectively effectuate: 1) Determine the scope of the universal service, 2) Determine possible providers of the universal service, and 3) Determine the compensation scheme for the universal service providers.

International Information Policy

By realizing the BcN (Broadband Converged Network) based on the Integrated Services Digital Network, the unbalanced problem of international information flow and cultural dependency are so serious.

The Major Issues

The rapid advancement of information and communication technology such as fiber optical communications, electronics, satellites, etc or the rapid development of technology systems such as computer network is to increase the distribution and exchange of information between countries to overcome the temporal and spatial constraints of information distribution.

The combination of highly developed communication network, satellite, and broadcasting technology is able to connect the every world in a matter of seconds. However, Due to the unbalanced information distribution, information sovereignty issues have been raised. In addition this, due to the outflow of domestic data, privacy concerns between countries also has been raised. The development of information technology and the increase in information data distribution have an advantage working for information developed countries. As a result, the Information Gap between developed and developing countries are likely to be extended more.

In this circumstance, it is necessary for Korea to establish policy and institutional solutions to reduce technological and industrial gap with the developed countries. On the other hand, international cooperation is needed to respond actively to these problems.

Policy Strategy

The policy challenges of international Information Policy issues are participation and market-opening problems.

1) Information User Centered Thought

Knowledge Information Society is epistemologically based on maximizing the benefits of personal freedom and convenience. The main subject of the Information Society is citizens who use information communication. The information utilization of citizens will be the key to the transition to a knowledge information society.

2) The Information Industry Competitiveness

The basis of the bargaining power in the international field is competitiveness of the domestic industry. Therefore, the basis of the international information policy has to be focused on promoting the competitiveness of the domestic industry.

3) The Balance between Competitiveness and Cooperation

In the international issues, the rule of partnership and cooperation is very important. Through the principle of co-existence and co-prosperity, the cooperative global governance should be managed and the consensus of the member states should be carefully drawn.

Summary and Conclusion

The unfolding of the 21st century has brought the world into a new and different turn. It's an era of speed and change. The swirl of change is blowing fiercely. There is a need to change to effectuate change, and therefore change management and innovation is indispensable to achieve transformation of governance. As new information technology combines broadcasting, telecommunications and mobile images, the new space, called cyber-space has been created by using the SMART technological innovations such as Smartphone, PC Tablet, and internet.

The combination of ICT and Smart SNS(Social Network Services) is also creating new growth engine for national competitiveness.

In this global open-system era, secrets or fluke does not work. All the elements including policy, law, rule and regulation has to be performed in a total transparent way. Furthermore, policy environment is rapidly changing due to the smart ICT development, combined with globalization; it requires information communication industry should be operated by the strict rule of market mechanism of competition and autonomy. In an open global economy, international information policy must encourage market-based competition which vitalizes the creativity and autonomy of the private sector. In addition, government should manage e-policy corresponding to the open economy in a transparent way to encourage competition and cooperation in global political economy.

The prosperity of next generation and the opportunity of world business do not come easily without policy strategies. The policy environment should be established to support business creativity and entrepreneurial innovation. Clear vision and paradigm change should be followed by the blue print of e-Government. Government should also accelerate to realize the high-tech information community by rearranging law and regulatory framework for the new era of e-Government. Finally, strong leadership and commitment should also be supported by the people's awareness and educational capacity building.

Key Point!

◎ Information Gap

Concept of Information Gap

- Information gap refers to the phenomenon that access and use of information does not progress on the same level among the various social groups. Information Gap is defined by unequal situations of digital divide in information society.

Theories of Information Gap

- Information Diffusion Theory: Shrinking Information Gap
- Digital Divide Gap Theories: Phenomenon of Widening Digital Divide Gap
- Information Gap Reality Theory

Problems of Digital Divide

- An intensified social gap between the rich and the poor
- Hinders development of democracy and building of the humanity-centered civil society in information society.

Policy Strategies:

- Support and supply technologies for the information disadvantaged groups
- ICT education for improving digital literacy
- Offering information systems and contents for information disadvantaged groups
- Solution of regional information disparity through Local Information Policy
- Providing opportunities of information access for the disadvantaged groups through the construction of information facilities.

◎ Universal Service

- Concept
    - Universal Service means the condition that quality information and communication services are provided to all users at affordable rates, anywhere and anytime.

▸ Strategy

- Determine the scope of the Universal Service provided.
- Determine the Universal Service providers and their obligation.
- Determining of compensation methods to subsidize the Universal Service provider.

International Information Policy

▸ Major Issues

- International communications and information systems
- Open systems and information and communication
- Information technology and the internationalization of the industry
- Internationalization of information distribution

▸ Policy Strategy

- Information User Centered Thought
- The Information Industry Competitiveness
- The Balance between Competitiveness and Cooperation

Key Question!

◎ Think about the concept of the digital divide and the assumptions of information gap.

◎ What are the factors on the occurrence of digital divide and the problems resulting from information gap?

◎ What are the challenges and strategic policies for bridging the digital divide?

◎ Explain the universal service concept and policy challenges.

◎ What are the challenges and strategic policies of international information policy?

Chapter 21

CIVIL SOCIETY DIMENSION OF E-POLICY(III): ETHICS AND REFLEXIVITY DOMAIN

Digital technology, like every other technology, has negative aspecst. We have to face cyber terrorism, digital vandalism, and hacking issues.

- N. Negroponte

Objectives

This chapter will give light on the ethics and reflexivity element of e-Policy in the standpoint of civil society. E-Policy must contribute to make a trustful and matured society beyond the dimensions of productivity and democracy. In this background, this chapter will discuss issues to be considered in the context of ethical e-Policy which includes privacy and personal information protection, issue of anonymity in the internet, and cyber crime policy.

First, the discussion will focus on the protection of personal information and privacy rights.

Second, it will discuss the emerging issue of anonymity in the information society and the needed policies and strategic mechanisms to respond on possible problems relating to this.

Third, it will highlight on the issue of cyber crime, understand how it works, and identify what are the possible policy safeguards to be adopted in this regard.

Fourth, the vital factors of information ethics and culture will be discussed, which includes: 1) Cooperation through international organization, 2) Utilization of mass media and education, 3) The role of transformational leadership, and 4) The role of NGO and citizens.

Privacy and Protection of Personal Information

Definition

Privacy is "the right to be let alone" has the meaning passive until 1960 before. Then, with the development of information society, it was changed into something that indicates "the right to control information about the self" in the positive sense.

Features

The following are the important features of Privacy.

1) Privacy as an exclusive human right

The right to demand protection against infringement of privacy is a prerogative right that every person must enjoy.

2) Rights of natural persons

In order to remedy the emotional distress of the individual, the right to privacy does not apply to the corporation.

3) Means of ensuring self-realization

Privacy gives the feeling of control and freedom against intrusion or external coercion to one's individual behavior. The absence of such outside forces intruding to one's calmness is tantamount to reaching self-realization.

4) Fungibility (Trade-off)

The right to privacy though an exclusive and inherent natural right is not an absolute right. There are circumstances that calls for some trade-offs such as legal or practical conditions. For example, there are laws that defines freedom of information, speech, access to public documents and other practical and reasonable circumstances such as an employer that requires information about job applicants.

5) Prerequisite

Privacy is s pre-requisite for a reliable and trustful society

The Protection of Personal Information

The right to protection of 'Personal Information' is a wider concept than the conventional concept or passive definition of right to privacy; it is the right to include self-determination and self-correction. 'Personal information' is the information about specific individuals which enables to recognize by name, social security number, and video. This is to say the whole information regarding any person representing the individual's mental and physical, wealth and social status and identity.

Protection Provisions of Personal Information: Security Technology

PKI (Public-Key Infrastructure) is important information technology that prevents problems and provides the trust between government and the public. It is divided the cryptographic techniques which assures the confidentiality of contents on the electronic trade and e-signature techniques which assures the identification, confidentiality and non-repudiation of transaction facts.

1) Hierarchy of PKI

(1) Root Certification Authority

The root certification authorities established the policies and procedure used in whole PKI, monitor the state and property of subordinate's policy-observance. Also they certify subordinate agencies' public key and manage authentication certificates and its revocation lists.

(2) Subordinate Certification Authorities

The subordinate certification authorities publish the public key certificate, abolish it as occasional demands, and deliver the public key certificate to the higher agencies. Also they manage the database which has personal information and keep the public key certificate, its revocation lists, and audit-review files.

(3) Registration Authority

The registration authorities are essential to join to use the electronic signature. But because only several certification authorities cannot handle a lot of member, the subordinate agencies are needed to have the registration authorities. The registration authorities check user's status and affiliation on behalf of the certification authorities.

After checking user's status, the registration authorities signature user's request and submit it to the certification authorities, and certification authorities check registration authorities' signature and send certification to the registration or to the user directly.

2) Government Public Key Infrastructure

(1) Definition of GPKI

GPKI is core infrastructure of e-Government to secure the method of trust and certificate for governmental documents. In the other words, GPKI plays a role in building the security of electronic approval and electronic document distribution to realizing e-Government for improving government service and government productivity. Also sometimes government electronic signature is needed to prevent to leak the national secrete and personal information through computer network, at this moment, GPKI is necessary for its certification.

(2) Purpose of GPKI

First, GPKI provides the efficiency for e-Government. Because its purpose is the electronic government performance, it establishes the effective infrastructure through the certificate issuing for government agencies and public officials.

Second, GPKI provides the transparency for e-Government. Its purpose is to provide online administrative service to enterprises and the public. Therefore users can find governmental official documents at any time, and can process all kind of certification and licensing on-line. GPKI improves the transparency of government procurement and contract.

Third, GPKI reinforces the competitiveness for e-Government. It provides various civil affair public services by interworking with private sector. Because GPKI can improve the quality of service significantly, reduce standby cost, break the limitation of time and place and enhance the administrative clarity, it improves government competitiveness.

Forth, GPKI provides the reliability for e-Government. Because it assures the identification, integrity and legal force of electronic documents, and personal information protection through internet, GPKI provides the trust of trading between government and the public in the cyber-space.

3) Government Electronic Signature

When users use e-documents of e-Government, they need the administrative electronic signature for the security. Especially in the private sector, users use electronic signature and in the public sector, the users use administrative electronic signature to make an identification.

Summary and Conclusion

The application of personal information at the government office in Korea has been swayed by logic of efficiency. Most e-Government projects prioritized efficient business process and effective control. But now government must seriously take care of the personal information protection. Especially because much personal information is potential to be spilled in the future, this issue about personal information protection becomes more and more important. Also the government must never forget that the most significant goal of e-policy is for not only simple government efficiency, but also realizing of the dignity of human and human rights.

Problems of Anonymity on the Internet

Significance

Namelessness or facelessness nature of users in the internet is called anonymity or anonymous users. Communication with non-face-to-face contact creates the problems for personal identity and trust issues. It raised the issue of trust between the users in the information society.

In modern society dominated by disconnected and impersonal relationships, trust promotes the formation of the ontological stability, social stability and coherence as well as creates a healthy social order. Due to the lack of face-to-face contact or personal relationship in information society, the trust will be formed through a reflexive and long-term process, which emerged as an increasingly important policy challenge in information society. In short, trust based on mutual openness in the process of cyber communication has emerged as an important issue.

1) Trust

Personal trust, stability and reliability are the necessary conditions for the development of a healthy self-identity. Trust based relationships are formed on the basis of the 'ontological stability' of individuals. Without building basic trust, people feel the permanent existential anxiety and lack of confidence about the identity. These personal issues lead to the problem on social order.

Before, trust was thought as cultural aspects of the theoretical approach, but now it considers itself as a political and economic entity. It has emerged as a key concept across the social sciences, such as the understanding of the strategic elements of national power. Participatory civic culture based on trust established the healthy democracy(Almond and Verba, 1963). Scholars such as Fukuyama (1998) and Nye (1998) argued that trust has emerged as the most important element of national development.

2) Anonymity, Mutual Openness and Trust

Due to the advancement of information society, cyberspace is activated; social relations on the basis of anonymity are formed. Such anonymity provides feedback to individuals without responsibility and causes delay or block the mutual openness that is the basis of human relations. The lack of mutual openness and trust hinders the healthy development of cyberspace and it will be important policy issues in the information society.

Information Society and Anonymity

1) Case of Cybercrime

Hidden crime within the traditional legal system now appears as a crime by using cyberspace. Unlimited dissemination of pornography, mail bombs, defamation or insult, undermine the credit of the ethical issues, which occur on cyberspace is known as cyber crime.

2) Features of Anonymity

(1) Virtual Reality

Cyberspace creates virtual reality which separates the real world from virtual world, which leads to problems such as confusion of identity, the emergence of cyber-ego, dualization of daily life, and loss of conscience.

(2) Lack of Sense of Guilt

In Cyberspace, problems such as un-ethical language-violence, invasion of privacy, hatred for a particular ethnic group, and the diffusion of spam mails can be taken place because each individual is able to hide their physical appearance in cyberspace, which may increase the cyber crime.

(3) ID

ID appears as a sign of identification of the individual activities in cyberspace but wrong or artificial identity creates problem of anonymity.

Policy Direction

Because of anonymity in cyberspace, the degree of moral and ethical corruption is getting worse, but the legal and institutional mechanisms to regulate them are still incomplete. Legal and institutional mechanisms as well as awareness program are necessary for solving this problem. Also, through education of ethical conscience, government should enhance the civic consciousness to enforce the functions of anonymity of cyberspace.

Cyber Crime

Definition

Cyber crime was not yet defined clearly. Cyber crime is closely related to the Internet and computer media. In this regard, cyber crime can be defined associated with the following two features. One is a cyber crime that is relating with network or internet; the other is cyber crime as a broad concept that includes all the computer crime in the cyber space.

Features

1) Anonymity and non-face-to-face

In cyber space, people can act anonymously with hiding the identity like real name, age, and gender. The anonymity and non-face-to-face are likely to increase cyber crime.

2) Unlimited space

Cyber space is an unlimited space and very large compared to the reality. It is an attractive space for those who want to cause a lot of problems to the world.

3) Expertise

Cyber crime requires a high level of expertise, compared to other crimes. As a result, computer crime is also referred to as the 'white collar crime'. Most of the production and dissemination of malware, hacking, and data manipulation or cyber-gambling needs to have highly specialized knowledge about the computer programming.

4) Hidden crime

Cyber crime is a hidden crime; it is hard to detect. The features of cyber crime, i.e., anonymity, a high level of expertise, and unlimited space cause a lot of difficulties to detect the cyber crime.

Types of Cyber Crime

There are two type of cyber crime: 1) Cyber crime with network invasion, 2) Cyber crimc without network invasion.

1) Cyber Crime with Network Invasion

(1) Information Invasion

Information invasion are the activities like hacking and Cyber spay. Hacking is a way of invading or compromising other's system through computer network. Cyber spay is an act of collecting other company's information or national confidential information in order to take advantage of economic interests of the certain companies or country.

(2) Cyber Terror

(A) Concept

Cyber terror is a compound of cyber and terrorism. A Cyber terror is an organization act that uses unpredictable harm to the government, public, and private for the political purpose. Cyber terror uses an unpredictable violence and is a form of terrorism in cyber space.

(B) Policy Response to Cyber Terror

Cyber terror all over the world are beginning to recognize the dangerous threat to national security. Therefore, the maintenance organization and response system for cyber terror, as well as for the international response effort should be in order(Kim, Jeong-Tai et al, 2004).

First, it is necessary to prepare the international organization of organic activity. International organizations such as the Asia-Pacific Economic Cooperation (APEC) and Development Organization for Economic Cooperation (OECD), recently maintain an organic relationship to the cyber-terrorists.

Second, it is necessary to have a program of responding cyber terrorism. The corresponding techniques for ensuring cyber terrorism, cyber-terrorism investigation and analysis techniques, should be developed organically among the related international agencies.

Third, it is necessary to support the R&D activities of enhancing the computer system for detecting a threat to computer network of national defense, transportation and critical national infrastructure.

2) Cyber Crime without Network Invasion

Cyber crime without network invasion indicates piracy and illegal distribution, cyber sex crime, cyber defamation, spam mail and so on.

(1) Illegal Copy and Distribution

Unauthorized copy and distribution does not eradicate as it is an uncovered act.

(2) Cyber Sex Crime

Cyber sex crime refers to the sexual abuse that can occur on the cyberspace. It includes sexual harassment in the chat rooms of the Internet or mobile communications.

(3) Cyber Defamation

In the case of defamation in cyberspace, it comes under rules and theories of the honor and credit of the Criminal law. This can be applied in the case of defamation in Internet chat rooms or mobile communications.

(4) Spam Mail

Spam means to advertise one's own site or product via e-mail. Spam is primarily used as a means of advertising products; however, in severe cases, it causes server down and communication problems.

Policy Strategy

1) The response system in the legal aspects

For punishing cyber crime and making it elements of a crime, the most basic way is to amend the Criminal law. There are many difficulties to punish cyber crime, because the proper regulation for punishment does not exist under old criminal law which does not bring in cyber crime. Therefore, legal action is necessary to amend some controversial provisions and make rules such as computer-related crime of business interference, fraud by using computer, and infringement on secrecy etc.

2) The response system in the technical aspects

In the technical aspects, response techniques should be developed to block any cyber crime by analyzing the technique of cyber crime. For example, the technology needs to be developed to cope with Hacking, Computer Virus, and Code Breaking etc.

3) The response system in the social aspects.

Government is necessary to ensure a systematic response system such as the Cyber Crime Task Force consisting of prosecutors and police experts. Especially, due to the spatial non-constraints, international cooperation should be required.

Information Ethics & Culture

Once deployed, it is hard to undo its momentum as information technology has its logic of self-replication. One should think seriously before it's too late to reflect the rightful way of its development.

Cooperation through International Organization

The international community should support research on the impact of science and technology to human life. These studies should include efforts to establish the direction that the new technologies should bound for. Furthermore, organic perspectives and balanced philosophy will be reorganized about the issue of human, nature, and technology.

The Use of Mass Media and Education

Through the use of mass media and education, it is necessary to increase public awareness of the fundamental common ethics and to teach the importance of moral values to the students. Through the regular curriculum of education system, students should be taught the importance of moral values, self-discipline, frugality, and a value system that emphasizes respect for the rights of others.

Transformational Leadership

Transformational leadership must be able to provide a practical vision on the basis of the moral force. The only new leadership armed with a common value system can open a new era. Leaders should get the people's trust and moral legitimacy. Leaders must have a firm belief in the universal basic values such as freedom, justice, and peace. If leaders themselves do not have a clear understanding about these principles, the people do not trust them anymore.

The Role of NGO and Citizen

It is critical to have the spontaneous consciousness and civic awareness of the citizens in the world. The new world and the natural order require ethics of the whole world. The dedication of law and freedom presupposes a sense of responsibility and obligation. Therefore, it should appeal to the hearts and minds of the people.

The world cannot be changed in the better direction without changing the individual's consciousness. The changes in the collective consciousness are so critical. Fundamental change should require a certain degree of risk and sacrifice. However, what is equally important is a firm belief and commitment. The solution will be found, if we maintain the collective awareness to face the challenges and have the real courage to open a new world.

Key Point!

◎ Privacy and Personal Information Protection

Definition

- The right to control private information.

Features

- Exclusive human rights
- Rights of natural persons
- Means of ensuring self-realization
- Fungibility(Trade-off)
- Prerequisite: Privacy is a right prerequisite to produce a reliable and trustful space required for the community is maintained.

The Protection of Personal Information

- It is the right to include self-determination and self-correction.
- It is the information about specific individuals which enables to recognize by name, social security number, and video.

Protection Provisions of Personal Information: Security Technology

▸ Hierarchy of PKI

- Root Certification Authority
- Subordinate Certification Authorities
- Registration Authority

▸ Government Public Key Infrastructure

- Definition of GPKI: GPKI is core infrastructure of e-Government to secure the method of trust and certificate for governmental documents.

- Purpose of GPKI

- GPKI provides the efficiency for e-Government.
- GPKI provides the transparency for e-Government.
- GPKI reinforces the competitiveness for e-Government.
- GPKI provides the reliability for e-Government.

◎ Problems of Anonymity on the Internet

Significance

- Trust
- Anonymity, Mutual Openness and Trust

▸ Information Society and Anonymity

- Features of Anonymity
- Virtual Reality
- Lack of Sense of Guilt
- ID: ID appears as a sign of identification of the individual activities in cyberspace but wrong or artificial identity creates problem of anonymity.

◎ Cyber Crime

▸ Definition

- Cyber crime that is relating with network or internet.
- Cyber crime as a broad concept that includes all the computer crime in the cyber space.

▸ Features of Cyber Crime

- Anonymity and Non-face-to-face
- Unlimited Space
- Expertise Required
- Hidden Crime

▸ Types of Cyber Crime

- Cyber Crime with Network Invasion
- Information Invasion
- Cyber Terror

- Cyber Crime without Network Invasion
- Illegal Copy and Distribution
- Cyber Sex Crime
- Cyber Defamation
- Spam Mail

▸ Policy Strategy:

- Legal aspects: Government is necessary to amend the Criminal law.
- Technical aspects: Response techniques should be developed to block any Cyber Crime by analyzing the technique of Cyber Crime.
- Social aspects: Government is necessary to ensure a systematic response system such as the Cyber Crime Task Force consisting of prosecutors and police experts.

◎ **Information Ethics & Culture**

- Cooperation through International Organizations
- The Use of Mass Media and Education
- Transformational Leadership
- The Role of NGO and Citizen

Key Question!

◎ Explain the concept of privacy and the passive and active privacy.

◎ What are the kinds of Privacy Statement of security techniques and cryptographic techniques PKI, GPKI, NPKI?

◎ What are the problems of anonymity on the Internet and restrictive identification system(the Internet real-name system)?

◎ What are the policy strategies to cope with Cyber Crime?

SUMMARY AND CONCLUSION

Policy wisdom of society in 21 Century should base on human respect and dignity

- Daniel Bell

Future Vision of E-Government

In the 21st Century, the key issues of competition are "overcoming time and space", through reinforcement of national competitiveness and improvement of the people's quality of life. The high speed of the SMART information technology((IT) will be key means of a national strategy to become an advanced country. The integration of SMART Information Technology (IT) and Green Revolution lifts up the economic development. The full integration of knowledge and skills stacked in thousands of human history, by dint of digitization and the advancement of Smart information technology, enables the paradigm of e-Government different from the traditional model of government bureaucracy.

The concept of time and space was totally obliterated due to the innovation of the Smart revolutions. The current form of governing paradigm is completely changing due to the creation of new social network (SNS) such as Twitter and Face book, so that the relationship between government, market, and civil society will be changed.

How these kinds of an enormous change and innovation, swirling from the high-technological environmental changes such as SMART revolution and SNS development, will impact the traditional study of public administration and public policy in the governance studies? What are the focal issues to be discussed in e-Government and e-Policy in this era of the comprehensive paradigm shift? What should be the new theoretical principle and philosophy to break-away the so-called criticism of the '*impoverished professionalism*' facing the science of public administration and philosophy?

How could we academically link the theoretical principles of the knowledge-created e-Government with the traditional administrative, policy, and network governance theories? Could the e-Government be the most effective, transparent, and accountable democratic governance model facing the turbulence of the upcoming Smart knowledge revolutions, especially in the developing countries? What would then be the effective strategies and tasks to face and solve the related, presumably enormous, policy challenges and thereby realizing such kind of democratic e-Governance?

This book is written as an attempt to answer these kinds of academic as well as practical questions, searching for a new paradigm of e-Government and e-Strategy facing the Smart revolution and knowledge society in this 21st century. The author utilizes the theories from the field of public policy, new public management, and new governance to link the gap between e-Governance and the traditional model of public administration.

E-Government and Policy Theory

The author discussed e-Government and e-Policy based on the framework of public policy process. From the theoretical perspective of policy process, e-Government and the knowledge government is the newly emerging policy decision-making mechanism in the overall governance scheme.

As shown in 〈Figure A-i〉, the policy input which is comprised of demand and support from civil society will be transferred to the policy decision-making models, composed of e-Government and knowledge government. Through a transforming process, e-Policy as a policy output are to be produced(see Figure A-i).

E-Governance and E-Government

There are three significant areas and features of e-Governance: 1) *Economic Area,* in which government productivity and national competitiveness are the most critical, 2) *Political Area*, in which civil participation and participatory democracy are the most crucial, 3) Finally, *Social Area*, in which trust building and reflexivity are the most critical for a healthy civic community.

Figure A-i E-Government(Policy System) and E-Policy(Policy Outcome)

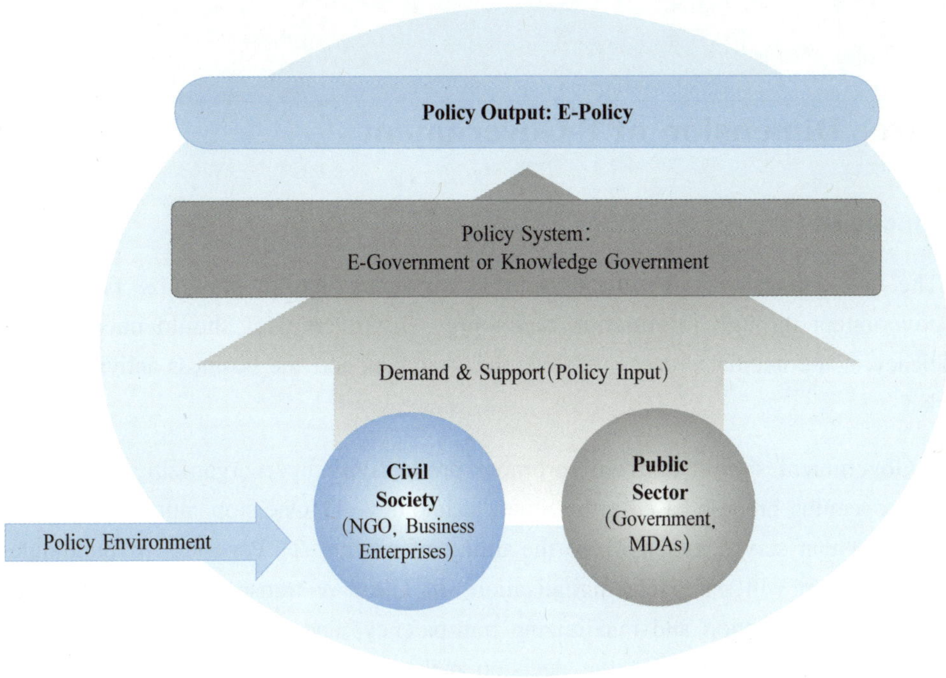

Figure A-ii Analytical Model: E-Governance and E-Government

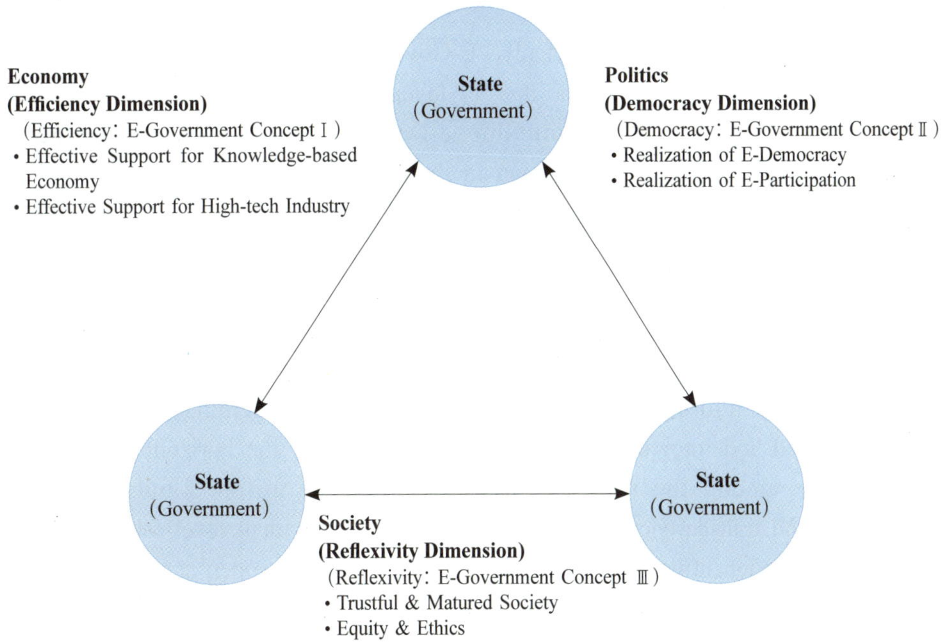

Along with this, the three dimensions of e-Government model was highlighted in this book.

Three Dimension of E-Government

Productivity

The first dimension is **Productivity**. E-Government has to maximize productivity of government through information technology. E-Government should maximize the efficiency of the internal process of government and support the business activities of the market.

E-Government should and will promote productivity by reorganizing government internal operating process base on the Smart technology. 1) One stop, non-stop, any stop government that serves to maximize the utility of citizen, 2) Paperless & buildingless government that will maximize digitalization, 3) Clean & transparent government that will minimize corruption and maximizing transparency, and finally, 4) Digital nervous government that will optimize the decision making process of the entire governance system.

Democracy

The second dimension is **Democracy**. E-Government has to realize e-Democracy through information technology. To do this, e-Government should encourage participatory e-Democracy(e-Policy) and accountable e-Democracy(e-Politics). Democratic government has to enhance e-participation in the policy process and promote e-politics using e-voting or e-legislation in the political process.

Reflexivity

The third dimension is **Reflexivity**. E-Government has to realize a healthy civic community through information technology. To do this, e-Government should achieve the trust, matured and integrated society through revitalizing the horizontal and vertical communication among the members of the community utilizing public space or e-Forum(trust and transparency). E-Government, at an individual level, should enhance human dignity through utilizing human-based e-policies such as open access, e-education and universal service to minimize digital gaps, while guaranteeing e-Security(equity and

Figure A-iii Three Dimensions of E-Government

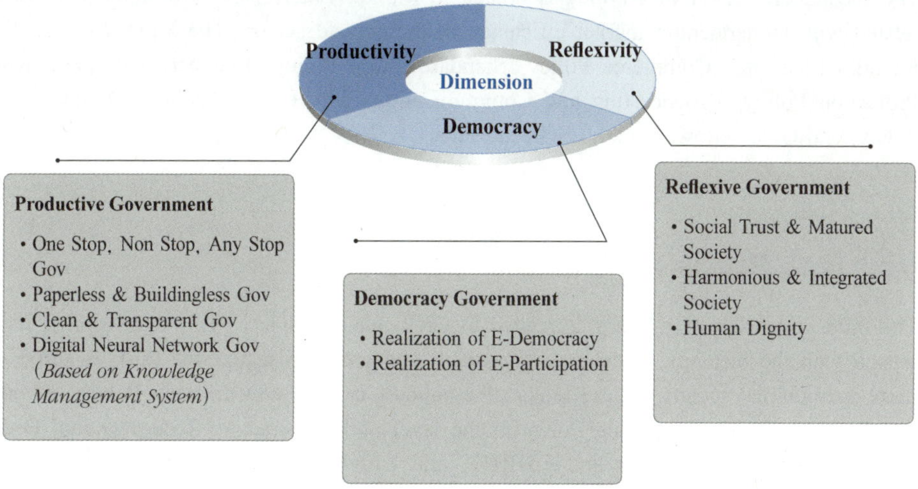

ethics).

Three Dimension of E-Policy

In the dimension of e-Policy, the unit of analysis of these three dimensions can also be applied. E-policy can be analyzed by the dimension of Productivity, Democracy, and Reflexivity, and their main agents are state/government, market/enterprise, and civil society/NGO.

Productivity(I)

The first dimension of e-Policy is the matter of productivity or efficiency at the government level. The government should effectively use e-policy as a strategic instrument for upgrading national competitiveness. These kinds of e-policies include the next-generation Broadband ICT Infrastructure Policy(Super-high Speed BcN Policy), Strategic Industrial Policy(High-tech Industrial Policy), Local Information Policy(e-Village Policy), and U-City Policy(Smart-City Policy).

Productivity(II)

The second dimension of e-Policy is related to Market(Enterprise). This dimension is also related with strengthening market efficiency in the private sector. These kinds of e-policies includes Electronic Commerce Policy, Standardization Policy, Intellectual Property Rights Protection Policy, Broadcasting and Communications Convergence Policy, Digital Content Policy, and Green Growth Policy(e-Green Policy).

Democracy & Reflexivity

The third dimension of e-Policy is related to Civil Society(NGO). This dimension is deeply related with the ideology of democracy, equity, and ethics to realize the trust, matured, and more harmonious society. These kinds of e-policies include e-Democracy Policy, e-Voting, and Public Informaton Opening Policy(at the level of Democracy); Reduce Digital Divide, Digital Literacy(e-Education and e-HRD), and Universal Service Policy(at the level of Equity); Personal Information Protection Policy, Internet Real Name Policy, and Cyber Crime Prevention Policy(at the level of Ethics).

Figure A-iv Three Dimensions of E-Policy

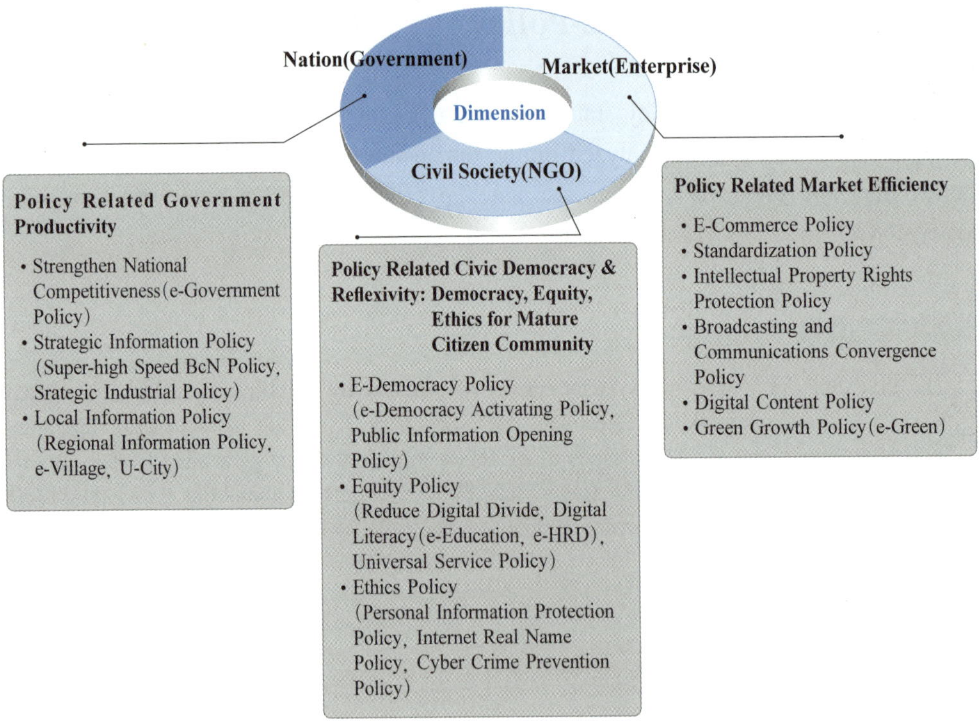

E-government and Governance Theory

In this book, we looked into the limitation of state centric bureaucracy, and various types of governance model. Cyber governance can be understood as the one of these types with spreading of the smart ICT and the Internet. E-government is the policy mechanism of Cyber governance; actually it is the backbone of Cyber governance.

Governance theory is an alternative one to make up for the limitation of state centric controlling model. It is the model which government, market and civic sector have the same position equally in the networked-based relations. In other words, it is the new governance model which turns up for efficiency, effectiveness, democracy, transparency, and accountability of governance by restructuring the relationship among three actors, government, market and civil sector.

The governance mentioned in this book is beyond just discourse of efficiency of government. It is because government can and should strengthen democracy and trust-based and mature civil society. It was emphasized that information policy, which means a policy outcome, is for not only for efficiency but also for democracy, equity, and ethics of civil society. In short, it is required that state centric government is being changed into horizontal network governance. It should be the basic thought of the new

Figure A-v E-Government and Governance Theory

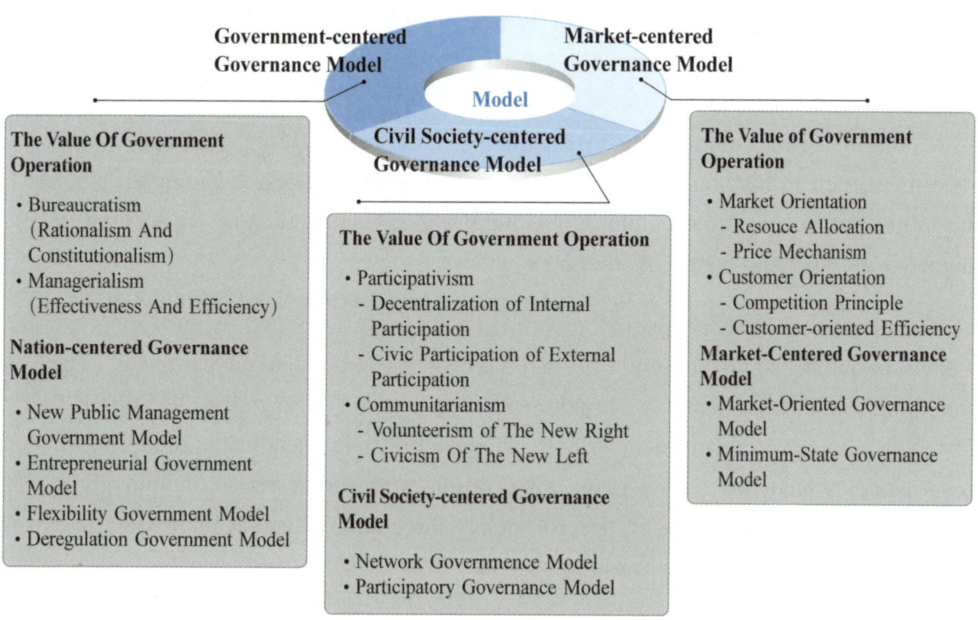

paradigm for the new vision of E-Government with advancement of the smart information technologies.

Epilogue

A real insight into the future is seeing what is invisible.

Beyond the Industrial Age of the 20th century, a new chapter of the history of the information age of the 21st century has been unfolded. Industrial age based on mass-production and mass-consumption simply lowered the curtain, knowledge age with a smart information technology has been progressing.

The concept of time and space was totally obliterated due to the innovation of the Smart revolutions. The current form of governing paradigm is completely changing due to the creation of new social network (SNS) such as Twitter and Face book, so that the relationship between government, market, and civil society is changing.

Under the turbulent changes of information technology, we are facing a new task of establishing the new paradigm of e-government. It is very crucial to building an e-governance system that could effectively implement humanistic ideal.

The developmental history of science and technology has not always been in the right direction. The role of the government is important in setting the ideological paradigm and control measures to the direction of science and technology. We should remember that we are still within the

realms of a shady experience in a capitalist industrial society. As Robert Heilbroner once mentioned in his book, "Crisis of Vision in Modern Economic Thought," society in the future must put more emphasis on moral and ethical standards. This perspective is aligned with the basic theme of this book.

Turbulent swirls of information revolution require an unsullied evaluation of existing models of public administration, the paradigm of e-Government in particular. The new paradigm of e-Government, as Thomas Kuhn once stated, is facing a "Paradigm Shift." The New, smart e-Government should suggest the next generation blueprint of new governance, which can lead a new globalization with a new spirit of innovation. The new innovation should suggest a specific policy direction and action plan which could be embedded in people's mind and action system.

The new e-Government should build up a new governance system that promote communication and participation from a citizen's voluntary basis by utilizing the new smart information technologies. It also should suggest on/offline policy mechanisms corresponding to these directions.

Mankind is not the owner of the earth, nor can leave here eternally; we just stay here for a while. Hence, a sustainable earth, and realization of a civilized society, and the new logic and policy for the humane information society, should be the focal point for the 21st century and beyond. The e-Government of the future should continuously create the new possibilities of Smart creativity with the spirit of New Frontier, while wisely and swiftly corresponding to the current turbulent changes of ICT Revolutions.

REFERENCES

INTERNATIONAL LITERATURE

Bangemann, M. (1994). Recommendations to the European Council – Europe and the Global *Information Society*. Brussels.

Bates, B. J. (1989). "Evolving th an Information Society: Issues and Problems." In J. L. Salvaggio(ed.), *The Information Society: Economic, Social, & Structural Issues*. Hillsdale, NJ: Lawrence Erlbaum Associates, Publishers.

Bell, D. (1973). *The Coming of the Post-industrial Society*. New York: Basic Books.

______. (1989). "Communication Technology: For Better of for Worse?" In Salvaggio, Jerry L. ed. *The Information Society: Economic, Social & Structural Issues*. Hillsdale, NJ: Lawrence Erlbaum Associates, Publishers.

Beniger, J. R. (1986). *The Control Revolution: Technological and Economic Origins of the Information Society*. Cambridge, MA: Harvard University Press.

Bill, Gates. (1996). *The Road Ahead*. Penguin Books.

Castells, Manuel. (1996). *Information age: Economy, Society and Culture, Volume I: The Rise of the Network Society*. Oxford, Blackwell Publishers.

Crane, B. (1967). *A History of Civilization*. New Jersey: Prentice-Hall.

Deming, W. E. (1986). *Out of the Crisis*. Massachusetts Institute of Technology, Center for Advanced Engineering Study, Cambridge, Mass.

Dizard, W.P. (1984). *The Coming Information Age*. New York: Longman.

Drucker, P. F. (1980). *Managing in Turbulent Times*. New York: Harper and Row.

Dutton, W. H. & J. G. Blumer. (1989). "A Comparative Perspective on Information Societies", In J. L. Salvaggion (ed). *The Information Society: Economic, Social & Structural Issues*. Hillsdale, NJ: Lawrence Erlbaum Associates, Publishers.

Ellul, J. (1962). "The Technological Order," *Technology and Culture*. Volume 3(4): 394-421.

Gandy, O. H. (1989). "The Surveillance Society: Information Technology and Bureaucratic Social Control", *Journal of Communication*.

George P. Huber. (2001). "Transfer of Knowledge in Knowledge Management System: Unexplored Issues and Suggested Studies," *European Journal of Information Systems*. Volume 10(2): 72-79. Palgrave Macmillan.

Giddens, A. (1989). *Sociology*, Cambridge: Polity Press.

Jessop, B. (1998). "The Rise of Governance and the Risks of Failure: the Case of Economic Development," *International Journal of Social Science*. Volume 155: 29-46.

Kellner, D. (1990). *Television and the Crisis of Democracy*, Boulder: Westview Press.

Kelly, G. & Muers, S. (2002). *Creating Public Value – An Analytical Framework for Public Service Reform*. London, Cabinet Office Strategy Unit(www.strategy.gov.uk).

Lasswell., H. D. (1951). "The Policy Orientation," *The Policy Sciences: Recent Developments in Scope and Method*. CA: Stanford University Press.

Lenk, Uta. (1998). *Marking Discourse Coherence: Functions of Discourse Markers in Spoken English*. TubingeN: Narr.

Loader, Brian D. (1998). "How Democracy Can Be in Reality?: A Strategy for Political Inclusion? *Paper Presented for 1998 Korea Association for Public Administration(KAPA)*, International Symposium on Electronic Government. Hotel Shilla(Oct, 17, 1998).

Marcuse, H. (1964). *One Dimentional Man*. Boston: Boston Press.

Mark, H. M. (1995). *Creating Public Value: Strategic Management in Government*, Harvard University Press.

Martin-Lof, J. (1984). "Some Policy Issues in the International Debate", In L. Bannon, U. Barry & O. Holst(eds.), Schiller, H. I. (1989). "Information for What Kind of Society: *Economic, Social, & Structural Issues*. Hillsdale, NJ: Lawrence Erlbaum Associates, Publishers.

Masuda, Y. (1981). The Information Society as Post-industrial Society. Bethesda, MD: WorldFuture Society.

_______. (1982). "Vision of the Global Information Society." In L. Bannon, U. Barry & O. Holst(eds.), *Information Technology Impact on the Way of Life*. Dublin: Tycooly International Publishing.

McLuhan, M. (1964). *Understanding Media*. London: Routledge.

Naisbitt, J. (1982). *Megatrends: Ten New Directions Transforming Our Lives*. Warner Books: New York.

Naisbitt, J. (1990). *Mega-Tendances*, 1990-2000. Ce qui va changer, First, Paris.

Negroponte, N. (1996). *Being Digital*. New York: Coronet.

OECD. (1992). *Telecommunications and Broadcasting: Convergence or Collision.*

______. (1998). *New Technologies in the 1990s: A Socio-Economic Strategy.*

Ostrom, E. (1990). *Governing the Commons: The Evolution of Institutions for Collective Action*, Cambridge University Press.

Rheingold, H.(1993). *The Virtual Community: Homesteading on the Electronic Frontier*. Reading, Massachusetts: Addison-Wesley.

Rhodes, R. A. W. (1996). "The New Governance: Governing without Government," *Political Studies*, 652-667.

Salvaggio, (1983). *The InformationIindustry's Strategy to Promote the Image of the Information Society.*

Schement, J. R. (1989). "The Origins of the Information Society in the United States: Competing Visions". In J. L. Salvaggio(ed.), *The Information Society: Economic, Social, & Structural Issues.* Hillsdale, NJ: Lawrence Erlbaum Associates, Publishers.

______. (1989). The Origins of the Information Society in the United States: Competing Visions.

Schiller, H. I. (1989). "Information for What Kind of Society?" In Salvaggio, L. Jerry (ed.), *The Information Society: Economic, Social,& Structural Issues*, Hillsdale, NJ: Lawrence Erlbaum Associates, Publishers.

Schindler, C. & G. Lapid. (1989). *The Great Turning: Personal Peace and Global Victory*, Santa Fe, New Mexico: Bear.

Simon, H. A. (1987). "The Steam Engine and Computer: What Makes Technology Revolutionary," *Computer and Society*.

Smythe, D. (1985). "A Historical Perspective on Equity: National Policy on Public and Private Sector in the U.S.A", *Paper Presented to the Thirteenth Annual Telecommunications Policy Research Conference*, VA: Airlie House.

Toffler, A. (1989). *The Third Wave*, Bantam.

______. (1990). *Powershift: Knowledge, Wealth and Violence at the Edge of the 21st Century*, Mass Market Paperback.

Weinberg, S. (1996). *The Quantum Theory of Fields*, Cambridge University Press.

Wilson, W. (1887). The Study of Administration, P*olitical Science Quarterly Volume* 2(2): 197–222.

KOREAN LITERATURE

Ahn, Moon Seok. (1992). Management Information System. Hakhyunsa.

Bae, Kang-Won. (2009). "A Study on the Similar Characteristics between 'Poong-Ryu Space Image' That is Native to Korea and Ubiquitous-Space", *Journal of Korean Society of Design Science*, Vol. 22, No. 4: 143-154.

Cho, Ui-Seol. (1971). *Brith of Civilization*. Hyeonamsa.

Cho, Yeong-Sik. (1996). *Outopia*. Kyunghee University Press.

______. (1997). *Reconstrunction of Human Society*, Kyohak.

Go, Seon-Gyu. (2006). *E-Democracy: Effects and Future Challenges of E-Voting System*, Korea Local Information Research & Development Institute.

Jang, Young-Chul. (2001). *Knowledge Management for Human Resources Development and Management System*, Jipmundang.

Jeon, Seok-Ho. et al. (1995). *A Study of the Information Policy System and Policy Issues*. Electronics and Telecommunications Research Institute.

Jung, Chung Sik. (1997). *Theory of Electronic Government*, Seoul: Nok Du.

Jung, Jung Gil. (2000). *New Public Administration*. Seoul: DaeMyung.

Kang, Hwang Sun. (2002). *Knowledge Management: Seoul Action Plan*. Seoul Development Institute.

Kim, Dong Wook. (1995b). "The Informatization in Public Sector for the Policy Information Sharing." *The Journal of National Basic Information System*. 2(4).

Kim, In-Su. (1991). *Macro-organization Theory*. Muyok-Kyungyoung Sa: 597-602.

Kim, Seok-Joon. et al. (2000). T*he Study of New Governance*. DaeYoung-Publication Corp.

Kim, Sun Kyung. (2003). "The Appearance of U-Government and the Direction of Service," *Digital Adminstration*. Ministry of Government Administration and Home Affairs.

Kim, Jin Hee. (2002). "The Information Technology Architecture: The New Paradigm of Enterprise Information Technology Management," *The Information and Communication Focus*, 18: 23-27.

Kwon, Gi-Heon. (2000). "The Theoretical Model of Knowledge Government," *Information Society*, 1: 28-47.

______. (2008a). *Theories of Policy Science*. Seoul: Parkyoungsa.

Lee, Jae Sung.et al. (2010). "A Study on the Activation of Smartwork," *The Journal of Korean Association for Regional Information Society*. 13(4): 71-96.

Lee, Tae Young. (2008). *A Study on the Types of e-Corruption and Control Strategies*. Doctoral

Dissertation, Hankuk University of Foreign Studies.

Min, Jin. (2004). *Management in the Organization*. DaeYoung-Publication Corp.

Mook, Jin Hue. et al. (1998). "The Impact of Information Technology in Policy Making Process". *The Journal of Korean Association for Public Administration*, 32(3).

National Computing & Information Agency. (2010). *Mobile Government Service Manual and Use the Casebook*. Ministry of Public Administration and Security.

National Information Agency. (2013). *Information Divide Index and Status Survey in 2012*.

Oh, GwangSeok. (2003). "Strategies and Construction of Ubiquitous e-Government," *Digital Government*, Special Edition for Ubiquitous and E-Government Ⅱ, Government Computer Information Management Office in Ministry of Administration and Home Affairs.

Park, JaeHee. (1996). "Enhancement of the Central Government's Decision-making Capacity," *KIPA Research Report*, 95-17, Korea Institute of Public Administration.

Samsung Economic Research Institute. (1999). "*Knowledge Management and the Future of Korea.*"

Seo, Sam-Yeong. (1996). "Direction of the Search for Information and Communication Policy for the Construction of an Advanced Information Society," *Role of Informatization*, Government and Media, Joint Symposium of Korea Communication Association and Korean Association for Public Administration.

Sin, Jung-Seop. (1992). *Philosophy of Science of K.* Popper, Seogwangsa.

INDEX

the Index of Persons

☙ CURRICULUM VITAE ❧

Gi-Heon Kwon, Ph D

Dean/President

GePeGi (Global e-Policy & e-Government Institute)
Graduate School of Governance, SKKU
Samsung Foundation

President

KAPS(Korean Association for Policy Studies, 2015)

Commissioner

Prime Minister Office
Policy Evaluation Committee
Republic of Korea

Dept./Professor

Graduate School of Governance, SKKU
Public Administration, SKKU
Samsung Foundation

Information

[Research Room] Law School B/D Room 320
SKKU(SungKyunKwan Univ.)
53 Myung Ryun Dong 3-Ga,
Jong Rho-Gu, Seoul
P.O.BOX 110-745
[E-mail] gkwon77@empas.com
[TEL] +82-2-760-0363(office)

ACADEMIC BACKGROUNDS

- 1991-1994 Ph. D in Public Policy,
  Graduate School of Arts & Science, Harvard University
- 1989-1991 Masters in Public Policy (MPP),
  John F. Kennedy School of Government, Harvard University
- 1983-1985 Masters in Public Administration (MPA),
  Graduate School of Public Administration, Seoul National University
- 1979-1983 Bachelor's Degree in Public Administration (BA),
  Han Kook University of Foreign Studies

AWARDS

- Prime Minister's Award
  (Ranked Top among the 26th Senior Government Entrance Exam)
- Fulbright Scholarship
- Best Thesis Award, APPAM
  (America Public Policy Analysis & Management Association)
- Best Thesis Award, Korea Association for Public Administration
- Academic Scholarship, MPP & Ph.D. in Public Policy, Harvard University
- Fulbright Visiting Scholar, Maxwell School, Syracuse University, USA
  (Lecture: e-Government/National Innovation)
- Best Book Award (two times), Korea National Academy of Science
- Best Book Award, Ministry of Culture & Tourism
- Passed the 26th Senior Government Entrance Exam (1982)

ACADEMIC ACTIVITIES

- 2015-2016 President
  Korean Association for Policy Studies
- 2009-2010 Editor in Chief,
  Korean Association for Policy Studies
- 2008 Chairman,
  Special Research Committee, Korean Association for Policy Studies
- 2005-2007 Editorial Committee,
  Korean Association for Policy Studies
- 2005 Chairman,
  Academic Information Committee, Korea Association for Public Administration
- 2004 Chairman,
  Special Policy Case Committee, Korean Association for Policy Studies
- 2003-2005 Editorial Committee,
  Korean Association for Public Administration

PUBLICATIONS

Monographs

- 2014 E-Government and E-Strategies: Explaining Successful Conditions of Korean e-Government
- 2014 Lectures on Public Administration
- 2014 Lectures on Policy Science
- 2014 How to Reform Public Enterprises?
- 2013 Electronic Government
- 2013 What is the Justice Nation?
- 2013 Public Administration Concert
- 2010 Theories of Policy Analysis
- 2009 Theories of Public Administration
- 2008 Future Foresight
- 2008 The Logic of Public Policy
- 2008 Theories of Public Policy
- 2004 Public Management Information System

Teaching/Consulting/Research Areas

- e-Government & e-Policy
- Policy Analysis
- Theories on Policy Science
- National Innovation
- Policy Foresight
- Policy Making

E-Government & E-Strategy

Printed the first edition in 2014. 9. 25
Published the first edition in 2014. 9. 30

Author Gi-Heon Kwon
President Jong-Man An
Publishing Company Parkyoung Publishing & Company
Saemoonan-Ro 3 Gil 36, 1601 Jongrogu, Seoul
Registered in 1959.3.11. 300-1959-1
Phone 82-2-733-6771
fax 82-2-736-4818
e-mail pys@pybook.co.kr
homepage www.pybook.co.kr
ISBN 979-11-303-0131-0 93350

28,000 ₩(Korean Currency)